WORLD HYPOTHESES

WORLD HYPOTHESES

A Study in Evidence

BY

STEPHEN C. PEPPER

UNIVERSITY OF CALIFORNIA PRESS

Berkeley, Los Angeles and London

UNIVERSITY OF CALIFORNIA PRESS
BERKELEY AND LOS ANGELES, CALIFORNIA
UNIVERSITY OF CALIFORNIA PRESS, LTD.
LONDON, ENGLAND
COPYRIGHT, 1942, BY
THE REGENTS OF THE UNIVERSITY OF CALIFORNIA
COPYRIGHT RENEWED, 1970, BY
STEPHEN C. PEPPER

ISBN 0-520-00994-0
LC CATALOG CARD NO. 42-37134

9 0

PRINTED IN THE UNITED STATES OF AMERICA

Preface

THE ORIGIN *of this book goes 'way back to a consuming personal desire to know the truth. As a boy I sought it in what was nearest at hand in the doctrines of a church and struggled with what I later found were the perennial issues of theology. Then for a time I sought it in physics. But physics seemed interested chiefly in measurements and formulas and impatient with what might be the bearing of these on the problems, like perception, that make one want to know the truth. Later I discovered philosophy. First I tried, under the guidance of Palmer and of T. H. Green's writings, to believe in idealism. But the arguments of this theory were then little better to me than verbal formulas. I tried to make them mine, used to repeat them in the hope that they would take, feeling, rather than knowing, that if they did take they would save something of my old theology. They did not take and I had a revulsion against them and turned dogmatic materialist. This I remained for many years, till I began to feel the impact of Gestalt psychology and pragmatic doctrines. And then the empirical grounds for that idealism which I had not previously understood began also to make an impression. All this was a slow, and as I look back upon it, a maturing process.*

Meanwhile the violent changes that were taking place in social values were having their effect. Individualistic democracy, which through the first quarter of the century

I naïvely accepted as the unquestionable social ideal, met with severe jars, and became subject to criticism. As an ideal it obviously required revision. It was in active competition with other political ideals. What were the grounds and evidences for any of these political creeds?

Having been shaken out of one dogmatism, I was on guard against falling into another. It was, moreover, a specially vivid revelation to discover the evidential force of a theory I had once verbally mumbled and utterly failed to comprehend. It was also pretty clear that materialism and idealism would not consistently go together. For a time I tried to find an adjustment of the evidences of both of these theories in a third, pragmatism. But I soon came to the conclusion that pragmatism was just one more theory, probably no better nor any worse than the other two. I began to wonder if there were not still more theories, not sufficiently worked over, containing grounds of evidence as convincing as these.

By now my old drive for the truth was directed toward the study of evidence and hypothesis—toward a reliable method rather than a reliable creed. And at this moment the logical positivists appeared on the scene with a nostrum made to order just along these lines. My immediate reaction to them was suspicious and hostile. I felt from their attitude and the tone of their statements, even before critically studying them, that they were not meeting the problem that needed to be met. I doubted if many of them had ever fully felt the problem. This was a question of truth and of the justification of human values. To think that this question could be met in the manner of a puzzle and in terms of correlations, statistics, mathematics, and language struck me as fantastic. Here was method running away with issues, evidence, and value itself. It was, as Loewenberg once remarked, methodolatry.

But the attack of the positivists on world theories did bring out the fact that there was more in physics which stood on its own feet without support of theory than I had previously been willing to allow.

Now all this material seems to have come to a sort of stability in the book that follows. Here I believe is the truth about these things, as near as we can get at it in our times. Or rather, here is the attitude and here are some of the instruments that can bring it to us.

At the very least, here is the solution that seems best to one man, living in the first half of the twentieth century, who has passed through most of the cognitive experiences we have been subject to: religious creed, philosophical dogma, science, art, and social revaluation.

Possibly here is also a present crystallization of some twenty-five centuries' struggle and experience with the problem of how men can get at the truth in matters of importance to them. S. C. P.

Table of Contents

PART ONE

The Root-Metaphor Theory

Chapter I : The Utter Skeptic

§1. *World hypotheses as objects in the world.*—Among the variety of objects which we find in the world are hypotheses about the world itself. For the most part these are contained in books such as Plato's *Republic*, Aristotle's *Metaphysics*, Lucretius' *On the Nature of Things*, Descartes's *Meditations*, Spinoza's *Ethics*, Hume's *Treatise*, Kant's three *Critiques*, Dewey's *Experience and Nature*, Whitehead's *Process and Reality*. These books are clearly different in their aim from such as Euclid's *Elements* or Darwin's *The Origin of Species*.

The two books last named deal with restricted fields of knowledge and can reject facts as not belonging to their field if the facts do not fit properly within the definitions and hypotheses framed for the field. But the other books deal with knowledge in an unrestricted way. These unrestricted products of knowledge I am calling world hypotheses, and the peculiarity of world hypotheses is that they cannot reject anything as irrelevant.

When certain inconvenient matters are brought to a mathematician, he can always say, "These are psychological [or physical, or historical] matters. I do not have to deal with them." Similarly with other students of restricted fields. But students of world hypotheses can never have that way out. Every consideration is relevant to a world hypothesis and no facts lie outside it. This peculiarity has extensive consequences.

[1]

I wish to study world hypotheses as objects existing in the world, to examine them empirically as a zoölogist studies species of animals, a psychologist varieties of perception, a mathematician geometrical systems. These are all in some sense facts. And the analogy between world hypotheses as actual facts or objects now present in the world and the facts or objects studied by zoölogists, psychologists, or mathematicians is worth holding in mind. For we all have and use world hypotheses, just as we have animal bodies, have perceptions, and move within geometrical relations. It is just because world hypotheses are so intimate and pervasive that we do not easily look at them from a distance, so to speak, or as if we saw them in a mirror. Even the authors named in my first paragraph do not fully succeed in looking at their results as things to be looked at.

World hypotheses are likely to be studied as creeds to be accepted or rejected, or as expressions of highly individual personalities, or as expressions of epochs, or as objects of historical scholarship to be traced to their cultural sources or given their philological or psychological interpretations. They are rarely treated as objects in their own right to be studied and described in their own character and compared with one another. Yet it is this last sort of study that I wish to make.

We cannot, however, enter immediately into this study. Even in the most earnest attempt to be faithful to the nature of the objects observed it is inevitable that the study should include some theory of its own. We must try to reduce this to a minimum and to be aware of the minimum. We shall accordingly begin with two attitudes toward such a study which purport to be entirely free from theory of any sort. These are the two opposite extremities of cognitive attitude: utter skepticism, and dogmatism. My intention is to show that these extremities, in their efforts to avoid the uncertainties of theory, actually lay themselves open more widely to theory and to unjustifiable interpretations and assumptions than the moderate middle course of partial skepticism which we shall pursue.

The term world hypothesis connotes this middle course. It signifies that these objects, which we are about to study, are not final products of knowledge and yet that they do contain knowledge. Unless we first considered the attitudes which from one extreme or the other deny this moderate judgment, our term would be question-begging. Moreover, we should logically find ourselves either with no objects to study (for such would be the contention of the utter skeptic) or with only one (for this is the usual belief of the dogmatist).

In the present chapter we shall consider the claims of utter skepticism and in the next those of dogmatism, and shall undertake to show that there is nothing cognitively legitimate in these claims which is not accepted also by our attitude of partial skepticism.

§2. *The position of the utter skeptic.*—In one of Berkeley's Dialogues, Philonous inquires, "What is a skeptic?" and Hylas answers, "One who doubts all things." This is supposed to describe the attitude of an utter skeptic.

For some strange reason this attitude is often popularly regarded as particularly impregnable. It is also frequently regarded as a particularly easy attitude: Knowledge is hard, but doubt is easy. Both of these ideas are mistaken and probably have their source in the common analogy between knowledge and building. It is hard to construct, but easy to destroy; yet if a structure is utterly razed to the ground so that no stone stands upon another, then there is at least the security of utter ruin in which no more stones can fall.

But actually in cognition it is generally easier to construct than to destroy, for the cognitive imagination is eternally active and a tremendous fabricator. Belief is the naïve attitude, while doubt is an acquisition won through long and hard experience. As for the impregnability of the position of the utter skeptic (he who doubts all things), it is so far from secure that it is difficult on scrutiny even to determine what it means.

What can the utter skeptic himself mean? Does he mean that all facts are illusory and all statements false? But this position is not one of doubt, but of downright disbelief. It is disbelief in the reliability of all evidence and in the truth of all statements; or, contrariwise, it is belief in the unreliability of all evidence and the falsity of all statements. For every instance of disbelief is simply the reverse of belief; it is belief in the contradictory of what is disbelieved. If a man disbelieves in the existence of God, he necessarily believes in the nonexistence of God. A dogmatic atheist is as little of a doubter as a dogmatic theist. It is the agnostic who completely doubts the existence of God. He genuinely doubts. That is, he finds the evidence on both sides so evenly balanced in this matter that he neither believes nor disbelieves, but holds the proposition in suspense.

Is the utter skeptic, then, one who holds all propositions in suspense? On this supposition, "one who doubts all things" is one who never believes nor disbelieves anything.

Now, this attitude is commonly enough held in isolated instances of uncertainty. Will a penny fall heads or tails? Will it rain tomorrow? Did I tell the gardener to water the flowers? Have I a nickel in my pocket? For different reasons, the available evidence is here so balanced that I would not risk a judgment either way—except for fun or out of practical necessity. I am genuinely in utter doubt in all these instances.

But to generalize the attitude forced upon me in these instances into an attitude to be taken toward everything in the world is quite a different matter. I feel certain that I see blue, and very sure that it is the blue of the sky I see, and rather sure that the stimulus for the blue is not light reflected from a hard surface, and fairly open to the idea that light is electrical in nature, and willing to entertain the hypothesis that electromagnetic vibrations are as real as the waves of the sea. To put all these sensations, data, ideas, and hypotheses on one level and assume an utterly skeptical attitude toward them is not easy, and does not feel very sound. In none of these instances does the evidence come equally balanced *pro* and *con*. To doubt at all that I now see blue seems utterly out of the question; the balance of evidence available to me in favor of believing that the blue I see is that of what we call blue sky is very great as against slight negative possibilities; and as for the hypothesis that electromagnetic vibrations are real, here the evidence is so complicated and so interconnected with masses of other evidence that the image of a balance with two trays, one receiving the evidence *pro* and the other the evidence *con,* seems to break down entirely. Summarily, in point of fact, men do not find all things at a balance of evidence. If by doubt is meant a sense of balance of evidence, nobody lives who "doubts all things." Such a man would simply fade away and die. He could not stand up, for the floor might not support him; nor sit down, for there might be no chair; nor eat, for the food might be cinders; nor speak, for he might not be heard. A consistent utter skeptic of the kind here supposed exhibits his beliefs and disbeliefs and denies his balanced doubts every time he takes a step or says a word. To avoid self-contradiction, he should never speak nor act.

But, it may be suggested, the utter skeptic is not referring to practical beliefs, but to the grounds of ultimate belief. In practice we must make decisions, and we do make them as we make guesses on the flip of a coin, or say "Yes" or "No" to an insistent lawyer in order to avoid "contempt of court." The world forces irrational decisions upon us, and irrationally we believe in what we decide. But if we are rational and study things to the bottom we shall find that we must "doubt all things." At bottom the evidence is evenly balanced for all things.

It is barely possible that such may be the nature of things. But note that this is a theory about the nature of things. This is no simple, naïve, easy, or secure attitude.

It is forced, sophisticated, and very insecure. For now the utter skeptic is making a statement about the nature of all things. And a most peculiar nature on this view all things must have. For take any statement: on this view the evidence for that statement must be evenly balanced; but so also must be the evidence for the evidence for the statement; and so on *ad infinitum.* For if there were ever any evidence for a statement that was not itself divided into two equally balanced parts of *pro* and *con,* there would be more evidence for something in the universe than against it, which would refute this position of the utter skeptic. So this position is that of a positive theory to the effect that the universe is infinitely divisible into dichotomous parts *pro* and *con.*

This theory may be put forward as dogmatic truth or as a hypothesis to be examined on the basis of its evidence and in comparison with alternative world hypotheses. If the former, we have the utter skeptic converted ironically into an utter dogmatist—with whom we shall be concerned in the next chapter. If the latter, we have the utter skeptic converted into a partial skeptic, with whom we can have no quarrel in principle since his is then the position we shall hold.

The utter skeptic, moreover, in presenting any sort of positive theory is always placed in an embarrassing position. For whatever that theory may be, it must, on his own assumptions, be utterly doubted. So again, it appears that the position of the utter skeptic either contradicts itself or turns into something else. His only safety lies in silence, and then nobody listens to him.

But perhaps the utter skeptic is one who doubts on principle the value of any kind of knowledge. He turns to faith, or action, or emotion and sets his back against knowledge. Perhaps he finds the structure, or form, or method of knowledge itself deceptive. This is possible. But again this involves belief and disbelief. To doubt utterly the products of knowledge, one must believe implicitly the deceptive structure of knowledge. And apparently one must dogmatically believe this, for otherwise some products of knowledge may be more credible than others. And again an utter skeptic turns into a dogmatist.

What other meaning can we give to "one who doubts all things"? The attitude is contrary to apparent fact. When ascribed to ultimate fact, it contradicts itself or turns into some other attitude. When ascribed to knowledge as a whole, it fares no better. Could it have any value as a mere method for clearing away false certainties, superstitions, word magic, and the like? So Descartes used it as a *method of doubt,* and in a modified way so have many other philosophers, and lately F. H. Bradley in his *Appearance and Reality.* But this is usually a device for dogmatism and far from the aims of skepticism. For the rest, the method which consists in trying to doubt (or, sometimes, to disbelieve) every sort of thing one can think of from God and Space to self and sense perception, is simply a convenient mode of philosophical exposition. It is a way of clearing the field of old doctrine and giving the appearance of starting afresh. It is often full of logical pitfalls, and not especially to be recommended. In a mild way we are, I suppose, using this method of doubt here as a means of clearing utter skeptics and dogmatists from our path. We doubt them, and that forces them to exhibit their presuppositions to the light of evidence.

The utter skeptic does not, it would seem, fare very well with this treatment. He does not appear able to establish even a settled position or to make himself clear. For we have tried in every way to find a position on which an utter skeptic could stand without falling into dogmatism on one side or partial skepticism on the other. One might be an utter believer, an utter disbeliever, or an utter unbeliever. There seem to be no other "utter" positions in knowledge. An utter skeptic is obviously not a believer. Nor is he a disbeliever, since a disbeliever is simply a negative believer. He must, then, be an unbeliever. An unbeliever could be either a partial or an utter unbeliever. But a partial unbeliever is only a partial skeptic. Some things he holds in suspense, but others he believes or disbelieves in various degrees. An utter skeptic must, then, be an utter unbeliever. But we find this utter unbelief sets demands upon the nature of fact and judgment and indeed of the whole universe which must be believed to guarantee the possibility of utter unbelief. An utter skeptic thus turns into a dogmatist.

The position of the utter skeptic is, we find on careful scrutiny, impossible. It amounts to the self-contradictory dogma that the world is certainly doubtful. If this thesis is taken seriously, it is not a skeptical position, but a dogmatic one. And to the dogmatists we shall soon turn.

If the utter skeptic is not a dogmatist, therefore, he must mean to be a partial skeptic. As a matter of fact, he is a good deal of a myth. Nothing is more common than to find men holding in imagination and with conviction what turn out to be logically or physically impossible beliefs. There may be men who honestly regard themselves as utter skeptics, but if there really are such they are hard to find. A solipsist is, of course, far from an utter skeptic; he *believes* in his solitude in the universe. Perhaps the sophist Gorgias was an utter skeptic, if we may credit tradition. But for the most part utter skeptic is merely a disagreeable name which we are likely to stick on a person who persists in doubting something which we prize and for which we cannot find adequate cognitive support. So, as we saw, Hylas called Philonous a "skeptic" ("one who doubts all things"), because Philonous cast some serious doubts on Hylas' precious belief in "matter."

The utter skeptic has apparently no firmer substance than an empty name, nor any good use. If there is anything in his position to be saved, it will be found in that of the dogmatist, and in that of the partial skeptic.

Chapter II : Dogmatists

§1. *Definition of a dogmatist.*—The dogmatist is a more serious character than the utter skeptic. He is the dictator of cognition. He will put you down by main force. And he is no myth.

We shall define a dogmatist as *one whose belief exceeds his cognitive grounds for belief.* By this definition, dogmatism is a cognitive error, that is, a fallacy. Our aim in this chapter is to find the extent of the fallacy—for there appears to be no question of its existence. It is clear from our remarks in the previous chapter that belief here covers also disbelief, since the latter seems to be simply belief in some negative condition; or if one demurs at this statement, he may simply add "disbelief" to "belief" in the definition. Our coming remarks will be unaffected by this change.

§2. *The constituents of belief.*—Now, we cannot proceed to study the dogmatist without analyzing some of the constituents of belief more carefully than we did in the first chapter. We have a more serious problem on our hands here and we must proceed with more circumspection.

Let us take some ordinary, everyday instance of belief to guide us by way of illustration. Take my judgment that it will rain tomorrow. There appear to be three rather obvious constituents of this judgment: (1) a *content,* or what I believe, in this example "It will rain tomorrow"; (2) an *attitude,* in this instance a positive attitude with some degree of intensity, which may vary all the way from a maximum called certainty to a minimum just above that balance of judgment called unbelief, and which may pass through unbelief and shift into a negative attitude of disbelief with a corresponding series of intensities up to an opposite maximum of certainty of disbelief; (3) *grounds* for belief, in this instance consisting of such items as my experience with weather conditions in this vicinity, the appearance of the sky today, the wind, the barometer, the weatherman's prediction in the newspaper, and my conception of the weatherman's reliability. This set of three constituents we are now calling belief in the broad sense, and it appears that belief in the narrower sense as contrasted with disbelief and unbelief is a matter of attitude in relation to content. The utter skeptic, we now see, was a dogmatist in respect to the attitude of unbelief which he insisted on maintaining without regard to content or the grounds of belief.

A reasonable man, we see, is one whose attitude in respect to content is guided by the grounds of belief. If the grounds weigh heavily for the content, he will believe; if against it, he will disbelieve; if evenly on either side, he will maintain an attitude of suspense and unbelieve. Moreover, he will seek to make his attitude exactly proportional to the balance of weight in the grounds of belief. A dogmatist is one whose attitude is not in proportion to the grounds of belief—one who believes, or disbelieves, or unbelieves too much in terms of the grounds of belief.

Moreover, a reasonable man is eager to find more grounds for belief if more are available, and to modify his attitude constantly in relation to these. A dogmatist often begins as a reasonable man; but, having struck an attitude, he resists the search for new grounds, and even when these are presented he refuses to change his attitude accordingly.

A dogmatist described in these terms is, without much question, an unprepossessing cognitive character. But while nearly everyone will agree that a tyrant in the abstract is an undesirable person, some of us nevertheless become indignant when we find that our benevolent neighbor fulfills the description, and possibly even our city magistrate and our national idol. The same with the dogmatist. So it is well to impress upon ourselves the cognitive undesirability of the character in the abstract before we begin to look about and see to whom the description applies.

§3. *Conviction and credibility.*—This caution is particularly necessary in view of the fact that what seems to be a dogmatic attitude is often practically advisable. The practical or ethical justification of an attitude of belief must not be confused with the cognitive justification. The one should probably follow after the other, wherever time for reflection occurs, but the two should not be confused. Perhaps, for instance, it is important for me to judge now whether it is likely to rain tomorrow, for I do not want to be bothered with a raincoat on an overnight trip if it is not going to rain. My action must be completely positive or negative, that is, I must act as if I were certain. I do not help the practical situation at all by taking half a raincoat if the chances of rain are even, or two-thirds if the chances are two to one. Nor do I help it if I worry on the trip because I did or did not take it, or adjust the intensity of my worry to the successive probabilities of the weather as I go along. The reasonable practical decision is to take the coat or not to take it, and, having made the decision, to act with assurance as if the judgment were certain.

But this action in no way requires me to judge it certain that it will or will not rain tomorrow. As far as this cognitive judgment is concerned, the only reasonable thing is to accept the attitude which the evidence justifies. So, on the slight probability that it will rain tomorrow, I act with utter decision and take my raincoat. I act with conviction on a highly dubious cognitive judgment. There is no contradiction in this situation; on the contrary, there is complete clarity of understanding. Confusion arises only when the practical attitude is merged with the cognitive, or vice versa. Because of the pressure of time it is usually necessary to act before all the evidence one could wish for is in. The attitude of belief *in the act* is usually stronger than the justifiable attitude of belief *in the judgment* on which the act is founded. This discrepancy is not only natural; it is correct. For the criteria which determine the proper attitude for action are ethical, whereas those which determine the proper attitude for cognitive judgment are cognitive.

The two attitudes can easily be confused because they are closely interrelated. It may help to call the practical attitude "conviction" and restrict "belief" to the cognitive attitude. So, our point is not to confuse conviction with belief. A man who acts with conviction is not necessarily a dogmatist. It may be that dogmatists as a rule act with more conviction than reasonable men. But that only shows that they are socially more dangerous than might have been supposed. And it may be that reasonable men do not always act with as much conviction as they should. But that only shows that reasonable men should be still more reasonable and realize the necessity of conviction where action demands it.

But all these matters are irrelevant to our inquiry, which is primarily cognitive. Only as conviction may itself, as some pragmatists say, be in some circumstances a ground for belief do we need to concern ourselves with conviction. And even then conviction functions not as a cognitive attitude but only as a ground for an attitude of belief. The pragmatists' point here is that occasionally conviction produces the very evidence which gives good ground for belief. So a sick man who is convinced of his recovery has better grounds to believe in his recovery than he would have if he were not convinced. But even in so close a relationship as this there is no need of confusing the two.

If, then, belief is distinguished from conviction and the dogmatist as a misbeliever is distinguished from the man of justifiable conviction, the dogmatist may be regarded as a completely undesirable character. A man of conviction is one whose attitude is justifiable (if it is justifiable) on practical grounds. He appeals for justification not only to the grounds of belief, but also to the criteria of practice. A dogmatist, however, is a man of belief. He appeals only to cognitive criteria, and yet maintains an attitude which these criteria will not justify.

One may ask, How is this possible? How could anyone in his senses appeal to cognitive criteria and then refuse to accept their verdict?

This question brings us to a more careful consideration of the grounds or criteria of belief. We do not at this point wish to specify what these grounds may be. They constitute one of the chief concerns of world hypotheses, and are somewhat differently determined, or discovered, or described by each hypothesis. We must be careful not to prescribe to these hypotheses or prejudge the nature of things. We should like it best if we could start at once upon a study of them without any precarious preliminaries. But it is just because we must be on our guard against certain typical kinds of prescriptions that the preliminaries are necessary.

§4. *Criteria of belief.*—If a man is called a dogmatist, he is judged so in reference to certain grounds or criteria of belief. Who determines those grounds? The accused himself, or another? It seems incredible that a man could be a dogmatist in the face of cognitive criteria which he himself has acknowledged. It seems unjust that he should be called a dogmatist in relation to criteria which he has not acknowledged. All dogmatists appear to be relative dogmatists, and who is to judge among the alternative grounds of belief?

The temptation arises to say that all grounds of belief are equally good. But that is precisely the doctrine of utter skepticism. Thus the circle becomes complete. Utter skepticism leads into dogmatism, and dogmatism leads into utter skepticism. For a generalized dogmatism is simply an utter skepticism with the accent changed. If in the one everything is certainly doubtful, in the other everything is doubtfully certain.

The fact is that a dogmatist never will generalize, and that is precisely where his dogmatism has its birth. Among his acknowledged criteria of belief is one which if generalized would lead to his acceptance of beliefs or degrees of belief which he refuses to accept. He explicitly acknowledges cognitive criteria which he implicitly denies.

There are two cognitive criteria which have been historically the principal breeding grounds for dogmatists, namely, infallible authority and certainty. Both are psychologically much stronger in their appeal than any other criteria of belief, for all others suggest caution, some degree of doubt, and some insecurity. An ultimate appeal to authority takes all responsibility off the mind of the knower and affords him a feeling of protection. An appeal to certainty does not remove from the knower his responsibility to find out what is certain, but, having found it, he feels assured of security. What is certainly true cannot by definition be doubtful. I wish to show that both of these criteria are inadmissible because they are inevitably productive of dogmatism, and that even if they are admissible they are not necessary, because they add nothing to the content or the grounds of legitimate belief.

Historically there has been a regular transition from authority to certainty and thence to hypothesis or probability as the dominant grounds for belief. In the Middle Ages authority was dominant; in the Renaissance, and even into the present day, certainty has been dominant;

only recently and not yet by many is hypothesis or probability regarded as properly dominant.

It is worth noting that all, or practically all, the knowledge of primitive societies is based on authority either in the form of mythology or of practical skills passed along as cultural tradition. The strength of tradition, and the feeling of security which it assumes, could hardly be immediately supplanted by anything so delicately balanced and apparently so flimsy as a hypothesis or a probability estimate. It would take the claims of certainty to meet the claims of authority with any power of conviction. Tradition would have to be already pretty well shattered for hypothesis and probability to enter successfully without an intervening period of battering by certainty—a condition, incidentally, which seems to have been present at Athens in the fifth century. Our own period has not been so fortunate. The authority of a long organized and powerful ecclesiastical tradition had to be beaten down by several centuries of claims to immediate personal certainty before the gentle influences of hypothesis and probability, guiding and not compelling knowledge, could make themselves felt without other aid.

Since the claims of authority as an ultimate criterion of knowledge are today almost entirely abandoned, I shall begin by pointing out the reasons for this abandonment. These will be found both convincing and credible for nearly everyone in our generation. The reasons should be marked well, for exactly the same reasons hold for abandoning the claims to certainty as an ultimate criterion of knowledge. Many of our generation in many fields are not yet willing to give up the claims of certainty. My argument, therefore, is in the form: Since we acknowledge the weakness of the claims of infallible authority, and since the claims of certainty have those same weaknesses, we ought to give up the claims of certainty.

§5. *The dogma of infallible authority.*—The difficulties with authority as an ultimate criterion of knowledge are: (1) that supposedly infallible authorities often conflict, (2) that the competence of an infallible authority is often seriously questioned in terms of other criteria, (3) that in the event of conflicting authorities or questioned authority, an appeal is customarily made to other criteria, which often attain what can scarcely be denied to be cognitive success. In view of these three deficiencies it is urged that authority is not an ultimate criterion of knowledge, or, what is the same thing, that infallible authority is not a legitimate cognitive criterion.

Illustrations of these difficulties are hardly necessary. But let us take the Bible, which at various times has been regarded as a divine revelation and therefore an infallible authority. Now the first and second chapters of the Book of Genesis seem to give two conflicting accounts of the creation of man and woman. In the first chapter both man and woman seem to have been created by God directly out of the earth in God's image. In the second chapter God seems to have created man first out of the dust of the ground and then later to have created woman from one of Adam's ribs. As a cognitive problem, how is this conflict to be resolved? It is true that the first account is very brief, and it might be argued that the second account is a detailed amplification of the first. But a literal reading of the first chapter without the second would surely be interpreted in the manner above stated. And to reinterpret the first account as not exactly literal so as to make it harmonize with the second account is to introduce principles of interpretation humanly devised and not to accept the literal implications of the words. From this admission of a freedom of interpretation, it is only a few steps to the treatment of these stories as mere allegories, and the principle of infallible authority becomes dissolved in principles of interpretative reasonableness, which latter gradually supplant authority altogether. That has actually been the history of the Biblical stories in cognitive criticism. The conflicts within the Bible have led to cognitive criticism, which has led to doubt concerning its infallibility, which has led to the consideration of the Bible as a mere human document recording Hebrew mythology and history and subject to all the failings of human chroniclers. Infallible authorities cannot conflict with themselves or with one another without mutual loss of their claim to infallibility.

But what has conduced more to the loss of infallibility for the Bible than internal conflicts or conflicts with other supposedly infallible authorities is conflicts between the Biblical accounts of natural events and the apparently much weaker empirical inferences concerning these events developed by geologists, biologists, chemists, and physicists. The questioning of infallibility by other cognitive criteria has actually done more to break down the claims of infallibility than its own internal dissensions.

Moreover, it is not simply particular infallible authorities such as the Bible that have been discredited, but the very principle of infallibility itself as a cognitive claim. For if a well-acknowledged infallible authority such as the Bible breaks down, how can we reasonably credit any other proposed infallible authority? Infallibility is put forward as an absolute security against doubt. If a good instance of infallibility has once failed, how can we ever trust a claim to infallibility again?

§6. *The dogma of self-evident principles.*—Exactly the same situation holds with respect to cognitive certainty. Here also the difficulties with the claims to certainty are: (1) that claims to certainty often conflict, (2) that a claim to certainty is often questioned in terms of other cognitive criteria, (3) that in the event of conflicting claims to certainty or of a questioning of certainty an appeal is customarily made to other criteria which often attain, as can scarcely be denied, some degree of cognitive success.

Claims to certainty are made with regard to two types of content, namely, principles and factual evidence. At present there is a prevailing willingness to abandon claims of certainty for principles, but not for factual evidence. The axioms of Euclidean geometry were for centuries the mainstay for claims of certainty with respect to principles. Since mathematicians have unanimously given up those claims, acknowledging that the primitive propositions of a mathematical system are not self-evident truths but only postulates for deductions which may or may not be true to fact, or true in fact, the claims of certainty for principles have in large part been abandoned.

The reasons for doubting the self-evidence of the axioms of Euclidean geometry are exactly the same as those for doubting the infallibility of Biblical statements. Other self-consistent geometrical systems were developed from sets of primitive propositions which were in conflict with the Euclidean set. There was as much reason to claim the self-evidence, or the certain truth, of these novel sets as of the Euclidean. Since these claims to certainty were in conflict, the mathematicians gave up all claims to certainty with respect to primitive propositions, and changed the names of such propositions from axioms to postulates.

Secondly, to clinch this decision, come the experimental results of recent physics which lead to the theory of relativity and a description of physical space in non-Euclidean or partly non-Euclidean terms. Empirical criteria come into conflict with the self-evidence or certainty of the Euclidean axioms, and the claim of self-evidence or certainty gave way to the claim of probability with regard to the structure of physical space.

Moreover, as in the case of infallible authority, it should be noted that the breakdown of the claim to self-evidence for this outstanding instance carries with it all other supposed instances. The criterion of self-evidence itself is discredited. For if in one good instance the criterion of self-evidence fails, how can it ever be trusted again? The criterion could not have been better tested than in the example of the Euclidean axioms. These for centuries were accepted as self-evident by the keenest minds. If the claim must be abandoned for these, how can it be legitimately offered for the truth of any other principles?

But surely the Laws of Thought, or at least the most indispensable of them, the principle of contradiction, must be self-evident. Surely "A is not non-A" is certain. I answer; "Quite surely it is a true principle, but not because it is self-evident. My knowledge of the fate of many dozens of principles once dignified with the claim of self-evidence makes me doubt the reliability of that claim. And if apparent self-evidence were all that could be offered as a ground for the truth of the principle of contradiction, I should be nearly justified in disbelieving its truth. I do believe that it is true, but only on empirical and hypothetical grounds."

"But," continues my shocked mentor, "thinking would be impossible without it and logic would be destroyed." "It may be that thinking would be impossible without it," I reply, "but is not that fact the chief empirical ground for believing the principle true?"

"But its contradictory is inconceivable and implies a self-contradiction. For who can conceive the principle 'A is non-A'? And note that this very statement itself is self-contradictory. For if 'A is non-A,' then you can substitute A for non-A and you find that 'A is A,' whence it follows that A is not non-A, which demonstrates a self-contradiction." I reply, "As for conceivability, the contradictory of the principle of contradiction seems to be conceivable at least in the sense that it can be symbolized as 'A is non-A.' And as for this principle's implying a self-contradiction, what is more to be expected? There are empirical grounds for believing it to be false, but that the contradictory of the principle of contradiction should imply that self-contradiction is itself an expression of self-contradiction does not appear remarkable nor any ground in itself for considering it false or its contradictory true. The argument seems to beg the question by assuming the truth of the principle of contradiction. Moreover, the claim of self-evidence is automatically lost the moment it must be argued for. If self-evidence must find evidence for itself elsewhere, it is no longer self-evidence. When the certainty of the truth of a principle can only be established on the grounds of the certainty of the falsity of another principle (its contradictory), it has relegated its claim of self-evidence to its contradictory. It is hard to see how the falsity of self-contradiction is any more self-evident than the truth of noncontradiction."

So let those logicians, and others who will, juggle with this principle, which is likely to be the last pillbox of defense for the supporters of self-evident principles. Let us simply repeat and again repeat the one telling fact on this matter: that many time-honored and highly credited self-evident principles have been found to be in conflict either with one another or with empirically established principles, and have accordingly been discredited as false or later recredited as only probable or postulable. When there are so many instances of error in the products of a criterion of knowledge which purports to be free from error, there would seem to be adequate grounds for discrediting the criterion itself.

§7. *The dogma of indubitable fact.*—We turn next to the claims of certainty for factual evidence. These are the claims of certainty for intuitions of content, sense immediacy, sense data, the offerings of common sense, the stubborn facts of science, or anything supposedly given. The continental rationalists of the seventeenth and eighteenth centuries tended to lean most heavily on the self-evidence of principles, but the English empiricists tended to lean on the indubitability of the facts given. A so-called empiricist may consequently be just as dogmatic as a rationalist. The dogmatic empiricist discredits the self-evidence of principles, believing that these are only inductions from facts. Principles are accordingly subject to the errors of induction, which may be either slips of reasoning or hasty generalizations from inadequate evidence. But as for the facts, at least the ultimate facts upon which inductions are based, these are certain. This type of empiricism is probably the prevalent view on all sides today. It is exactly as unjustifiable, and on exactly the same grounds, as dogmatic authoritarianism or dogmatic rationalism.

First, descriptions of indubitable facts conflict with one another. Second, descriptions of indubitable facts conflict with hypothetical descriptions of facts supported by corroborative evidence. Third, when doubt is cast upon a description of an indubitable fact as a result of either of the preceding types of difficulty, there is no recourse except to considerations of corroborative evidence; and such recourse has been apparently successful so often as to suggest that the criterion of factual indubitability is not a reliable criterion.

The history of science and philosophy is full of "indubitable facts" which have been discarded as false or have been reinterpreted in more conservative ways. We shall meet many of these in the succeeding chapters. Probably no extensive hypothesis has ever been put forward but some of its ablest proponents have sought to support it on grounds of indubitable evidence. Subsequently the evidence has shown signs of being colored by the concepts of the hypothesis it was supposed to support. As with the criteria of infallible authority and of self-evidence, when the criterion of factual indubitability fails in one fair instance, how can it ever be trusted again? It has, as we shall see, failed repeatedly and under the fairest conditions. Indeed, the principal cognitive issues of the present day center about the problem of what are the facts rather than about the problem of what inferences can be drawn from them.

Let us take one instance of conflicting descriptions of indubitable fact by two of the ablest philosophers of the present day.

When I see a tomato there is much that I can doubt. I can doubt whether it is a tomato that I am seeing, and not a cleverly painted piece of wax. I can doubt whether there is any material thing there at all. Perhaps what I took for a tomato was really a reflection; perhaps I am even the victim of some hallucination. One thing however I cannot doubt: that there exists a red patch of a round and somewhat bulgy shape, standing out from a background of other colour-patches, and having a certain visual depth, and that this whole field of colour is directly present to my consciousness. What the red patch is, whether a substance, or a state of a substance, or an event, whether it is physical or psychical or neither, are questions that we may doubt about. But that something is red and round then and there I cannot doubt. Whether the something persists even for a moment before and after it is present to my consciousness, whether other minds can be conscious of it as well as I, may be doubted. But that it now *exists,* and that *I* am conscious of it—by me at least who am conscious of it this cannot possibly be doubted. And when I say that it is "directly" present to my consciousness, I mean that my consciousness of it is not reached by inference, nor by any other intellectual process (such as abstraction or intuitive induction) nor by any passage from sign to significate. There obviously must be some sort or sorts of presence to consciousness which can be called "direct" in this sense, else we should have an infinite regress. Analogously, when I am in the situations called "touching something," "hearing it," "smelling it," etc., in each case there is something which at that moment indubitably exists—a pressure (or prement patch), a noise, a smell; and that something is directly present to my consciousness.

This peculiar and ultimate manner of being present to consciousness is called *being given,* and that which is thus present is called a *datum.* The corresponding mental attitude is called *acquaintance, intuitive apprehension,* or sometimes *having.* Data of this special sort are called *sense-data.*[1]

The crucial phrases in this passage are, "that something is red and round then and there I cannot doubt. . . . that it now *exists,* and that *I* am conscious of it—by me at least who am conscious of it this cannot possibly be doubted. And when I say that it is 'directly' present to my consciousness, I mean that my consciousnes of it is not reached by inference, nor by any other intellectual process." These phrases are repeated so as to show Price's italics as they stand.

I think anybody familiar with the analytical methods of Price's general school of thought will be amazed at how much he indubitably knows whenever he looks at a tomato, and how highly articulated and itemized his knowledge is! It appears that we indubitably know (1) an entity

---

[1] H. H. Price, *Perception* (London: Methuen, 1932), p. 3.

that may be called "something," (2) existence, (3) qualities like "red" and "round," (4) temporal location like
"then," (5) spatial location like "there" (cf. footnote,
" 'There' means in spatial relations to other colour-patches
present to my consciousness at the same time"), (6) "I,"
(7) consciousness. Possibly in a different way the "peculiar and ultimate manner of being present to consciousness called *being given*" is also indubitable. But we are
assured that "we may doubt about" the question whether
the red patch which we see is "an event."

With this assurance concerning what we may doubt we
turn with some interest to Dewey, who in his first chapter
of *Experience and Nature*[2] offers quite a different picture
of the indubitable.

The experiential or denotative method [he affirms] tells us
that we must go behind the refinements and elaborations of reflective experience to the gross and compulsory things of our
doings, enjoyments and sufferings [p. 16]. . . . *Being* angry,
stupid, wise, inquiring; *having* sugar, the light of day, money,
houses and lands, friends, laws, masters, subjects, pain and joy,
occur in dimensions incommensurable to knowing these things
which we are and have and use, and which have and use us. Their
existence is unique, and, strictly speaking, indescribable; they
can *only be* and be *had*, and then pointed to in reflection. In the
proper sense of the word, their existence is absolute, being qualitative. All cognitive experience must start from and must terminate in being and having things in just such unique, irreparable
and compelling ways [p. 19]. . . . A man may doubt whether he
has the measles, because measles is an intellectual term, a classification, but he cannot doubt what he empirically has—not as has
so often been asserted because he has an immediately certain
knowledge of it, but because it is not a matter of knowledge, an
intellectual affair, at all, not an affair of truth or falsity, certitude,

---

[2] *Experience and Nature* (Chicago: Open Court, 1925).

or doubt, but one of existence. He may not know that he is ailing, much less what his ailment is; but unless there is something immediately and noncognitively present in experience so that it is capable of being pointed to in subsequent reflection and in action which embodies the fruits of reflection, knowledge has neither subject-matter nor objective. In traditional epistomologies, this fact has been both recognized and perverted; it is said that while we can doubt whether a particular thing is red or sweet, we have an immediate or intuitive cognitive certitude that we are affected by redness or sweetness or have a sensation of sweet and red. But as cognized, red and sweet are data only because they are *taken* in thought. Their givenness is something imputed; they are primary and immediate relatively to more complex processes of inquiry. It required a high degree of intellectual specialization, backed by technical knowledge of the nervous system, before even the concept of sensory data could emerge. It still taxes the resources of investigation to determine just what are 'immediate data' in a particular problem. To know a quality *as* sensation is to have performed an act of complicated objective reference; it is not to register an inherently given property. The epistomological sensationalist and the epistomological rationalist share the same error; belief that cognitive property is intrinsic, borne on the face [pp. 21–22].

According to Dewey, then, "we must go behind the refinements and elaborations of reflective experience" such as Price indulges in, "to the gross and compulsory things of our doings." According to Dewey, we may doubt about these reflective refinements and elaborations, "their givenness is something imputed," but what we cannot doubt and what alone we cannot doubt is the denoted event. This is the gross compulsory thing of our doing that goes behind all analyses and is so incapable of being doubted that it is "not an affair of truth or falsity, certitude, or doubt, but one of existence."

Now, it is quite clear that in some sense Price and Dewey are looking at the same tomato. And yet what one finds certain and indubitable in the situation, the other finds dubious or downright false. The event character of everything in the situation is indubitable for Dewey; it is confused, uncertain, and dubitable for Price. As to the indubitability and dubitability of everything in the situation, there is complete disagreement. This disagreement is, moreover, based on causes which I believe I can show later are endemic to the methods of thinking of the two men. All I wish to show now is the unreliability of the criterion of factual certainty. Here are conflicting claims of indubitability made by two of the best-recognized thinkers of the present day. If one or the other or both have been mistaken about what is indubitable, how can we ever be sure that other claims of indubitability are not mistakes? If we cannot be sure, then the criterion of indubitability is automatically discredited, since its purport is precisely that we can be sure.

"But," it may be contended, "you must not discredit a criterion just because it is sometimes misused. Everybody makes mistakes. Dewey perhaps senses that there is something indubitable about the perception of a tomato, but fails to analyze the grounds for his feeling. If he traced his feeling to its source, he would perhaps find that Price is right and the disagreement would be dissipated." "Yes," I reply, "my whole point is that everybody makes mistakes, and therefore nobody's claim of indubitability is utterly reliable. Such claims must always be checked up with corroborative evidence. Consequently, nothing is indubitable, for we mean by indubitable a self-sufficient cognitive criterion. My criticism holds whether Dewey can ever be brought to agree with Price or not."

"But surely," insists the champion of indubitables, "there must be some indubitable facts or there would be no knowledge. Notice that Price and Dewey both agree about that. For Price says that 'there obviously must be some sort or sorts of presence to consciousness which we call "direct," else we should have an infinite regress,' and Dewey: 'All cognitive experience must start from and must terminate in being and having things.' Facts obviously are what they are, and to doubt every fact on the ground that it contains or may contain some interpretation is to make it impossible ever to reach a fact. We should then never have any evidence for anything."

"This infinite-regress argument," I reply, "is more plausible than credible. In the first place, when persons are earnestly in pursuit of the facts, is it ever safe to smother doubts? To argue that we must accept somebody's claims of indubitability because we might otherwise be left without any evidence is like arguing that we ought to accept counterfeit bills for fear we might otherwise be left without any money. All we need to do when such fears attack us is to consider the position of the utter skeptic. That position, we saw, is untenable. There is no danger of our becoming destitute of facts. But when we take up any fact to examine it, how pure a fact is it? That is the problem. And the hypothesis is not, so far as one can see at the present moment, a ridiculous one to suppose that every fact we pick up has some impurities in it. Now the criterion

of indubitability virtually asserts that there are some pure
facts which men can take up and that these can be credited
on sight without further test or corroboration with other
facts. I have suggested reasons for doubting such an assertion. There may be no pure facts in our reach, and if there
are I doubt they can be distinguished on sight from impure facts. Certainly past history has not given us much
encouragement on that score."

"I begin to understand the source of our difficulties,"
says the proponent of indubitables. "You have been talk-
ing not about facts, but about descriptions of facts. Of
course, descriptions will disagree and all descriptions are
dubitable. Price describes the perception of a tomato one
way, Dewey another. But the fact is just what it is. What
happens in an experience is just what happens. There can
be no question about that. And that naturally is what is indubitable."

I answer: "This observation does not remove the difficulty. As we shall see in due time, there is great divergency
of competent opinion concerning where to find what happens. Where do we draw the boundaries of what happens?
At the outskirts of my consciousness, or at the ends of the
universe? Too often men have excused themselves from
examining their ideas about what happens, or about what
is, by leaning on the pleasant maxim of 'What happens,
happens,' or of 'Whatever is, is.' But our problem is, 'What
does happen?' and precisely 'What is?' and the history
of thought seems to indicate that we never exactly know,
or, at least, know that we know. We do have to describe
and interpret, and even Dewey's innocent-looking 'denota-

tions' are actually descriptions and interpretations, for he distinctly denotes matters different from Price's matters and disparages Price's matters as subsequent reflective interpretations false to the gross doings they were supposed literally to be. Both of these men believe that they are transparently exhibiting what happens or what is. Both, I am quite sure, are deceived. The result is that under the cover of 'What is, is' and 'What happens, happens' these men fail to notice that what they offer as pure facts are actually descriptions with (who knows how much) distortive interpretation. Let me put the matter the other way about: Show me any way of presenting evidence that does not contain the possibility of some degree of interpretation."

"Just now you said," retorts the champion of indubitables, "that 'what they offer as pure facts are actually descriptions.' What did you mean by 'actually' if not the actual fact that occurred there—in this instance the fact of a man making a description? You cannot deny that that fact is just what it is and not anything else."

I reply, "Do not forget that we are discussing criteria for evidence. Now, show me the indubitable fact about that fact."

"Why," the retort continues, "the fact that it is precisely that fact."

"Is that a fact," I ask, "or is it not rather a statement of an ideal regarding facts?"

"But what can be ideal about fact? Is not a fact a fact?"

"I should never wish to deny that," I reply, "for I have not forgotten the ironical fate of the utter skeptic. We are surrounded and immersed in facts and we can never get away from them nor out of them, for even the escape from facts would be a fact, if that were possible. But our problem is to know what is a fact and by what criteria it can be known. There is little comfort for this inquiry in the discovery that whatever we do, or say, or doubt, or deny is itself a fact."

"But that is indubitable, is it not?" interrupts the champion of this criterion.

"I do not think so," I reply. "It seems to me to be a discovery arising from reflection over what we mean by ultimate evidence, supported by observations of cognitive procedure. And that is just why I believe that your principle, 'A fact is a fact' (and note that it is a principle and not a fact, and so, in the terminology into which we have drifted, might be self-evident but not indubitable), is a statement of a cognitive ideal. As a statement of principle offered as true—something to the effect that the aim of all empirical cognitive procedure is to grasp, intuit, denote, describe (what you will) something that purely is or happens, and that this aim is theoretically if not practically attainable—as a statement of this sort, your principle is as much an empirical principle as Euclid's axioms or Newton's three Laws of Motion, and is just as dubitable or corrigible or whatever you accept as an opposite of indubitable or self-evident."

"Of course, an ideal," interposes our critic, "is never either true or false. It is in the nature of a volitional injunction or an emotional hope."

"If that is so," I answer, "it is obviously irrelevant to our present purpose of seeking reliable cognitive criteria.

But your statement sounds to me a good deal like something that purports to be true and indubitably so. On the basis of our discussions, I am doubtful of its truth, apart from supporting evidence."

"It is merely a definition," our critic informs us. "It is consequently meaningless to attribute truth or falsity to it. It is an analytical expression stating, as pertinent to our discussion, what we shall mean by an ideal. Whether any ideals exist or not is irrelevant to the definition. So, you see, one cannot doubt it, since it does not say anything."

"And since it does not say anything, it is meaningless?" I ask, just a bit maliciously.

"Oh no," I am informed, "in a definition the predicate supplies the meaning that is to be given to the subject. The subject term is to be used in the manner prescribed by the predicate term in the expression. A definition merely prescribes a meaning. It is purely analytical and arbitrary. As such, it cannot be significantly doubted."

"But are you not," I ask, "denoting a class of facts and even describing them when you assert that definitions are injunctions of the sort you specify? Are you not describing definitions as facts? And do you not need evidence for this description?"

Thus, this simple criterion of the indubitable fact spreads into an argument over all the issues of logic. For I have simply been summarizing the current argument on this topic. We suspect that the champion of the indubitable fact must himself have become a little uncertain. Why else should he present so many reasons for what by definition needs none? His dilemma is extreme. For if he argues for his criterion of indubitability, he implicitly admits a dubitability; and if he does not argue for it, his criterion is unsupported. The dilemma arises from the fact that highly credited "indubitable facts" have frequently conflicted with other highly credited "indubitable facts." When this happens, the opponents may silently glare at each other or call each other names, the contradiction acknowledged by both remaining unresolved; or they may bring forward reasons and corroborative evidence, but then the appeal is away from indubitability to probability. In either case, indubitability as a reliable criterion of fact is discredited. And once this criterion has been discredited in a well-authenticated instance such as that of Price and Dewey, how can it be credited again?

In practice these dogmatic criteria which we have been reviewing—infallibility, certainty, self-evidence, indubitability, and their latest allies definitional prescription or injunction, and the analytic proposition—have only the effect of blocking cognitive progress for a while. The evidence finally breaks through if the questions involved are important—unless some powerful authoritarian social institution imposes its dogmatism, and even then the evidence eventually seems to break through. Meantime, these dogmatic criteria may be, as they have been, prodigious obstacles to cognitive progress and clarity of judgment.

Men may be dogmatists without employing the above-named criteria, for dogmatism is any belief in excess of the available evidence, but when hereafter I mention dogmatism as a cognitive fallacy I shall mean (unless I state otherwise) the use of these criteria in support of belief.

§8. *Legitimate uses of authority and certainty.*—In thus sweeping away the criteria of infallible authority and cognitive certainty, it must not be assumed that there is no ground for belief in authority or the feeling of certainty. Authority is a legitimate and socially indispensable secondary criterion of cognitive belief. But we legitimately credit an authority, not because whatever he utters is true, but because he utters, we trust, only what he believes to be true. We legitimately credit an authority, not because he is an ultimate source of knowledge, but because he is not. We believe he is a reliable mediator and transmitter of knowledge the ultimate validity of which lies elsewhere.

Similarly with the *feeling* of certainty. This feeling is an excellent sign of factuality and even of the probability of empirical principles. What we feel certain about is generally very trustworthy. But the feeling is not what constitutes its trustworthiness. The feeling is something which accrues to experiences that are habitual or particularly consonant with our mental and physical make-up. So far as we are well adjusted to our environment the things we feel certain of are very likely to be true. In practice we probably trust this feeling more than any other cognitive criterion. But it is not an ultimate criterion and it frequently leads to error. As a contributory cognitive criterion it is not only acceptable, but by no means lightly to be ignored. We ourselves shall not ignore it.

Authority and the feeling of certainty properly understood are legitimate cognitive criteria, but never infallible authority nor utter certainty. The importance of emphatically noticing these fallacies at the start is that hereafter we shall need only to name them to dispose of them. They crop up in cognitive inquiries so often and in such subtle and oblique ways that unless their illegitimacy is pointed out as a general fallacy of method at a time when no vital issue is immediately pending, much time and effort would have to be spent in exposing them on each occasion at which they should occur. Moreover, their illegitimacy is rarely apparent in the single case, though clear enough in a survey of their uses over a broad field of knowledge.

Lastly, before leaving this subject, we must observe that these criteria of infallibility and certainty add nothing to the cognitive grounds or content to which they are applied. If I assert that I perceive a red tomato, nothing is added to the material of my perception by my putting "certainly" in front of the assertion. This adverb does not add even the evidence of the "feeling of certainty," for that feeling is implied in the verb "perceive." If I had not "felt certain" that I saw a red tomato, I should not have asserted that I "perceived" it, but only that I "thought I saw" it. The "certainly" in "I *certainly* perceive a red tomato" or in "I *certainly* think I see a red tomato," has only one effect, and that is to forbid us to question the assertion or to seek other evidence for its truth. And this prohibition is unavailing to a man who has had considerable cognitive experience, for he will question it anyway, if much depends upon it. What is the use, then, of adding it?

These dogmatic criteria, therefore, are not only illegitimate; they are useless. We shall, accordingly, ourselves never appeal to them, nor shall we permit ourselves to be imposed upon by others who do appeal to them.

Chapter III : Evidence and Corroboration

§1. *Common sense.*—If the conclusion of the last chapter is correct, namely, that there is no certain evidence of any kind, then where shall knowledge begin? The pathos of the question betrays the assumption behind it. For why should knowledge begin with certainties? Why should it not dawn like day out of a half-light of semiknowledge and gradually grow to clarity and illumination?

There appear to be two broad types of evidence: uncriticized, and criticized or refined evidence. Socially and individually, knowledge begins with the former and gradually passes into the latter. So let us begin by considering uncriticized evidence.

We often call this sort of evidence common sense. Plato called it "opinion." It has been called "preanalytical data," and "middle-sized fact." All these terms are useful; but no term could be wholly satisfactory, because "satisfactory" here tends to mean critically sound and what we wish to denote is something precritical and probably not critically sound.

Uncriticized, common-sense facts are the sort of things we think of when we ordinarily read the daily papers or novels depicting the ordinary life of men or the sort of things we see and hear and smell and feel as we walk along the street or in the country: that is the sound of a bird;

it is three thousand miles across the continent; trains run every day on schedule, except in case of accident; there is space and there is time; the laws of nature have to quite a degree been discovered by scientists and the world runs according to them and scientists can predict by means of them; astronomers can predict eclipses with perfect accuracy; dreams are not true; three is a lucky number; it is perhaps wiser not to go under a ladder, because paint or something might fall on one; God exists quite certainly, or, at least, probably; science says that I am made up of chemicals; my soul may be immortal; I can make free choices; pleasures are good and pains are bad; do to others as you would be done by; turn the other cheek; an eye for an eye and a tooth for a tooth; men are born equal; the best man wins; bigamists are immoral, unless they are Turks; Turks are funny people and probably immoral—and so on. Something like this is the material of present-day common sense in America.

If we examine material of this sort, we note certain traits. First, it is not definitely cognizable. Any attempt to exhibit, or describe, or specify any of this material definitely in detail generally carries us out of the material. What was uncriticized fact immediately turns into criticized fact, and generally a transformation of the material takes place as a result of the attempt. We cannot at this moment tell whether the transformation is distortion or realization of the material, but in terms of common sense the material does often change in appearance.

We have already had a good example of such transmogrification in Price's red tomato. When he first mentioned the object it was a typical example of a common-sense fact, but by the time he finished his paragraph describing the tomato in detail it had become a highly criticized fact. Deducting from the description its dogmatic elements, we see that it was a penetrating critical hypothesis of the factual perception of a tomato. To remove any doubt of our judgment, we have contrasted Price's description with one by Dewey of similar facts. Here, then, under our eyes we have seen how an uncriticized common-sense fact became converted into two criticized uncommon-sense facts. There is the common-sense tomato, Price's criticized tomato, and Dewey's criticized tomato. Price and Dewey, moreover, agree that they are both accurately exhibiting the common-sense tomato. But their two exhibitions of that tomato are incompatible—to a degree which we shall fully realize only many pages farther on. And the uncriticized red tomato of the man in the street is not (except rarely) identifiable literally with either Price's or Dewey's tomato.

Which is the real tomato? Any one of them might be. Probably none of them is. To declare for any one of them without full consideration of evidence—that is, without criticism—would be dogmatic. But all we desire to note at present is that the common-sense tomato is evidence. It is not certain evidence. It is probably well loaded with more or less hidden interpretation. But it is a fact of a sort, though not (as a rule) definitely describable. Indeed, it is a fact of a sort because not definitely describable, for that trait alone separates a common-sense fact from any carefully described criticized fact. And to ignore the difference would be to ignore some available evidence.

The first trait of a common-sense fact, then, is that it is not definitely cognized and generally not definitely cognizable. For such definite cognition immediately converts it into criticized fact. The same is true of all common-sense material, whether we should care to call it roughly fact, principle, belief, feeling, or what not. There is no implication in this assertion, of course, that whatever is the fact or the truth in a common-sense matter is not what it is. We simply cannot have any assurance that we know what it is without criticism. But then the matter ceases to be uncriticized and generally considerably changes in appearance.

A second trait of common-sense material is its security. Critical cognitions of the red tomato may come and go, diverge and conflict, but the common-sense tomato or something there, call it what you will, insists on cognition. This does not imply that some items of common sense do not disappear in the course of history. A great deal of common-sense material, we may be quite sure, is ancient or modern myth, science, and philosophy that has seeped down to an uncritical level, so that a highly criticized belief such as that water is H_2O may be an item of common sense, as also that water is one of the four elements. One of these beliefs is a very recent accession to common sense, the other very ancient. Both came out of highly criticized cognition, and both may yet disappear from common sense. Common sense is not stable. But it is secure in that it is never lacking. It is, as we have noticed, an ultimate rebuke to the utter skeptic. Water may not be H_2O, nor an element. Price's and Dewey's tomatoes, and dozens of other tomatoes, may be critically full of holes. The very word, tomato, may be abandoned. Nevertheless, common sense will not let us down. Water somehow and tomato in some way will always be waiting to receive the weary cognizer, however discouraged he may be in his search for perfect cognition. Even though in the anger of despair he loudly denies the existence of either water or tomato, the one still quenches his thirst and the other nourishes his body. No cognition can sink lower than common sense, for when we completely give up trying to know anything, then is precisely when we know things in the common-sense way. In that lies the security of common sense.

But, thirdly, common sense is cognitively irritable. Secure as common sense is, and grateful as we may be to it for its limitless store of materials for cognition, still as cognizers the more we know it the less we like it. This attitude, I believe, is true even for men like Dewey, who profess to champion common sense, for in their careful critical defense they do not quite take common sense at its word. The materials of common sense are changing, unchanging, contradictory, vague, rigid, muddled, melodramatically clear, unorganized, rationalized, dogmatic, shrewdly dubious, recklessly dubious, piously felt, playfully enjoyed, and so forth. One may accept common sense and thoughtlessly roam in its pastures, but if one looks up and tries to take it in, it is like a fantastic dream. To the serious cognizer it is like a bad dream. For the serious cognizer feels responsible to fact and principle, and common sense is utterly irresponsible. It accepts the principle of contradiction and ignores it. It insists upon a fact and equally insists upon its contrary. It is vague and clear without reason, capriciously, and seemingly in the wrong places—clear about a superstition, for instance, and vague about a tomato,—or it may be both at once, as with water. Sometimes it will stand up to unlimited criticism, and then again break down at the first critical probing. It is unreliable, irresponsible, and, in a word, irritable.

§2. *Tension between common sense and refined knowledge.*—This is a strange set of traits for an important mass of cognitive material—to be not definitely cognizable, to be not cognitively responsible and so irritable, and yet to be cognitively secure. The first two traits in the order just indicated are negative in the eyes of knowledge; only the last is positive. The first two traits are, in fact, so displeasing to experts of cognition that the material of common sense has very frequently been ignored as a respectable factor in cognition. And so, on this side, we find common sense, the opinions of the man in the street, disparaged and ridiculed in comparison with the definite and responsible knowledge of science and philosophy. Yet, on the other side, the security of common sense does not wholly escape the attention of men, nor can men wholly ignore an insecurity in the abstract concepts, the hairsplitting definitions, the speculative hypotheses of expert critical knowledge. So, on this score, common sense becomes an object of praise for its simple homespun wisdom and plain practical sense.

This tension between common sense and expert knowledge, between cognitive security without responsibility and cognitive responsibility without full security, is the interior dynamics of the knowledge situation. The indefiniteness of much detail in common sense, its contradictions, its lack of established grounds, drive thought to seek definiteness, consistency, and reasons. Thought finds these in the criticized and refined knowledge of mathematics, science, and philosophy, only to discover that these tend to thin out into arbitrary definitions, pointer readings, and tentative hypotheses. Astounded at the thinness and hollowness of these culminating achievements of conscientiously responsible cognition, thought seeks matter for its definitions, significance for its pointer readings, and support for its wobbling hypotheses. Responsible cognition finds itself insecure as a result of the very earnestness of its virtues. But where shall it turn? It does, in fact, turn back to common sense, that indefinite and irresponsible source which it so lately scorned. But it does so, generally, with a bad grace. After filling its empty definitions and pointer readings and hypotheses with meanings out of the rich confusion of common sense, it generally turns its head away, shuts its eyes to what it has been doing, and affirms dogmatically the self-evidence and certainty of the common-sense significance it has drawn into its concepts. Then it pretends to be securely based on self-evident principles or indubitable facts. If our recent criticism of dogmatism is correct, however, this security in self-evidence and indubitability has proved questionable. And critical knowledge hangs over a vacuum unless it acknowledges openly the actual, though strange, source of its significance and security in the uncriticized material of common sense. Thus the circle is completed. Common sense continually demands the responsible criticism of refined knowledge, and refined knowledge sooner or later requires the security of common-sense support.

Why cannot the two merge? No doubt, that is the inherent aim of cognition. For what the question amounts to is, Why is there any ignorance? It is clear that the answer to such a question can only be given with any specificity in terms of refined knowledge. We shall presently have several answers in terms of the best cognitive hypotheses we possess. But it seems fairly obvious that as long as refined knowledge is not complete, so long at least will there be a discrepancy between the material of common sense and that of critical cognition. For, considering the situation at its worst, even the extremest efforts of dictatorial propaganda cannot stop those insistent questionings that well up in the most innocent as also in the most sophisticated minds.

Whence do these questionings well up, which are the signs of the obstinate security of common sense? For though man reason himself into a machine, into a solipsism of the present moment, into Nirvana, or into Nothing, life still breaks out in hunger and craving, and nature affirms itself in the strong pressure of the ground and the heat of the sun. There is no doubt of these common-sense insistences, but if we seek the reasons for them we can find them only in refined critical knowledge. We shall find several good reasons in terms of our best critical hypotheses. But until ignorance completely disappears we cannot expect a specific and fully adequate answer.

Such, then, is the basic polarity of cognition, which we may expect to continue as long as we fall short of omniscience. On the one side, irresponsible but secure common sense; on the other, responsible but insecure critical cognition. We therefore acknowledge the importance and legitimacy of common-sense facts as evidence even in the face of the most polished critical evidence. We regret the instability and irresponsibility of common sense and shall therefore weigh it judiciously, but we shall not ignore it. Because of its need of criticism, we shall find it convenient to call a common-sense fact a *dubitandum,* an item of evidence that ought to be doubted.

§3. *Types of corroboration in refined knowledge.—* From uncriticized evidence we now turn to criticized evidence. Uncriticized evidence, as the term itself suggests, is accepted without reflection. It is not taken as certain or self-evident, for such cognitive evaluations are reflective additions. It is simply accepted. Even if an item of common-sense evidence is taken as doubtful, like tomorrow's weather, it is simply accepted as such. Reflective or critical certainty and doubt are quite different from the unreflective, uncritical assurance or canniness of common sense. If we drop the dogmatism of reflective certainty, then all critical evidence becomes critical only as a result of the addition of corroborative evidence. The work of legitimate criticism in cognition, then, is corroboration. And the value of the evidence is in proportion to its expected corroboration.

There are two types of corroboration and accordingly two types of critical evidence. There is corroboration of man with man, and corroboration of fact with fact. Let us call the first "multiplicative corroboration" and the second "structural corroboration." And let us call the products of multiplicative corroboration "data," and the products of structural corroboration "danda." We shall justify these names later.

Now, these two types of corroboration can be found in common sense, or very close to common sense. For there is no sudden leap from uncriticized to criticized fact. Common sense has the germs of criticism in it and performs some degree of criticism by itself. Or rather, viewed from the perspective of highly criticized fact, rough criticism appears closer to common sense than to science, mathematics, or metaphysics. To refer to this factual material which lies between highly criticized data and danda at one extreme and wholly uncriticized dubitanda at the other, we may use the terms "rough data" and "rough danda." We shall find this distinction between data and danda proper, and rough data and rough danda, very useful in avoiding certain cognitive pitfalls.

But to give a simple preliminary idea of the contrast between multiplicative and structural corroboration it will be helpful first to exemplify these in terms of rough data and rough danda, that is, essentially in common-sense terms.

Suppose I want to know whether a certain chair is strong enough to take a man's weight. I may sit in it myself. Perhaps I sit in it several times, taking this posture and that and dropping down in it with some force. And then, to be quite sure, I ask several of my friends to try sitting in it. If we all agree that the chair supports us firmly, we may feel justified in believing that the chair is a strong chair.

Or I may use another method. I may examine the relevant facts about the chair. I may consider the kind of wood it is made of, the thickness of the pieces, the manner in which they are joined together, the nails and the glue employed, the fact that it was made by a firm that for many years has turned out serviceable furniture, the fact that the chair is an item of household furniture at an auction and shows evidence of wear as if many people had successfully sat in it, and so on. Putting all this evidence together, I should again feel justified in believing that the chair is a strong chair.

Whichever I do, my belief is clearly based on a cumulative corroboration of evidence. But the nature of the corroboration differs with the two methods employed. In the first trial, it consists in what may be roughly called a repetition of the same fact. I agree with myself in many repeated observations, and my friends agree with me that the chair was strong. In the second, the corroboration comes from an agreement of many different facts in the determination of the nature of one central fact. In the first, the persuasive force of the corroboration comes from the number of observations and even more from the number of men who agree about them. It is a social force. In the second, the persuasive force comes from the massiveness of convergent evidence upon the same point of fact. It is the structural force of the evidence itself and is not peculiarly social.

The first method seems to be predominantly one of observation; the second, one of hypothesis. This is roughly correct, though the further criticism is carried the less does this distinction count, and at the very end the situation appears almost reversed. The highly refined data are observations sharpened to so fine an edge that the highly refined danda seem to contain much more observation. We shall presently have many occasions to notice this.

It may seem also from these two instances that the first has unquestionable priority over the second. If one can get a number of corroborating observations, it seems foolish to spend time over a hypothesis. This also is roughly correct, though again the further criticism is carried the less are we likely to insist on this priority. A highly refined datum would probably never have to give way to a highly refined dandum, but only because the datum has been thinned to such a degree that it does not commit itself to very much. And as for rough data, they constantly give way to established hypotheses. Ghosts, for example, are repeatedly observed by earnest persons, and consistently doubted by most scientists and philosophers. Ghosts are doubted because as observed facts they do not fit into the structure of accredited theories and because in terms of these theories they can be easily explained away as highly interpreted perceptions. Take even our example of the chair, and slightly change the circumstances. Suppose a considerable structure of evidence had converged upon the belief that the chair was not strong, but weak, and then suppose somebody had sat in it and the chair had not broken down. Would we be more likely to doubt the hypothesis, or the observation? Wouldn't we be more likely to interpret the observation to fit the hypothesis? Perhaps the person who sat in the chair was unusually light, or didn't put his whole weight on it, or sat in such a way as not to put a strain on the weak parts, or perhaps he never sat in it at all, but only gave us the illusion that he had. Of course, if a number of persons sat in the chair without its breaking, we should discard the hypothesis. But the question is one of proportion, and it appears that structural evidence does not give way to multiplicative evidence, unless the latter is based on very considerable agreement among many observers and unless it cannot be interpreted to fit the hypothesis which organized the structural evidence.

It appears, then, that between the two types of critical evidence there is a tension somewhat comparable to that between critical evidence as a whole and uncritical common-sense evidence. Data and danda vie with each other in somewhat the same way that these together vie with dubitanda. The issue between data and danda, however, is entirely open to view, because both are critical and refined, and agree in seeking a solution by carrying criticism and refinement to the maximum. The common-sense indefiniteness of such rough data and danda as appeared in our example of strong chair or weak chair drives thought to criticism and refinement. What do these produce? What is the nature of highly refined data and danda?

§4. *Data.*—The standing criticism to which rough data are subjected is that they are not pure observations, but are loaded with interpretation, or, in a word, that they are danda. A datum, as its derivation indicates, is supposed to be something given, and purely given, entirely free from interpretation. The search for multiplicative corroboration is the effort on the part of a datum to confirm its claim to purity. It is as though a datum turned from one observer to another and asked, Am I not just what I said I was? The technical name now being employed to denote the sort of purity here sought after is "invariancy."Are there not some data that never vary, no matter who the observer, and, if possible, no matter what his point of view? If such there are, these are ideal data.

Absolutely ideal data are probably not available, but close approximations to them have been developed in the course of cognitive history. There are two genuses of refined data, and these may be called empirical data and logical data. Refined empirical data consist of pointer readings and correlations among pointer readings. A pointer reading is such a fact as the observation of the position of the hands on the dial of a watch, the position of the top of a mercury column along a scale of temperatures, and the like. A correlation of pointer readings is the observation that two or more pointer readings repeatedly occur in some precisely statable relation. In other words, refined empirical data are precise physical measurements together with their observed relations to one another.

It should be especially noticed that what the measurements are about is not data. The hypotheses which interpret the data are often highly conjectural, and far removed from multiplicative corroboration. For, where data are concerned, the aim is to attain cognitive items so clear and distinct and simple that disagreement about them among men can scarcely arise. That is what has driven multiplicative refinement to pointer readings, and what gives these data such great reliability. No special skill or erudition is needed to note what mark on a dial a black needle rests upon. Anyone with a pair of eyes and a most elementary capacity for following instructions can take a pointer reading. The most brilliant scientist and his most stupid student both easily agree about the reading. Everybody who can look at it can see for himself where the pointer comes. That excessive naïveté, and just that, is what makes the evidence so credible and so refined.

Nothing else in the world has such a degree of credibility in terms of multiplicative corroboration. Tastes, smells, pressures, colors all lack the precision and the publicity of a mark on a rod or pointer on a scale. The pointer reading is a remarkable cognitive development, the importance of which we are just beginning to realize.

A careful study of the refinement of empirical data has been made by Lenzen in the field of physics, where this sort of refinement has reached its apex. He follows the steps of refinement of all the principal physical concepts from their origin in common sense to their highest stage as empirical data. We shall find it worth our while to examine one of his instances:

I first consider the concept of *temperature* and shall begin with a qualitative analysis. The original qualitative basis of this concept is the sensation of hotness or coldness: we touch a body and declare it to be hot, warm, cold, etc. I first explain the concept of equality of two bodies with respect to hotness. At first glance it might appear that the concept of equality with respect to intensity of heat could be based upon the experience that two bodies appear equally hot to touch. This basis is unsatisfactory because the sensation depends upon the kind of material, hence the criterion would lead to contradictions. Our concept of temperature will be defined in such a way that, of two bodies at the same temperature, one may appear colder to the touch than the other, as for example steel and wood.

We shall base the definition of equality with respect to hotness upon the empirical fact that it is possible to bring two bodies into contact and experience no change in hotness in either body. The relation between the bodies is symmetrical, if body A is as hot as B, then B is as hot as A. The relation is also transitive, for, if A is as hot as B, and B is as hot as C, then A is as hot as C. In virtue of this symmetrical and transitive relation between the two bodies we ascribe to them a common character, the same temperature. Thus the concept of temperature is defined on the basis of generalization from experiences of equally hot bodies. By definition, two bodies have the same temperature if, when they are brought into contact, no change in the hotness of either body is experienced.

One body is hotter than another if on contact the first cools and the second becomes warmer. This process will continue until both bodies are at the same temperature. We can arrange bodies according to a scale of hotness: very hot, hot, warm, lukewarm, cool, cold, very cold. Temperature is a nonadditive property: if one joins two bodies equal in temperature, one obtains a body of the same temperature.

The discussion thus far has yielded a concept of temperature, but one which is not satisfactory because of the impossibility of making discriminating and reproducible estimates of temperature by our temperature senses. A physical concept of temperature is based upon the empirical fact that as a body changes in hotness certain correlated measurable properties change; for example, the volume of a body generally increases upon heating. Hence one can define *changes* of temperature in terms of the changes of some more accurately measurable property. An instrument which embodies a definition of temperature in terms of some measurable property is called a *thermometer*. The first thermometer was Galileo's air thermometer, which consisted of an inverted bulb with a stem whose open end was in water. The air in the bulb was at less than atmospheric pressure, so that the water rose in the stem above the level in the outer vessel. Changes in hotness of the air in the bulb were indicated by a change in the level of the water in the stem. Such a thermometer defines the physical quantity temperature in terms of changes in volume of air.

There are various possible definitions of temperature in terms of different thermometers. In order to construct a thermometer one must choose: (a) a substance, (b) a property which varies with hotness and coldness, (c) the zero of a scale, (d) the standard unit of a scale. The international standard thermometer is the constant volume hydrogen thermometer. Temperature is defined in terms of the pressure of hydrogen gas at constant volume. Defining the temperature of a mixture of water and ice under a pressure of one atmosphere as 0° Centigrade, and the temperature of steam over boiling water under a pressure of one atmosphere as 100° Centigrade, fixes the zero and the standard unit of the scale. One calibrates the thermometer by noting the pressure of the gas for a given volume at these two fixed points. In determining the fixed points of the thermometer one must wait until temperature equilibrium is established between the gas and the medium in terms of which the fixed points are defined. The meaning of this procedure is based upon our initial definition of temperature and the empirical law that if a hot body and a cold body are placed in contact they gradually come to the same temperature. The definition of the physical quantity temperature is thus based upon a law the meaning of which depends upon a qualitative definition of temperature. Furthermore, the definition of a fixed point depends upon the fact that the pressure of the gas is always the same at the ice-point and steam-point. The definition of the ice-point as 0° C and the steam-point as 100° C is possible in virtue of the fact that ice has a definite melting-point and water a definite boiling-point. Temperature as a physical quantity may now be defined by the equation

$$t = \frac{P_t - P_0}{\dfrac{P_{100} - P_0}{100}}$$

where P_0 is the pressure of the hydrogen gas at 0° C,
P_{100} is the pressure at 100° C,
P_t is the pressure at some temperature t which is to be determined.[1]

---

[1] V. F. Lenzen, *The Nature of Physical Theory* (New York: Wiley, 1931), pp. 133–135.

The concept of temperature begins with the ordinary common-sense feelings of hotness and coldness, and the degrees of these as we touch various objects. These feelings, however, lead to contradictions which show them up as dubitanda. Objects such as steel and wood feel different in temperature and yet for other reasons are believed in common sense to be of the same temperature. The concept is therefore refined on the basis of a common-sense correlation, "the empirical fact that it is possible to bring two bodies into contact and experience no change in the hotness of either body." So, for the evidence of direct feeling is substituted the evidence that when a piece of steel, which feels colder, is brought into contact with a piece of wood, which feels warmer, no difference is felt in the coolness of the one or the warmness of the other. The partly refined fact is that two such bodies will be credited with the same degree of heat, in spite of the contrary evidence of direct touch. This fact, however, is not very discriminating of temperatures. A further refinement is accordingly made on the basis of another correlation (itself rather refined), the observed and measured fact that "the volume of a body generally expands upon heating." An instrument is constructed by means of which this correlation is controlled and standardized in such a way that a reading can be made on a scale. From now on, the refinement consists simply in the perfecting of instruments so as to produce the maximum of precision in the readings and the minimum of variability in comparative readings. To insure uniformity of agreement in temperature readings, advantage is taken of two critical occurrences in nature which are themselves as simply observable as pointer readings, namely, the freezing point and the boiling point of water. These are, so to speak, natural pointer readings. But these natural pointer readings are themselves highly refined in terms of another pointer reading—namely, pressure of one atmosphere—which is based on another refined correlation between freezing and boiling points, on the one hand, and a scale of pressures on the other. When all is finished, we have an instrument with a scale and a pointer (or the equivalent). To find the heat of any body, place this body in contact with the instrument and observe the position of the pointer on the scale. This pointer reading is the completely refined empirical fact.

The cognitive drive throughout is for the most completely invariant evidence possible. An item of evidence is wanted that will be completely free from such qualitative contradictions as the common-sense deliverances that neighboring bodies of wood and steel both are and are not of the same temperature, and that will be as free as possible from those quantitative contradictions which we call lack of precision. In short, an item of evidence is wanted that will be capable of precise corroboration by any and all men placed in a position to observe the evidence. The result is pointer readings and correlations among pointer readings. In a word, the result is empirical data.

Now, for the moment, let us leave these and turn to logical data. Logical data are the evidence for the validity of logical and mathematical transitions and for those organizations of such transitions which are called logical and mathematical systems. As with empirical data, so with logical data; the aim is to obtain types of transition so simple and obvious that any and all men observing them will agree that they are legitimate. These also have had their development out of common sense, and have reached their apex in symbolic logic just as empirical data have reached their apex in physics. The principal logical data have been named by Lewis as substitution, inference, and adjunction. He defines these as follows:

[Substitution:] Either of two equivalent expressions may be substituted for the other. Thus, if an expression of form $p = q$ has been assumed, or subsequently established, what precedes the sign of equivalence in this expression may be substituted for what follows it; or *vice versa*.

[Adjunction:] Any two expressions which have been separately asserted may be jointly asserted. That is, if p has been asserted, and q has been asserted, then pq [i.e., p and q] may be asserted.

[Inference:] If p has been asserted and p [implies] q is asserted, then q may be asserted. That is to say, a new theorem may be inferred from a previous principle which has been shown to imply it.[2]

Let us take an example:

To prove that p implies p—

It is a rule of substitution in the sort of system from which this theorem is taken that with certain exceptions any element, p, can be substituted for any other element q, r, s, or combination of elements if this is done consistently through a section of proof. (1)

Now, pq implies p [this is a postulate in this system] (2)

Let $p = q$ [by (1)] (3)

[2] Lewis and Langford, *Symbolic Logic* (New York: Century, 1932), pp. 125–126.

Then	pp implies p [by (2) and (3), *substitutions*]	(4)
Now	if p implies q, and q implies r, then it is implied that p implies r [postulate]	(5)
Let	$pp = q$ and $p = r$ [by (1)]	(6)
Then	if p implies pp, and pp implies p, then it is implied that p implies p [by (5) and (6), *substitutions*]	(7)
Now	p implies pp [postulate]	(8)
Hence	p implies pp and pp implies p [by *adjunction* of (4) and (8)]	(9)
Hence	p implies p [by *inference* since (9) asserts the antecedent clause of (7) which permits the assertion of the consequent clause of (7) alone][3]	

If there is any difficulty with this proof, it is that it is too plain. A layman would hardly think the theorem needed proof anyway. It is likely to seem obvious enough that p implies p in any sense of "implies" that he can think of— more obvious than the postulates on which the proof is based. But if anyone wants to prove this theorem and if the postulates are admitted, a layman will find the steps of the proof perfectly clear even though he might not be able to put any particular sense into the symbols. Just as the slave boy in Plato's *Meno* found he could follow the steps of a complex geometrical proof and see that the conclusions followed from the premises, so here, any man with an ordinary brain would admit the obviousness of the steps of substitution, adjunction, and inference, once the postulates and rules of substitution were granted. The cognitive strength of the proof is based on multiplicative corroboration, just as that of pointer readings is.

[3] Modified from Lewis and Langford, *Symbolic Logic*, pp. 127–128.

§5. *Data and positivists.*—We thus see that logical data have an affinity with empirical data in that their cognitive value is based on the same critical principle, namely, multiplicative corroboration. Now, there is a theory of knowledge called positivism which appears to amount to the proposition that ideally knowledge should consist of beliefs founded on data. Empirical facts should ideally be all empirical data (pointer readings and the correlations among these), and where empirical data turn out to be insufficient for the organization of knowledge, they should be supplemented with logical data. Knowledge, then, would be identified with science, and science would be conceived ideally as a mathematical or logical system in which postulates and propositions referred to empirical data and in which the connections among the propositions and their empirical references would be exhibited by logical data. It is the conception of knowledge as a deductive system validated throughout by logical data and referring to the empirical data, which are thereby transparently and completely organized.

There is no question about the cognitive attractiveness of this conception. The facts of the world and their connections would then be as obvious to all as a pointer reading or a logical substitution. Knowledge might still be complicated, but it would not be obscure or puzzling. It would be almost indubitable. For a pointer reading or a substitution is so highly refined for multiplicative corroboration that we hold it dubitable only, so to speak, methodologically and to avoid the traps of dogmatism. Within certain fields knowledge has already to a remarkable degree attained this positivistic form. And it would be dogmatic to assert that all knowledge might not attain that form.

But it would be equally dogmatic in the present state of knowledge to assert that all knowledge can attain that form, and still more dogmatic to deny cognitive value to beliefs that are not in that form, or, more loosely, to beliefs based on evidence that is not refined data. It would be dogmatic, that is, to deny the cognitive values of dubitanda, rough data, and danda so long as we are not omniscient in our possession of refined data.

Realizing that their ideal lies in the future, actual positivists differ a good deal in their restrictions upon the evidence they will provisionally accept. On the basis of our classification of evidence as dubitanda, rough data, refined data, rough danda, and refined danda, we might distinguish a number of different species of positivists, depending upon the range of evidence they would find acceptable and the amount of cognitive weight they would assign to each type. Still, the defining mark of a positivist is his bias for refined data, or at least for data—that is, for the principle of multiplicative corroboration. He tends to disparage the principle of structural corroboration and reduce it rather plausibly to logical system.

He is likely to express a good deal of respect for common sense and may insist that refined data are simply matters of common sense, so preparing for rather serious confusions between criticized and uncriticized knowledge, between data and dubitanda. He is likely to notice no difference between rough data and rough danda, which is excusable, seeing that the tension between the two modes of corroboration is not acute in the early stages of refinement. But he is traditionally emphatic in his disparagement of refined danda and of the world hypotheses which support them and are supported by them. For him metaphysics is mythology. It may have some aesthetic, emotional, or sentimental value, but no cognitive value, or at the most very little. Such is the traditional character of the positivist.

Our need to consider him at this point arises from his traditionally hostile attitude toward metaphysics. For world theories and the refined danda generated by them fall within the subject often called metaphysics.

The issue is this: Can't we in cognition get along without danda? Shouldn't we staunchly maintain that the only legitimate method of cognitive refinement is in the direction of refined data? Can't we dispense with structural corroboration? Isn't multiplicative corroboration the only reliable ground for cognition? The supporters of danda seem here to be thrown on the defensive. What can we who are about to study world theories say for ourselves?

Our final and only adequate reply, of course, is: Wait until the end of our investigation. How can one fairly estimate the value of world theories and their danda until he has studied them? Nevertheless, two preliminary comments at this point seem advisable.

First, it will be salutary to stress still more the actual state of affairs with respect to the positivistic ideal program: (1) the program is at present far from being realized; and (2) possibly it is inherently unrealizable.

1) The refined empirical data at our present disposal cover a very small field of nature. They are mainly limited to the data of physics and chemistry, and even in these sciences much of the evidence is of the type of rough data, and some of it is little better than dubitanda (not to mention frequent infiltrations of danda). Outside of the fields of physics and chemistry, refined data play a secondary role and are rarely capable of expression in the form of a deductive mathematical system. More serious than that, the more carefully we study the nature of the development of refined data the less convinced we become of their adequacy to absorb all evidence. Even a careful study of our illustration from Lenzen will raise up doubts. That refinement of thermal data depends upon a primitive correlation, one item of which is, it seems, unavoidably a rough datum or a dubitandum. And that primitive correlation with one end resting *not* on a refined datum is never entirely dispensed with. The pointer reading of a thermometer does not after all entirely dispense with the primitive feeling of hot and cold which generated the series of steps which culminated in the pointer reading. Refined correlations seem never quite to clear themselves of the crude correlations from which they started. Something in these crude correlations seems essential to give significance to the refined correlations at the end of the development (*unless some other kind of refinement can explain the process*). This inherent lack of significance in data alone is what we meant earlier by the thinness of refined data, a thinness which finally causes a return to common sense for a security and healthiness of fact that threatens to

disappear when data try to carry on cognition alone. So much for the first comment.

2) The second comment arises from the first. In order to bring it out in strong relief, we shall make a classification of positivists on the basis of the possible cognitive attitudes they may assume. We shall distinguish between the undictatorial and the dictatorial positivists, and the latter we shall divide into the undogmatic and the dogmatic positivists. We shall see that undictatorial positivists are inherently undogmatic and are also unconcerned with the present issue. The question will be whether undogmatic dictatorial positivists are possible, for they alone could legitimately deny the legitimacy of danda.

Now, the undictatorial positivist is simply a man who is more interested in data than in any other kind of evidence. He claims high cognitive value, quite rightly, for refined data and for data in general. He concentrates his interest on the refinement of data and the search for new data. He makes no remarks about other kinds of evidence. His is often supposed to be the proper attitude for the experimental scientist, though actually very few experimental scientists seem consistently to maintain such an attitude. Most of them appear more or less consciously to hold rather extensive theories about their data—so extensive, indeed, as implicitly to involve danda. Be this as it may, the undictatorial positivist creates no cognitive issues for us and may be left to his researches in peace.

But the dictatorial positivist is quite different. He sets up data, and especially refined data, as norms of evidence. The question is whether he can do this without either being dogmatic or basing his claims on a structural world theory, in which latter case his evidence is interpreted in the light of his theory and takes on the color of danda.

That a positivist can dogmatically dictate supreme claims for multiplicative corroboration and set up refined data as the ultimate norms of evidence is not to be denied. Such dictation has in fact been done repeatedly. On the basis of our examination of dogmatism in the last chapter, however, it can never be done legitimately. A refined datum is not, in fact, indubitable. Its high cognitive value depends on the precise, or relatively precise, corroboration of many observations, or upon the expectation of such corroborations. Any datum may be in error. Nor is the principle of multiplicative corroboration self-evident. Its cognitive value rests upon the observed reliability of the evidence gained through its use. It may occasionally be deceptive. The dogmatic dictatorial positivist, therefore, need be of no cognitive concern to us, since dogmatism is illegitimate.

But what of the undogmatic dictatorial positivist, he who claims that multiplicative corroboration and data are the sole reliable norms of evidence, and who makes these claims as a sound hypothesis on the basis of the consideration of all relevant evidence available? To him our answer is, "How can you make these claims except on the basis of an extensive theory in terms of which all proffered evidence other than data—namely, dubitanda and danda— are satisfactorily interpreted in terms of data?" If he replies, "There is no need of interpretation; the evidence comes as data and only as data," our answer is, "You can only say that in the role of a dogmatist. This is evident from our first comment on positivism, where we showed the relatively small range of refined data, and the apparent dependence of these for their cognitive foundations upon dubitanda."

An undogmatic positivist, therefore, would not after reflection make such a reply. Rather he would say: "I believe I can make reasonable interpretations of dubitanda and of danda in terms of the data already observed and of other data which I hypothesize may some day be observed, and perhaps of still other data which are unobservable because of the impossibility of constructing instruments that would render them observable, but which nevertheless may reasonably be called inferable data in the sense that if we hypothesize them they will render it possible to make explanations of fact consistent with the data we have observed."

To this we answer: "If you can carry out this program you have indeed presented a reasonable hypothesis and supported your claims for the adequacy of data as norms for cognition. But note that you have done this only through the adequacy of your hypothesis to interpret all types of evidence in terms of 'data.' That is, you so interpret the evidence that is not obviously data as to make it *corroborate* the evidence that is. For what are hypothesized 'data' and inferred 'data' but unobserved danda, the sort of evidence that *ought* to be given, if data are the sole norms of evidence? Moreover, you must find some means of converting all actually experienced dubitanda into data, as well as many insistent danda of other hypotheses such as we shall soon encounter. In a word, you may become undogmatically dictatorial about data, but only, as you see from your own admissions, by accepting the principle of structural corroboration along with that of multiplicative corroboration, as a result of which your original data take on the form of danda, the sort of evidence that *ought* to be if the hypothesis maintained can be carried out. And note, furthermore, once you have tacitly admitted the legitimacy of structural corroboration, you are under cognitive obligation to consider other hypotheses constructed on the same principle and to accept for your theory the position of one competitor among others. Your own hypothesis may be judged cognitively best, not because it is based on the principle of multiplicative corroboration, but because it exhibits a superiority on the basis of structural corroboration. In short, you cannot dictate cognitive values except on the basis of structural corroboration and of a hypothesis built up through this principle. The only way this dilemma could be escaped would be if all evidence actually were obviously data. As this condition is contrary to fact in the present or any future state of knowledge at present predictable, an undogmatic dictatorial positivist is a self-contradiction. For in order to dictate the sole value of multiplicative corroboration, you are forced to appeal to structural corroboration, thereby admitting a cognitive value in structural corroboration which denies the sole value of multiplicative corroboration."

The gist of the matter is this: In order to set up refined data as the sole norm of evidence, it is necessary to *deny* the claims of danda, derived from various structural world

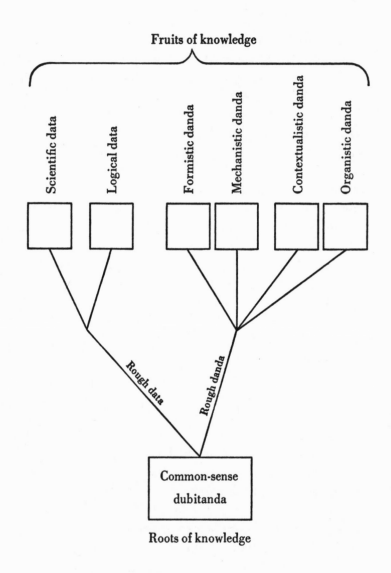

A TREE OF KNOWLEDGE

theories, as alternative norms of evidence. To back up this denial an undogmatic dictatorial positivist must so assemble his data as to drive out the claims of alternative danda. Multiplicative corroboration alone will not do this, for it only establishes the data it establishes, and neither affirms nor denies the claims of any facts other than those, like pointer readings, by which man corroborates man. In order to assemble data so as to drive out alternative danda, such a positivist must make a structural hypothesis, and a world-wide one, such that fact corroborates fact throughout and every fact is a "datum." Then, and only then, can no alternative danda squeeze in. But then this positivist has developed a structural world hypothesis, and his "data" become actually danda of a certain sort.

To add to the irony of the matter, the sort of "data" developed by this process have in the hands of many prominent positivists turned out to be the typical danda of well-recognized world theories. So with Hume, Comte, Mach, Mill, and Schlick. Their "data" are not data, or not for long, but the regular danda of some of the world theories we shall study. With such men the cognitive situation is generally much confused by this failure on their part to notice how they are dictating. In the end they generally turn out to be dogmatists.

But is it not possible for a positivist to organize his data without committing himself to a structural world theory? Yes, by means of conventionalistic hypotheses, as we shall see in the next chapter. But only if, or because, these hypotheses (if they may be so called) do not assert or deny anything. So far as such hypotheses can be made, they do not concern our present issue. For such hypotheses would not deny the cognitive claims of danda and structural corroboration.

The study of danda and structural corroboration seems, then, to be cognitively justified. We proceed, accordingly, to ask ourselves about hypotheses, since danda involve hypotheses. Danda are the facts that seem to be given as we note the extended corroboration of fact by fact. Or, better, danda are facts that *ought* to be given if the hypothesis which describes an extended mass of structural corroboration were true.

Chapter IV : Hypotheses

§1. *Views about hypotheses.*—There are as many views about hypotheses as there are about knowledge. In the most rudimentary common-sense view a hypothesis is identified with a guess or a hunch, and is considered good if it turns out right, bad if it does not. In this stage or corner of common sense the highest type of knower is the soothsayer or the prophet, a man who knows ahead. And the admiration of the man in the street for science is mainly due to science's many confirmed predictions, not only predictions of eclipses and arrivals of comets, but also those implied in planning skyscrapers, steel bridges, and ships that fly.

To the positivist a hypothesis is a human convention for the purpose of keeping data in order; it has no cognitive value in itself. He is, therefore, often cynical or gently indulgent with the wonder and admiration of the common man for scientific predictions. A prediction is nothing but an anticipated correlation, valueless if unconfirmed, and just one more multiplicative corroboration if it is confirmed. To wonder at it is childish. To accord it cognitive value for itself is a misunderstanding. Cognitive value belongs where knowledge is. And what we know are data. A hypothesis is not a datum; it is simply a symbolic scheme for the arrangement of data, so that men can easily find and use the data they know. Man has a limited memory and a limited attention. If it were not for these limitations he would not need hypotheses. He could just note data and their correlations and pick out the ones he needed when he needed them. But because of human limitations he does have to find convenient systems of organization for his data. Ideally, these systems are in mathematical symbols and are deductive in form. The same data can often be organized in different systems, depending upon the postulates or primitive concepts employed. As between two such systems, the one most economical of a scientist's thought is the best. And this is proof, if any were needed, that such systems or hypotheses have no cognitive value in themselves. Their sole value is as a means of facilitating human thought, like a memorizing scheme or an alphabet. All cognitive value resides in the data which these schemes conveniently order.

This interpretation of hypotheses is known as conventionalism. It has been excellently explained by Poincaré, who is quite surely the greatest of all positivists because of his consistency of attitude, his brilliance, his humanity, and his cognitive restraint. He is, of course, not a dogmatic nor a dictatorial positivist (or only rarely). He makes well-grounded assertions about the methods and achievements of physical scientists and mathematicians. He rarely makes denials regarding the methods of others. Conventionalism is unquestionably the proper interpretation for hypotheses on the basis of the refinement of cognition in terms of multiplicative corroboration only. We shall have more to say about conventionalism later.

Other interpretations of hypotheses arise out of the results of refinement of cognition in terms of structural corroboration. There are, accordingly, as many of these structural views of hypotheses worthy of consideration as there are relatively adequate systems of structural corroboration. We are, therefore, faced with a peculiar difficulty at this point. We wish to regard these systems of structural corroboration, which are, of course, world theories, as hypotheses. We feel justified in doing so, in view of our observation that there are several of them, each making effective cognitive claims. None of them can, we believe, support a claim of absolute truth, or certainty. They must, then, be hypothetical, be hypotheses. Yet we cannot enter into detail regarding the nature of hypotheses in terms of structural corroboration without finding ourselves involved in one of these world theories.

Hence we are forced to make only the most general statements regarding the nature of hypotheses in terms of structural corroboration. And to guard ourselves against an accusation of bias or of dogmatism even in what we do say, or in the very terms we use, we hereby reserve the right to retract anything we say in these preliminary pages, so far as anything here is found to be dogmatic or biased. The purpose of these pages is simply to lead us intelligently into an understanding of world theories, not to prescribe to them.

The only legitimate cognitive sources of prescription, I believe, are world theories, and the only legitimate critics of such prescriptions, other world theories. Common sense, as we have seen, cannot prescribe anything. It can vitalize, it can guarantee us against utter skepticism, but irresponsibility is one of its intrinsic traits. Nor can data in the guise of positivism legitimately prescribe anything beyond the undoubted cognitive value of their own mode of cognitive refinement. When positivism undertakes to prescribe for knowledge in general, it becomes, as we saw, either dogmatic or metaphysical and unpositivistic. Only world theories through structural corroboration acquire a cognitive right to prescribe concerning knowledge—a prescription which is of course not dogmatic, but a particular sort of refinement. We, therefore, standing now outside of world theories, cannot and would not attempt to prescribe to them. Yet, like men betting at a race track, we may perhaps make some shrewd observations about the horses that are to run, their condition, their build, their training, their jockeys, and the state of the turf, though what we say or think will mean nothing to the contestants and will have no effect upon the course of the race.

From now on, but for one brief comment, we shall be discussing only structural hypotheses. Common-sense hunches obviously need refinement, as all dubitanda do. Conventionalistic hypotheses growing out of the positivistic treatment of data make no cognitive claims. Our interest, therefore, will henceforth be focused upon structural hypotheses—of which world hypotheses are examples,—for these do make cognitive claims. They purport to inform us about the structure of the world.

§2. *Scope and precision.*—Our preliminary comments about hypotheses based on structural corroboration will be under two main headings: first (to be given in this chapter), general comments about the grounds of cognitive value for these hypotheses; and second (to be given in the next chapter), a general theory about the origin of such hypotheses.

The cognitive value of such hypotheses is generated directly out of the mode of cognitive refinement which requires them. Structural corroboration cannot get along at all except by the aid of hypotheses which connect together the evidence that is corroborative. Even in our earlier common-sense example of structural corroboration having to do with the strength of a chair, the evidence would not have been convincing but for a set of hypothetical connections, mostly causal, which brought together the evidence toward the belief in the chair's strength. For instance, take the evidences of wear on the chair which were accepted as evidences of the chair's strength. Consider what an amount of hypothetical construction based on what an amount of more or less rough observation was necessary to bring that perception forward as an item of evidence. Consider, furthermore, how weak this evidence would be if not supported by the other items of corroborative evidence. Notice how every item mutually supports every other through some sort of implied structure, so that each gains in weight as the evidence accumulates. And notice—what is particularly interesting after our discussion in the previous chapter—how, after all this circumstantial evidence has been accumulated and organized, the sitting of a man in the chair becomes simply one more (though certainly weighty) circumstance to be added to the structure of other circumstances justifying the belief in the chair's strength.

If we wished to increase the reliability of this crude hypothesis (and for the moment we shall minimize the aid of multiplicative corroboration), we could do so by developing it in either of two directions, either by discriminating more carefully the nature of a chair and its strength or by extending the range of circumstances which bear upon its strength. The first may be called the development of the *precision* of the hypothesis; the second, the development of its *scope*. These two marks of a good structural hypothesis are so closely allied that often they can scarcely be separated, and the greater the refinement of the hypothesis the less they can be separated.

For in increasing the precision of the hypothesis—that is, making it exactly fit, conform to, apply to, describe or in any other way strictly refer to the facts under consideration—these facts have to be discriminated in ever greater detail. "Chair" is a rough sort of term. Exactly what is a chair? And "strength" is a very complex matter. What does it consist in? The precise determination of these two terms is a factual study, which must be brought to bear on the facts observable in the so-called "chair" before us, in order to render the hypothesis precisely adequate. But the accumulation of these facts to increase the precision of the hypothesis automatically increases its scope. They constitute so many more circumstances organized and brought to bear upon the cognitive situation.

Similarly, an attempt to increase the scope of the hypothesis, to find more corroborative facts for it, will inevitably lead to more precise analysis of the individual facts and their connections. We find out what facts bear, or most strongly bear, on the situation, and automatically the precision of the hypothesis is increased. The further structural hypotheses are carried in their refinement the more these two gauges of a good hypothesis tend to coalesce.

§3. *World hypotheses demanded by structural corroboration.*—It thus becomes clear that, in the pursuit of reliability, structural corroboration does not stop until it reaches unlimited scope. For as long as there are outlying facts which might not corroborate the facts already organized by the structural hypothesis, so long will the reliability of that hypothesis be questionable. The ideal structural hypothesis, therefore, is one that all facts will corroborate, a hypothesis of unlimited scope. Such a hypothesis is a world hypothesis.

Thus structural corroboration inevitably leads to the conception of a world hypothesis. In terms of the corroboration of fact with fact one can never be quite assured that a hypothesis is precisely adequate to a fact under consideration unless he believes that no fact would fail to corroborate it. Now, one cannot without dogmatism draw arbitrary lines in nature and say that the facts within these lines bear upon our problem but the facts outside do not. Specialists may do that sort of thing, and in practice it proves useful, and facts gathered in a limited field may acquire a certain degree of autonomy through the aid of multiplicative corroboration; but in terms of structural corroboration the hypotheses covering such facts and even the facts themselves are only tentative and provisional. The hypotheses are adequate and the facts genuine *if* there are no disturbing facts bearing on them outside the arbitrarily limited field. And how can it be known that there probably are no disturbing facts outside of the limited field, unless the areas outside are explored to see? This does not mean that an utterly precise account could not be given of an isolated fact. It does mean that in terms of structural corroboration the only way of assuring ourselves of the isolation of a fact is to find that other facts are not connected with it and that they thereby confirm its isolation; and we can only believe that the fact is truly isolated if we believe that no other fact in the universe could affect it, which is the same as saying that we have a hypothesis of world-wide scope on the basis of which we judge that the description of this isolated fact as isolated is entirely adequate. However we turn it, structural corroboration drives us eventually to hypotheses of unlimited scope—to world hypotheses.

Tentative structural hypotheses with limited scope are, of course, not devoid of cognitive value, especially when partly supported, as they generally are, with some degree of multiplicative corroboration. The facts they generate are rough danda and are cognitively in the same condition as rough data. What may actually be their cognitive value (apart from a guess that it is pretty good) can only be established reliably in terms of the refined danda of world theories (or in terms of refined data). The strength of the chair in terms of circumstantial evidence and one or two experiences of sitting in it is a good example of a rough dandum.

§4. *World hypotheses include data.*—Of necessity, a world theory draws data within its scope as well as everything else. It, therefore, does not reject, but acquires the cognitive force of multiplicative corroboration as well as that of structural corroboration. In other words, the refinement of structural corroboration eventually draws in multiplicative corroboration.

But in a world theory multiplicative corroboration is not necessarily regarded as cognitively self-justified, though it may acquire high or even supreme cognitive value in terms of structural corroboration. Some world theories rate data high, others rather low. There have been dogmatic metaphysicians who have been as scornful of pointer readings and mathematical logic as dogmatic positivists have been of metaphysics. Data are as susceptible to the jibe of being mere records of the opinions of a vulgar majority, as danda of being mere fancies of a harebrained mystic. Cognition needs both types of refinement as much as a bird needs two wings. The relative claims of the two can never be settled short of omniscience, or at least of a highly adequate world theory. But within the domain of structural corroboration danda come first, and in that domain data must submit to the corroborative evidence of fact with fact and accept whatever consequences develop.

§5. *Evidence and interpretation merged in world hypotheses.*—Another matter that comes out is the queer way in which the distinction between hypothesis and evidence, interpretation and fact, tends to disappear the greater the refinement of structural corroboration. In a world theory it is impossible to say where pure fact ends and interpretation of fact begins. Within the theory itself the distinction is clear. The theory will tell you what in fact is fact and what in fact is theory. But another equally reliable theory will draw the line in another place.

It is characteristic of structural corroboration to try to resolve everything of cognitive value into fact. For one fact effectively corroborates another fact only if the structural bearing of the one upon the other is itself a fact. The aim is to make the very structure of the corroboration, so to speak, natural or causal, and to remove all arbitrary elements (except the bare symbols of verbal expression) from the hypothesis. So far as this aim is achieved, the hypothesis constitutes the very structure of nature and is not hypothetical or a hypothesis at all.

Ideally, through words on the pages of a book, a world theory illuminates the world for us, and the world stands revealed to us not in imagination but in fact just as it is. For the words of the book are supposed, so to speak, to put us in gear with the world, so that all we have to do is to guide the wheel and observe how things look as the headlights bring them in view. Actually this ideal is not attained, as the conflict of world theories with one another and the conflict of facts within world theories sufficiently prove. The gears grind, the lights flicker, and the lenses distort. Nevertheless, we do seem to get some idea of our world from these vehicles, and without them we should have to walk pretty much in the dark. But the better the cars we make, the harder it is to find out what is still wrong with them. When the lights obviously flicker, we know where to apply our ingenuity to make them steady, but when they steadily make everything, say, blue, it is hard for us to realize that natural objects are not themselves always blue and that it is only this car which makes them appear so.

This analogy must not be taken too literally. The likening of knowledge to an illumination is itself question-begging. But it is well to realize early how hard it is to guard against the apparent purity and innocence of highly refined danda. We have evidence that such facts are often highly interpreted. They seem through the lenses of a world theory to be the most obvious uncontaminated facts. The champions of such danda have almost always offered them as clearly certain and indubitable. We have had a good example in Price's description of the tomato. His analysis seems transparent, his danda indubitable as he tells us they are. Only a comparison with Dewey's sort of description made us wary. Price's facts are indeed good danda. Their cognitive value lies in the world-wide scope of the type of theory which supports them and the high degree of harmonious corroboration of evidence within that theory. But where the pure fact ends and the interpretation begins, no one in the absence of a completely adequate world theory, which would correct the errors of inadequate theories, could possibly tell. And the better a world theory, the less are we able to tell fact from theory, or pure fact from the interpretation of fact.

For this reason, it would be helpful if we could find some clue to the origin of world theories. For while it is true that the final development of anything cannot be legitimately judged in terms of its origin, still a knowledge or a shrewd guess regarding the origin of a world theory may be of assistance in showing where its factual strength or weakness is likely to lie. Such a theory of world theories I shall offer in the next chapter.

§6. *Structural versus conventionalistic hypotheses.*—
But before turning to that subject we should try to answer
a question that is frequently asked about world theories:
"In what way, if at all, does a structural world theory
differ from a scientific theory?" If by "scientific" is meant
the methods which present-day sciences employ and accept in practice, our answer must be: "There is no difference. At most there is only the difference of scope, and
even that does not hold since scientists today as always
have assisted in the development of structural world theories and have often ardently believed in them."

But the question may be reframed so as better to bring
out what is perhaps the motive for its being asked: "In
what way, if at all, does a structural world theory differ
from a conventionalistic hypothesis such as a positivist
naturally develops?" To this question the answer is: "A
structural world hypothesis differs markedly from a conventionalistic hypothesis. The latter is admittedly artificial
and clearly distinguishable from the evidence it system-
atizes. The greater the refinement of data and multiplicative corroboration, the more unmistakable the distinction
between evidence and hypothesis. The only gauges for the
value of a conventionalistic hypothesis are economy of
intellectual effort and aesthetic elegance—neither of them
gauges of cognitive value. In short, a conventionalistic hypothesis has no cognitive value, but only utility and beauty.

"In contrast, a structural world theory is not clearly
distinguishable from much of the evidence it organizes,
and the more highly developed it is, the less can the distinction be made. It follows that a structural world theory

is not conceived as artificial, but as the natural and inevitable reflection of the structure of the evidence organized, as if the references of the symbols passed directly
out into the natural structures symbolized, or suggested
the immediate intuition of them. It acquires, accordingly,
cognitive value in its own right, a cognitive value that is
practically indistinguishable from that of the evidence it
organizes.

"To state the contrast in brief: The data systematized
by a conventionalistic hypothesis provide no evidence
whatever for the cognitive value of the hypothesis, whereas
the danda organized by a structural hypothesis do constitute evidence for the cognitive value of that hypothesis.
If truth means the possession of a cognitive value, then
to say that a conventionalistic hypothesis is true (or false)
would be a self-contradiction, whereas to say that a structural hypothesis is not true (or false) would be a self-
contradiction."

From this, it will probably be generally admitted that
scientists make considerable use of structural hypotheses.
Philosophers are not the only men in pursuit of the truth,
nor scientists the only men collecting facts.

Chapter V : Root Metaphors

---

§1. *Root metaphors induced from world theories.*—The material of this chapter is on a different level from the level of those preceding. I believe that anyone taking a broad and tolerant view of the cognitive situation would sooner or later reach essentially the conclusions of the previous chapters. Those conclusions, and the evidence and reasoning on which they are based, are a sort of bedrock of cognition. That utter skepticism and dogmatism are self-defeating, that there is common sense, that we do have great confidence in data, which numbers of observations confirm, and in danda, which large masses of fact confirm—those seem to be minimum conclusions safely acceptable.

But one may accept those conclusions without accepting the suggestions of this chapter. Here I shall offer a hypothesis concerning the origin of world theories—a hypothesis which, if true, shows the connection of these theories with common sense, illumines the nature of these theories, renders them distinguishable from one another, and acts as an instrument of criticism for determining their relative adequacy.

Logically, this chapter should follow our study of such theories; for it purports to be no more than a summary of conclusions gained by studying them and the men who made them. But to serve the purposes of exposition the theory comes better first and the evidence afterward. I call it the "root-metaphor theory." Such a theory of world theories seems to me much less important than the clarification it introduces into the field of cognition it covers. Our interest is not so much in the truth of a certain theory about world theories as in the cognitive value of the world theories themselves.

Strangely enough, if this root-metaphor theory is correct, its truth could only be established by the adequacy of the theories which constitute its evidence. For this theory is itself a structural hypothesis—at least, it would be such in its ultimate corroboration—and, as we have seen, a structural hypothesis only attains full confirmation in a world theory. Hence, if this theory is true, an adequate world theory will support it. This theory would then, so to speak, become absorbed in its own evidence, that is, become an item in the very theory which it is a theory about. If this sounds like a dark saying, we reply that a world theory that cannot adequately explain it is not an adequate world theory.

But it is not a dark saying, though it does constitute a curious puzzle like that of the bottle carrying a label of the picture of that bottle, which picture of that bottle is pictured with a label which pictures the picture of that bottle, and so on—*if* so on. A bottle with a label like that is a fact of some sort in the world—a dubitandum, at least— and so is a world theory, and a theory about a world theory. And we know that the critical refinement of, at any rate, the second and third of the facts just presented lies in the direction of danda and world theories. There is nothing but dogmatism that can stop such criticism. To say, therefore, that a theory about world theories is something the cognitive value of which will depend ultimately on the value ascribed to it by an adequate world theory is merely to say that this theory, like any other criticizable cognitive item, is as valuable as the relevant evidence that corroborates it. And I stress this point at once to make it clear that our interest is not in a particular theory but in the nature and value of cognition itself.

This chapter and its root-metaphor theory, the purpose of which is to link dubitanda and data to danda, and indirectly to link different sorts of danda together, would therefore drop completely out of sight so far as it were true. Ideally, we should pass directly from dubitanda and data to fully adequate danda which would exhibit all things cognitively in their proper order. Unfortunately, danda are not at present nearly adequate. We are therefore prompted to ask ourselves why. The result of the inquiry is this root-metaphor theory, which in its content is in the nature of a rough dandum. This theory, therefore, definitely does not legislate over world theories except so far as these voluntarily accept it and thereby refine it. On the contrary, an adequate world theory by virtue of its refinement legislates over this theory or any like it. There is no reliable cognitive appeal beyond an adequate world theory. But when world theories show themselves to be inadequate we accept what makeshifts we can find. This root-metaphor theory is such a makeshift. Its purpose is to squeeze out all the cognitive values that can be found in the world theories we have and to supply a receptacle in which their juices may be collected, so that they will not dry up from dogmatism, or be wasted over the ground through the indiscriminate pecking of marauding birds.

§2. *Can logical postulates make world theories?*—How could world theories be generated? Barring the refined account from world theories themselves, and sticking to the levels of common sense and data, two suggestions emerge. One of these is typical of common sense, the other of data. The first suggestion is analogy; the second, permutations of logical postulates. The root-metaphor theory is an elaboration of the first suggestion. It has the advantage of being practically a common-sense theory and therefore inviting refinement and self-development along the lines of structural corroboration, so that each refined interpretation of the root-metaphor theory by a relatively adequate world theory appears as simply the natural and fully detailed exposition of precisely what a root metaphor is. Just as common-sense fact always calls for refinement, so a common-sense theory of world theories will call for refinement, and that refinement by the very nature of the material itself is bound to culminate in a world theory or in a number of alternative world theories.

But the suggestion that comes from the field of data would also seem worth considering. Coming as it does from a field of cognition already refined, it might seem more promising than the common-sense suggestion. So it has seemed to many men. And yet, that such is its source may be why it has proved less successful.

At the break of the century, when the potentialities of the new symbolic logic were dawning upon men, there were some who expected that mathematical logical systems would yield all that traditional metaphysical systems had, and more too, and would therefore in time completely supplant the traditional modes of metaphysical thought. These hopes have waned. But the possibility still remains of using the apparatus of symbolic logic as a means of generating world theories.

The idea is to conceive a world theory in the form of a deductive system with theorems derived from postulates. Once obtain such a system, and new world theories might then be generated like new geometries by simply adding or dropping or changing a postulate and noting the result in the self-consistency of the system and in the application of the theorems to *all* the observed facts of the world.

The idea is particularly attractive to the positivist. Suppose we conceive such a system as a summary of the facts of the world, that is, as a conventionalistic hypothesis. Something like this is being done with a degree of success in physical cosmology, both microscopic and macroscopic. Just conceive such mathematical speculation of physicists and astronomers expanded to cover all facts, and then we have a conventionalistic world hypothesis. By manipulating the postulates, hypotheses might be spawned by the dozens, and many of them might be adequate world hypotheses according to the conventionalistic standard of adequacy, namely, intellectual convenience.

Here we seem to avoid the difficulties of dictatorial positivism noted in chapter iii. Danda are not denied. They are not denominated false, nor even ignored, for by definition a conventionalistic hypothesis affirms nothing. It merely organizes the facts observed in such a manner as to be most conveniently used and perused. If no dictatorial claims are made, and these conventionalistic hypotheses are merely presented as alternative world theories to be considered along with the analogically generated world theories, what objections can there be?

None, if the proponents of this method do really maintain an undictatorial attitude. But it is to be noticed that no conventionalistic world hypothesis has ever been generated by the postulational method. The method, therefore, is quite speculative so far as it applies to world theories. It does not, therefore, actually exist as an alternative to the analogical method, which we shall develop. It is only a *possible* alternative. This fact in itself is noteworthy.

Can any reasons be given for this failure? We suspect that there is a good reason; which is, that the postulational method itself is not quite free from structural presuppositions. For this method is an application of multiplicative corroboration in terms of logical data. And all types of multiplicative corroboration seem to take for granted the fact of exact repetition or exact similarity. The corroboration of man by man seems to take it for granted that each man agrees with the others that their observations are the same.

But, from the standpoint of structural criticism, the unquestioning acceptance of the principle of multiplicative corroboration and its apparent assumption of exact repetitions of observation is rather naïve. The fact of repetition itself is something that needs refinement, and by the nature of the case multiplicative corroboration cannot give it; only structural corroboration can. From the standpoint of structural corroboration, a datum is barely more than a dubitandum—something very curious and problematic just because in its extremes of pointer readings it is so reliable.

Now, among the relatively adequate structural world theories which we shall study there is only one that accepts exact repetition of observations at its face value, that is, accepts a refined datum as a refined dandum. The other world theories, of course, accept the evidence of the reliability of data; but they account for this reliability not in terms of exact repetition, but in quite different terms. We therefore reach the curious result that so far as the postulational method is accepted at its face value (even as purely conventionalistic) the cognitive values it offers fall within only one of several alternative structural world hypotheses. In other words, the idea of a conventionalistic world hypothesis (even barring the consideration of chapter iii) is not so innocent as it sounds. It presupposes the danda of a certain structural world theory, namely, formism.

Hence it does not seem likely that adequate world theories will be generated in the postulational way. Subsidiary theories of limited scope can be generated in this way; but probably not world theories, for the cogent reason that an uncritical acceptance of data at their face value already commits a man to *one* structural world theory, and all the permutations of postulates he can make will never get him out of that theory. If he accepts the interpretation of data in terms of some other structural world theory the same condition will hold there.

The postulational method might accordingly be suggestive of alternative ways of presenting the categories of a single structural hypothesis already generated in the analogical way, or it might do other subordinate services, but it is unlikely to prove a fertile method of generating new sets of categories or new world theories.

§3. *The root-metaphor method.*—So we return to the traditional analogical method of generating world theories. The method in principle seems to be this: A man desiring to understand the world looks about for a clue to its comprehension. He pitches upon some area of common-sense fact and tries if he cannot understand other areas in terms of this one. This original area becomes then his basic analogy or root metaphor. He describes as best he can the characteristics of this area, or, if you will, discriminates its structure. A list of its structural characteristics becomes his basic concepts of explanation and description. We call them a set of categories. In terms of these categories he proceeds to study all other areas of fact whether uncriticized or previously criticized. He undertakes to interpret all facts in terms of these categories. As a result of the impact of these other facts upon his categories, he may qualify and readjust the categories, so that a set of categories commonly changes and develops. Since the basic analogy or root metaphor normally (and probably at least in part necessarily) arises out of common sense, a great deal of development and refinement of a set of categories is required if they are to prove adequate for a hypothesis of unlimited scope. Some root metaphors prove more fertile than others, have greater powers of expansion and of adjustment. These survive in comparison with the others and generate the relatively adequate world theories.

As a simple illustration of the growth of a root metaphor let us consider and imaginatively reconstruct the probable development of the Milesian theory, which was the first self-conscious world theory in European thought. Thales, wondering about the world, and dissatisfied with the explanations of mythology, suggested, "All things are water." He picked out a range of common-sense fact, water, which impressed him, a citizen of a seaport town, as likely to possess the secret of all things. Water stretches far and wide. It evaporates, generating fogs, and mists, and clouds, and these in turn condense in dampness and rain. Life springs out of its slime and mud, and the absence of water is death.

Anaximander followed Thales and thought the selection of common water rather crude. The substance of all things, metaphysical water, was not after all just common water. It was common water plus all its phases and acquired qualities. He accordingly emphasized the extensive category of infinity and a category of qualitative change which he called "shaking out." He gave the substance of all things the name *apeiron* or "infinite." In the "infinite" lay the "mixture" of all qualities: hardnesses, softnesses, shapes, colors, tastes, and odors. For any particular object in the world, such as a ship, a leaf, a pebble, or a fire, some of these qualities were "shaken out" of the "infinite mixture" as perhaps rain is shaken out of heavy clouds. These segregated qualities then congregated in the familiar forms we perceive.

After Anaximander came Anaximenes, who felt that Anaximander was very near to substituting an abstraction for the concrete substance of things, but apparently agreed that water did not connote the infinity which a world substance should have. He accordingly suggested air, denoting by this something more akin to what we should now call mist, which was, after all, one of the phases of Thales' "water." Anaximenes also added the clear discrimination of a category of quantitative change, namely, rarefaction-condensation, which seems to have been assumed by Thales and perhaps by Anaximander, but was not defined. It amounts to a category of the phases of matter: solid, liquid, and gas.

The root metaphor of this theory thus ultimately turns out to be the characteristics of a basic material out of which all the facts of the universe can be generated by certain processes of change. The set of categories may be listed as (1) a generating substance (or maybe several), (2) principles of change like "shaking out," and rarefaction-condensation, and (3) generated substances produced by (1) through (2). We might call this the "generating-substance theory."

It is not a very adequate theory, though its shadow falls upon the works of many men who developed much more adequate theories. It is periodically revived in practically pure form, but always by men of relatively small caliber. It was revived by Bernadino Telesio in the sixteenth century and by Büchner, Haeckel, and Herbert Spencer in the nineteenth. The trouble with the theory is that it lacks scope. There are too many facts that cannot be satisfactorily described in terms of these categories. We shall examine in detail one instance of this sort of inadequacy in this sort of theory when we study types of inadequacy in the next chapter.

When attempts are made to develop these categories further so as to render them more adequate and give them the scope required of a world theory, we discover either that they break down or that they break out into various types of cognitive fallacy, or that new sets of categories are in the making and men are seeking inspiration from new groups of common-sense facts, seeking new root metaphors.

So, after Anaximenes came Empedocles, who proposed in his perplexity over the inadequacies of water, *apeiron,* and air a plurality of generating substances and some new principles of change; and, in the same perplexity, but following another path, Anaxagoras; and also Parmenides and Zeno, who boldly but not so wisely proposed to solve the difficulties by believing only in elemental substance, denying generating change; and Heracleitus, who equally boldly and unwisely proposed believing only in generating change and apparently denying permanent substance. So we see how a world theory beginning promisingly with a root metaphor fresh from vital common sense grows for a while, meets obstacles in fact, is incapable of overcoming these obstacles, desperately juggles its categories, forgets the facts in the juggling of the categories, till these presently become so empty that some men can cast half of them overboard, devoutly believe the other half, substitute concepts for the facts, and deem it unnecessary to look back upon the forgotten facts. When an inadequate theory reaches such a state of intellectual chaos, there is stimulus for criticism and for new insight. Both came at once in Greece. The Sophists offered plenty of criticism, and two of the most adequate world theories came to birth: mechanism, through Leucippus and Democritus; and formism, through Socrates, Plato, and Aristotle. These theories were not sudden births, as the generating-substance theory seems to have been. There were germs of them in the disintegrating stages of the generating-substance theory itself, as if this disintegration of a promising theory turned men's eyes back toward common sense to find new sources of cognitive inspiration, that is to say, new root metaphors.

This brief account of the Milesian theory is a good parable for all of us who are interested in structural hypotheses and world theories. Never again do we see so simply and clearly the full course of a world theory—its promise, its bloom, its difficulties, its struggles, its collapse—and the type of men for every stage of it, exhibited almost in caricature. The genius Thales, who intuited the root metaphor and left only vague hints and a central saying, "All things are water"; the systematizers Anaximenes and Empedocles, who in different ways brought the theory to a high point of reasonableness by their careful reflection and extensive observation; Parmenides and Zeno, confident, brilliant, and clever jugglers of concepts, confounding to their opponents, uncompromising in their logic, who preserved some of the categories of the theory only by rejecting the others, and emptying all of them of the facts which generated them; Anaxagoras, observant again, but confused, reminiscent of Anaximander, full of promise, and yet disappointing to the young Socrates, for Anaxagoras was an eclectic bridging the way from a theory he could not make work to a theory which as yet, from lack of a clear intuition of its root metaphor, he did not comprehend. The counterparts of all these men reappear over and over again in the later history of thought, and it is a good thing to mark their type here where they are so simply seen, and judge their reliability and worth.

On the slim basis of this illustrative sketch of one root metaphor and its world theory let us make some critical generalizations. These will find their full justification, of course, only later. Once more, in the interest of clarity of exposition, we are led to state first what in the order of evidence should come last. Let us put these generalizations in the form of maxims:

§4. *Maxim I: A world hypothesis is determined by its root metaphor.*—When we speak of different world hypotheses, we mean the several developments of different root metaphors. The theories of Thales, Anaximenes, Empedocles, Telesio, and Spencer are all one world theory, because they are all derived from one root metaphor. The statements of the theory may differ in the degree of refinement of the categories, in terminology, in emphasis on certain details, in omission of some details, and even in omission of some basic categories. Still, all these statements will be reckoned as statements of one world theory in that they are all generated from and related to a single root metaphor.

Moreover, it is implied that there is some statement or number of statements which represent the world theory, its categories, and root metaphor, at the height of its development. So we suggested that Anaximenes and Empedocles represented the generating-substance theory at the height of its Greek development. It is always possible that a theory may develop farther than the best statement we have of it. In a sense, Herbert Spencer's statement was a development beyond the Greek. It was a development, however, chiefly in respect to the vast accumulation of factual detail over what the Greeks had, and hardly a development at all in respect to the refinement of the categories. It is the latter sort of development we chiefly have in mind when we speak of the development of a world hypothesis. For its adequacy depends on its potentialities of description and explanation rather than upon the accumulation of actual descriptions, though its power of description is never fully known short of actual performance.

This fact brings out that the unlimited scope essential to a world hypothesis is more a matter of intent and accepted responsibility than a matter of actual test. Obviously, all the facts in the world can never be described literally by any hypothesis. The testing of a world hypothesis consists in presenting to it for description types of fact or specimens from diverse fields of facts, and if it can adequately describe these we assume that it can describe the rest. Experience has made philosophers pretty well aware of what are likely to be the hardest facts for a world theory to handle, and these are at once respectfully presented for solution to any young hypothesis that ventures to claim world-wide scope. If the description of these facts tolerably well passes criticism, critics scour the universe for some other evidence which will break the theory down. The world-wide scope of a theory, therefore, is actually a challenge rather than an accomplishment.

Our best world hypotheses, however, seem to have this scope. They seem to handle fairly adequately any fact that is presented to them. Their inadequacies arise not so much from lack of scope as from internal inconsistencies, so that the minimum requirement nowadays for a world hypothesis is unlimited scope. We therefore speak only of the relative inadequacies of world theories, their world-wide scope being taken for granted.

§5. *Maxim II: Each world hypothesis is autonomous.*— This follows from our observation in the previous paragraph. If two or more world hypotheses handle their facts with the same degree of adequacy (so far as can be judged), and there is no world hypothesis of greater adequacy available, then there is no appeal beyond these hypotheses and each must be held to be as reliable as the other. The reason, of course, is that structural refinement reaches its culmination in world hypotheses, so that there is no cognitive appeal beyond the most adequate world hypotheses we have. Several important corollaries may be stated:

i) *It is illegitimate to disparage the factual interpretations of one world hypothesis in terms of the categories of another—if both hypotheses are equally adequate.* This disparagement is an almost universal procedure, very plausible and entirely fallacious. We believe that at the present time there are four world hypotheses of about equal adequacy. We shall call them formism, mechanism, contextualism, and organicism. Now, the very statement that these are relatively adequate hypotheses means that they are capable of presenting credible interpretations of any facts whatever in terms of their several sets of categories. Indeed, these interpretations are so convincing that a man who has not had an opportunity to compare them with the parallel interpretations of a rival hypothesis will inevitably accept them as self-evident or indubitable. The basic danda, that is, the refined evidence, of every one of these rather reliable world hypotheses has traditionally been presented and accepted as indubitable by the believers in these hypotheses, so obviously pure fact do the refined danda of any good world hypothesis appear through the lenses of its categories. Remember the danda of Price and Dewey. It is the apparent transparency of danda for cognition that makes dogmatism so easy to accept and so hard to dispel. The exponents of the theories which we are about to study have in the past, almost to a man, been dogmatists. They have believed their theories implicitly, accepted their danda as indubitable, and their categories generally as self-evident.

One reason they have been so sure of themselves is that whichever of these hypotheses they have espoused, they have been able to give relatively adequate interpretations *in their own terms* of the danda and categories of the other hypotheses. "You see," they say, "we are able to explain what these other mistaken philosophers have thought to be facts, and to show where the errors of their observations lay, how they rationalized their prejudices, accepting interpretations for facts and missing the real facts. Our hypothesis includes theirs and is accordingly the true account of the nature of things."

This would be a good argument if the other hypotheses were not equally well able to make the same argument. Among the facts in the world that a relatively adequate world theory must adequately interpret are, of course, other world theories, and a world theory that cannot reasonably interpret the errors of other world theories is automatically inadequate. By that much it lacks the requisite scope. The four world theories which we shall consider have no difficulty in explaining each other's errors.

It follows that what are pure facts for one theory are highly interpreted evidence for another. This does not imply that there are no pure facts in the universe, but only that we do not know where they are. The danda of the best world hypotheses, however, are our best bet. It is the cognitive obligation of a world theory to interpret the danda and categories of other world theories in terms of its own categories. Within the mode of interpretation of any world theory, the categories of that theory legislate without appeal. But this privilege belongs to any other equally adequate theory. One set of categories, therefore, cannot legislate over another set of categories unless the latter fails to reciprocate or in any other way indicates a lesser degree of adequacy.

ii) *It is illegitimate to assume that the claims of a given world hypothesis are established by the exhibition of the shortcomings of other world hypotheses.* This may be called the fallacy of clearing the ground. It assumes that if a theory is not perfect it is no good, and that if all other suggested theories are no good, then the ground is clear for whatever one's own theory can produce. This holds, of course, only if the suggested theory is more adequate than those rejected.

This is so obvious a fallacy that it is remarkable it should be so frequently used and to such persuasive effect. Yet a great proportion of philosophical—and not only philosophical—books give a large part of their space to polemic, finding the faults in rival theories with an idea that this helps to establish the theory proposed. The cognitive value of a hypothesis is not one jot increased by the cognitive errors of other hypotheses. Most polemic is a waste of time, or an actual obfuscation of the evidence. It is generally motivated by a proselytizing spirit supported on dogmatic illusions. If a theory is any good it can stand on its own evidence. The only reason for referring to other theories in constructive cognitive endeavor is to find out what other evidence they may suggest, or other matters of positive cognitive value. We need all world hypotheses, so far as they are adequate, for mutual comparison and correction of interpretative bias.

iii) *It is illegitimate to subject the results of structural refinement (world hypotheses) to the cognitive standards (or limitations) of multiplicative refinement.* Data cannot legislate over danda. Data must be accepted as evidence to be accounted for in a world hypothesis, but a world hypothesis does not have to accept data at their face value, or to exclude acceptance of any other sort of evidence than data. This point was discussed in detail earlier, in our examination of the positivistic proposals.

iv) *It is illegitimate to subject the results of structural refinement to the assumptions of common sense.* Dubitanda must be accepted as evidence to be accounted for, but, as we have seen, hardly ever at their face value. And this is without disparagement to the ultimate cognitive security of common sense.

v) *It is convenient to employ common-sense concepts as bases for comparison for parallel fields of evidence among world theories.* Dubitanda definitions of a group of facts are the best *test* definitions for the comparison of parallel danda definitions in different world theories. For instance, suppose we wanted to compare the interpretations of "red tomato" in the four relatively adequate world theories we are to study. From the brief earlier quotations from Price and Dewey on such a subject, it is pretty obvious that the field of fact covered by "red tomato" would, for Dewey and Price, not exactly correspond. Some items of evidence which for Price would be rather or quite irrelevant in determining what "red tomato" is, would for Dewey be vitally relevant. For Dewey, "red tomato" spreads over, so to speak, a different area of fact from what it does for Price. Yet the descriptions these two men give of "red tomato" are as nearly descriptions of the "same" fact as can be found from their respective points of view. If we want to compare the views of the two men, we can do no better than compare their different interpretations of what may be called the "same" fact. Yet the fact is never literally the same, because, if it were, the description or interpretation would be just the same, which never happens if the categories are really different.

If, let us imagine, there were an omniscient mind who looked upon the world with the "true" categories, which in such a case would, of course, be the actual structural order of nature and not interpretative conceptions at all, he could correct the interpretations of Dewey and Price, showing just where one perhaps took in too much fact here, and the other too little there. For such a mind Dewey's and Price's descriptions would be definitely two different facts of interpretation different from a third fact, which is the real red tomato truly intuited by this omniscient mind. (Any dogmatist of a theory other than Dewey's or Price's would also say just that, believing his *interpretation* of the red tomato to be the real red tomato.) But since we do not have (we find reason to believe) the fully adequate view of the world which definitely would tell us the difference in fact between the "same" red tomato interpreted by Price and by Dewey, how can we compare the two interpretations? Why, of course, as we have been comparing them—by noting the interpretation which each gives of the *same* common-sense fact.

We take a common-sense dubitandum, red tomato, and we note the structural refinement of that fact which culminates in Dewey's dandum, and also the refinement which culminates in Price's dandum. We then say that Dewey's dandum is the "same" fact in his world view that Price's dandum is in his. Though in any specific instance there is some risk in such ascriptions of equivalence, in the end (that is, in the comparison of all the ascriptions made by both theories) there is no risk; for within world hypotheses having unlimited scope, the *totality* of interpretations in any two world hypotheses must be literally equivalent since they both take in all the facts there are.

As a maxim of method, then, we find that there is no better way of entering upon the study of a field of fact than through common sense. Let the subject be perception, physical body, personal freedom, the law of gravitation, legal right, aesthetic beauty, myself, identity, space, yellow, saltiness, anger, air, action, truth—whatever you will, the essay or the book will most profitably begin with the common-sense meanings of these terms and then proceed to refinements of interpretation which can be compared with one another on the basis of their mutual points of origin.

§6. *Maxim III: Eclecticism is confusing.*—This maxim follows from the second. If world hypotheses are autonomous, they are mutually exclusive. A mixture of them, therefore, can only be confusing. We are speaking now as having cognition in mind, not practice, which often entails other than purely cognitive considerations.

When we say that world theories are mutually exclusive, we do not mean that they stand apart from one another like so many isolated posts. Each theory is well aware of the others, criticizes and interprets them and entirely includes them within its scope. It is only from the perspective of common sense, in the recollection of the different theories' diverse courses of critical refinement, that we are aware of their mutual exclusiveness.

More perspicuously, it is only through our study of their factual conflicts, their diverse categories, their consequent differences of factual corroboration, and—in a word—their distinct root metaphors that we become aware of their mutual exclusiveness.

It is not to be denied (especially after our perception that root metaphors become themselves refined in consort with the refinement of the very theories they generate) that the root metaphor of one theory may merge with that of another, and eventually all may come harmoniously together. But this idea itself is a principle derived from *one* world theory, and cannot be affirmed until, or if, that theory (organicism) should turn out to be completely adequate. For, contrariwise, it is barely possible that the world has no determinate structure, but that the past is being continually revised by the future and that the present is consequently utterly indeterminate and likely to change its nature without notice at any time, so that an indefinite number of structural hypotheses are all equally pertinent and equally impertinent. Though this latter proposal skims perilously close to the dogma of utter skepticism, something very like it is defended by some pragmatists and therefore receives some support from the categories of contextualism.

The point is, once more, that there is no way of obtaining better cognitive judgments than in terms of the best cognitive criticism we have. At present this criticism seems to be concentrated in four diverse modes of cognition or world hypotheses. While all sorts of things might happen to these diverse theories so far as abstract possibility is concerned, as a fact (in the best sense of fact we know) these four theories are just now irreconcilable. Any creditable attempt to reconcile them turns out to be the judgment of one of the theories on the nature of the others—as just now we saw was the case with the organic idea. This is a good idea, one of the best. But it would be dogmatic to accept it, when other equally adequate hypotheses have other ideas on the subject.

Yet it is a tempting notion, that perhaps a world theory more adequate than any of the world theories mentioned above (those bound to their metaphors) might be developed through the selection of *what is best* in each of them and organizing the results with a synthetic set of categories. This seems to be the deliberate principle of method used by Whitehead in his *Process and Reality*. It is the eclectic method. Our contention is that this method is mistaken in principle in that it adds no factual content and confuses the structures of fact which are clearly spread out in the pure root-metaphor theories; in two words, that it is almost inevitably sterile and confusing.

The literature of philosophy is, of course, full of eclectic writings. Moreover, it is probably true that all (or nearly all) the great philosophers were in various degrees eclectic. There are various reasons for this. One is undue faith in self-evidence and indubitability of fact, another the desire to give credit to all good intuitions with the idea that these all have to be put inside of *one* theory. But the best reason is that many of the great philosophers were not so much systematizers as seekers of fact, men who were working their way into new root metaphors and had not yet worked their way out of old ones. The eclecticism of these writers is, therefore, cognitively accidental and not deliberate, though psychologically unavoidable.

There are, then, two sorts of eclecticism: the static, deliberate sort; and the dynamic, accidental sort. Whitehead is mainly an example of the first, Peirce or James of the second. Both sorts are confusing and (I believe) can be clarified only by unraveling their eclectic tangles in terms of the different root metaphors that got mixed up. The dynamic sort, however, is obviously not sterile. This eclecticism contains the best creative work in philosophy. But its cognitive value comes not from the eclectic factor (which is entirely obstructive), but from the creative factor. The dynamic eclectic tries to divest himself of his eclectic encumbrances, and the drama of his struggle often produces great literature as well as great philosophy. But the greatness of his philosophy is not so much intrinsic as prospective. Peirce and James intuited the pragmatic, or contextualistic, root metaphor. But their intuitions were primitive, and they were in need of a technical vocabulary, and were constantly enmeshed in formistic categories. As pragmatists their cognitive achievements were probably inferior to those of Dewey and Mead, though as creative thinkers they were probably superior. Dynamic eclecticism is, therefore, the sort of exception that proves the rule. We honor its exponents above all other cognizers because of their keen scent for new facts. But it is not for their eclecticism that we honor them, for that is still only a source of confusion.

Static and deliberate eclecticism, however, cannot claim the discovery of new fact or insight, but only the merit of a method different from that of the root-metaphor method. The two methods are not in any way in contradiction with each other. The issue between the two is consequently not fatally serious. Nevertheless, it would greatly simplify the critical problem of estimating the value of world theories if we had reason to believe that eclectic theories were in principle less reliable than pure root-metaphor theories. The question is this: Does a deliberate eclectic theory add anything that is not better found in the alternative root-metaphor theories from which an eclectic theory must obtain its materials? If not, we can safely limit our attention to pure root-metaphor theories.

There are theoretically two ways of deliberately constructing an eclectic world theory. One is to combine all the adequate world theories we have into one synthetic whole. The merit of this way is supposed to be greater comprehensiveness. But clearly nothing could be more comprehensive than the complete comprehensiveness of a theory of world-wide scope. Every relatively adequate world theory is completely comprehensive. The reason that there are several root-metaphor theories is precisely that they are all fully comprehensive and their categories refuse to merge and their danda refuse to harmonize. So that way is impossible. The other alternative is to make selections, generally said to be of "the best," from the several theories, and then out of the combined selections to elicit a new synthetic set of categories. The merit of this way is supposed to be greater adequacy.

But the trouble with this second way is how to determine a reliable ground of selection. What shall determine "the best" in the various theories? If anyone can suggest any other mode of cognitive refinement (that is, mode of finding "the best" in cognition) than multiplicative or structural refinement, he is certainly to be listened to attentively. But if not, how can the selection be made? As we have seen, multiplicative refinement will not help us. As to structural refinement, there are as many "bests" as there are world theories on an equal footing of adequacy. What, then, or who determines the "best" that is better than the "best" guaranteed by the relative adequacy of each world theory? Apparently only the personal preferences of the eclectic selector.

But is it not true that some world hypotheses seem to be especially strong in some cognitive fields, others in others? And would not an eclectic theory which combined these strong fields be more adequate than any pure root-metaphor theory? For instance, is it not true that the mechanistic theory seems to be particularly effective in the field of the physical sciences and rather shallow in the field of values, and is not the organistic theory rather strained in the field of the physical sciences and strong in the field of values? Would not an eclectic theory which accepted the mechanistic interpretations of physical facts and the organistic interpretations of facts of value be a more adequate world theory than either pure mechanism or pure organicism?

But would it? We must not forget that the main strength of a world hypothesis comes from structural corroboration. That means that the greater the spread of corroborative fact, the greater the cognitive reliability of the interpretations of each separate fact and field of facts. Now, the cognitive strength of both mechanism and organicism lies in their relative adequacy of unlimited scope. If their scope were limited, their interpretations would lack full corroboration. We find them credible precisely because their scope is unlimited. But the eclectic suggestion amounts to a limitation in the scope of both interpretations. In the eclectic theory the interpretations of physical facts would not be corroborated by the interpretations of value facts, and vice versa. The eclectic theory would actually lack universal scope and would not literally be a world theory at all.

More than that, can we afford to sacrifice the mechanistic interpretations of value or the organistic interpretations of physical facts? These interpretations are convincing to many men, and they do have structural corroboration. There is refined cognitive evidence for them. On what cognitive grounds can we discard them?

There are indeed some grounds. It may be pointed out that the mechanistic root metaphor springs out of the common-sense field of uncriticized physical fact, so that there would be no analogical stretch, so to speak, in the mechanistic interpretations of this field, while the stretch might be considerable in the mechanistic interpretation of the common-sense field of value; and somewhat the same, in reverse order, with respect to organistic interpretations. Moreover, mechanism has for several generations been particularly congenial to scientists, and organicism to artists and to persons of religious bent. Also, the internal difficulties which appear from a critical study of the mechanistic theory seem to be particularly acute in the neighborhood of values, and contrariwise the internal difficulties with organicism seem to be particularly acute in the neighborhood of physical fact.

These are cognitive grounds, and they all converge on the suspicion that mechanistic interpretations are perhaps more trustworthy for physical fact, while organistic interpretations are more trustworthy for values. But can more be legitimately said than that? And is not this suspicion based on the universal structural adequacy of *both* theories? Is it not precisely because both of these theories generate unlimited factual corroboration, and because their relative adequacy is about the same, because, in short, they are cognitively of equal weight and reliability, that we are somewhat justified in considering these external grounds of criticism? We, as practical human beings having to make practical choices in a pressing world, may well take these suspicions into account when we make our choices—rely more confidently on the judgment of a mechanist, perhaps, if we are building a bridge, more on the judgment of an organicist if we are building a society. But can we do more than that with these grounds of suspicion?

For these grounds of suspicion cannot legislate over world theories, over the most highly refined cognitive criticism we have. The mechanistic interpretation of value has, after all, the powerful corroboration of the remarkably satisfactory mechanistic interpretations of physical fact. And the mechanistic interpretations of value are by no means unsatisfactory. Many men have been satisfied to be dogmatic about them. Those corroborative grounds are cognitively stronger than our grounds of suspicion in the previous paragraph. For in status these latter are little better than common-sense hunches—cognitive grounds all right, but dubitanda grounds, chiefly valuable in irritating us into the search for still better world theories.

But our proposed eclectic theory has by definition no root metaphor, and does not, so far as we can see, carry cognition forward at all. If such a combination of mechanism and organicism were proposed as a substitute for the two pure theories, the cognitive loss would be obvious. If it is proposed simply as another alternative, there is not so much objection. But why do it? As a flight of fancy it may be amusing, as men have fancied fauns, centaurs, angels, and dragons. But it can hardly be a genuinely creative cognitive achievement. If a man is to be creative in the construction of a new world theory, he must dig among the crevices of common sense. There he may find the pupa of a new moth or butterfly. This will be alive, and grow, and propagate. But no synthetic combination of the legs of one specimen and the wings of another will ever move except as their fabricator pushes them about with his tweezers. Moreover, what happens at the joints? What happens under the skin between the centaur's neck and body? How do the wings of angels fit into their shoulders? Either the eclectic glosses these difficulties over, or we perceive confusion.

How far such criticisms apply to Whitehead's *Process and Reality*, it is for each man to decide. There are many genuinely creative touches in the book, where Whitehead pushes forward now one mode of interpretation, now another, especially many insights into the implications of contextualism. But all agree that it is a hard book. The question is whether it is not an intrinsically confused book. When Whitehead writes in the Preface, "The history of philosophy discloses two cosmologies. . . . In attempting an enterprise of the same kind, it is wise to follow the clue that perhaps the true solution consists in a fusion of the two previous schemes, with modifications demanded by self-consistency and the advance of knowledge,"[1] the question is whether he is not proposing to himself something impossible. He has, I think, underestimated the number of cosmologies that he is about to "fuse." But to "fuse" even two and to have the fusion "self-consistent" is, on the evidence of our root-metaphor theory, impossible. All that can result is confusion, and I suggest that that is just what did result.

§7. *Maxim IV: Concepts which have lost contact with their root metaphors are empty abstractions.*—This fault is one stage worse than eclecticism, and is very likely to grow out of it. When a world theory grows old and stiff (as periodically it does and then has to be rejuvenated), men begin to take its categories and subcategories for granted and presently forget where in fact these come from, and assume that these have some intrinsic and ultimate cosmic value in themselves. The concepts are often pretty thin by that time, little more than names with a cosmic glow about them. Such has been the fate of many good terms and some not so good—substance, matter, mind, spirit, God, ego, consciousness, essence, identity, phlogiston, ether, force, energy, magnetism. As a fallacy this cognitive propensity is sometimes called hypostatization.

[1] Whitehead, *Process and Reality* (New York: Macmillan, 1930), p. ix.

The fallacy is somewhat tricky, however. Every world theory considers the danda and categories of other world theories as hypostatizations. Terms are only genuinely hypostatized, clearly, if some cognitive weight is given to their very emptiness, if the absence of evidence they have attained is actually used as evidence—word magic, in short. A term or concept is no better than the corroborative evidence it stands for. When it begins to demand respect in its own right, it is beginning to be hypostatized. The fallacy is often hard to detect because the process of hypostatization is gradual and rarely complete. It is for this reason all the more disturbing to cognition, for its detection depends upon a careful weighing of the cognitive evidence for a concept against its cognitive claims. The detection is easier, however, once the dogmatic claims of infallibility, self-evidence, and indubitability have been recognized as fallacious. All that remains to be done, then, is to find the concept's actual significance in terms of multiplicative or structural corroboration—or, for our immediate purposes, to trace it back to its root metaphor.

We must not forget, however, that there are many root metaphors. A concept or category derived from even an inadequate root metaphor is not a hypostatization. It is simply a concept of an inadequate hypothesis. That is, there is no cognitive trouble with the term, which is functioning as well as it can. The trouble is with the hypothesis which generates the term. Nevertheless, there is a strong tendency to hypostatize the terms of a weak hypothesis. For where cognitive claims cannot be legitimately produced they tend to be illegitimately sought.

Chapter VI : Examples of Inadequacies in World Hypotheses

§1. *Tests of adequacy.*—As we look back over the maxims presented in the previous chapter, we see that they constitute a canon of cosmological criticism based on the hypothesis that the most promising way of developing reliable world theories is by the root-metaphor method. These maxims do not, however, indicate how we may judge the relative adequacies of different pure root-metaphor theories. Since we believe that even our best world theories are somewhat inadequate, this question becomes rather serious. We have no assuredly adequate theory against which to judge the apparently inadequate ones. How, then, can we judge any theory claiming world-wide scope to be more inadequate than others? How can we legitimately restrict our study to four world theories, and reject others (like the generating-substance theory) as too inadequate for further consideration?

By the maxim of autonomy, we know that one world theory cannot be legitimately convicted of inadequacy by the judgment of another. How, then, do we discover that a theory is inadequate? By its own judgment of its own achievements in attaining complete precision in dealing with all facts whatever presented. A world theory, in other words, convicts itself of inadequacy. By its own logic, or refined canons of cognition, it acknowledges its own shortcomings in dealing with certain kinds of facts, or in dealing with them consistently with its dealing with other kinds of facts. These judgments, once made by the theories themselves, can then be compared externally. Theories which show themselves up as dealing much less adequately with the world-wide scope of facts than others are said to be relatively inadequate; the others, relatively adequate.

This is not an absolutely final judgment. It may be mistaken. A theory so judged to be relatively inadequate may not as yet have reached its full capacities of development. Nevertheless, a detailed study of a theory that has been long worked over generally leaves one pretty well convinced that it has done all that its categories can do, and that the inadequacies of which it convicts itself are permanent inadequacies.

It must be recalled that we make a sharp distinction between world theories and the men who develop them and write them out. The maxims of the previous chapter suggest ways by which the eccentricities of authors may be separated from the development of the theories themselves. It is not what any author thinks about his theory that counts in determining its inadequacy, but what the theory itself in terms of its own logic thinks of itself. The authors are generally confident and dogmatic. The theories themselves have better judgment, assisted thereto, of course, by the unrelenting criticism of the exponents of rival theories as much as by the honest work of their own exponents.

Men, in other words, come to agree with men under certain circumstances about the structural agreement of fact

with fact. The self-sufficiency of a world theory and its independence of any one man's judgment are based on a
qualified application of multiplicative corroboration superimposed upon structural corroboration. One honest,
clear-thinking man should be able to make a correct judgment of the adequacy or degree of structural corroboration of a world hypothesis. But every honest, clear-thinking
man is aware of his susceptibility to bias and to plain
mistakes in observation and reasoning, and therefore seeks
the corroboration of other men for his conclusions. So, the
two fundamental modes of cognitive refinement collaborate here; as actually they do also in scientific hypotheses
of limited scope, but there with the emphasis reversed,
structural corroborations being superimposed upon the
data of multiplicative corroboration. That is, we feel surer
of our data, as data, if they do fit together as a hypothesis.
In spite of the tension between these two modes of cognitive
refinement, we as cognizers demand in the end that they
shall collaborate. This demand shows itself within the
field of structural refinement in the expectation that a
structural world theory will stand on its own feet and make
its own judgments about its own inadequacies. In practice
this means that competent men will come to essential agreement about the shortcomings of a world theory, once the
claims of dogmatism have been set aside. To a considerable degree, competent men have agreed about the shortcomings of world theories, even under the embarrassment
of dogmatic claims.

These agreements come to light as the regular, or traditional, difficulties found in this or that type of theory—the

"perennial problems" of philosophy with which the text-books have made us familiar. Even with this explanation, however, the situation is likely to be regarded as sufficiently extraordinary to require exemplification. We shall, therefore, present two definitely very inadequate world theories, namely, animism and mysticism, and show how neatly they convict themselves of inadequacy.

We found earlier that the adequacy of a structural hypothesis depended upon its *precision* in dealing with individual facts and its *scope* of factual corroboration. A world hypothesis may, therefore, be inadequate in precision or in scope. It may, that is, on the one hand have world-wide scope but lack precision, this lack of precision showing itself either in an inability to come to close quarters with a fact (that is, cognitive vagueness), or in an overability to produce interpretations of a fact any one of which would be as consistent with the categories as any other (that is, cognitive indeterminateness); or, on the other hand, a world hypothesis may have apparent precision in the interpretation of many fields of fact, but lack world-wide scope through its inability to offer any interpretation of some field or fields.

The typical ruse in this latter case is to call the recalcitrant fields "unreality." It follows that whenever a world hypothesis makes an appeal to "unreality" (especially as an explanatory or interpretative principle), it unwittingly convicts itself of inadequacy, and the more definitely it locates its fields of "unreality" the more definitely it shows just where it falls short of world-wide scope and factual corroboration.

It follows, further, that in a completely adequate theory everything referred to would be "real" and there would be no "appearance" or "unreality" at all. Errors would be noted, but they would be "real" errors, facts fully explained or interpreted even if part of the explanation were in terms of pure chance, for then chance would be "real." Whence it follows, still further, that in a completely adequate world theory, even the term "reality" would disappear, since there would be no "unreality" to contrast it with. Or rather, "unreality" would be merely the name for the *fact* of inadequate interpretation suggested by hypotheses claiming, but not possessing, world-wide scope.

Even among inadequate world theories, the danda of one theory are likely to be called "unreal" in the interpretations of another. This detraction may often rebound to do more damage to the criticizing theory than to the theory criticized. For unless the criticizing theory can convert the "unreal" danda of the criticized theory into "real" danda of its own, it convicts itself of lack of scope in its inability to absorb and interpret the danda of the rival theory.

"Reality" and "unreality" and "appearance" are red-hot words. A very prudent thinker will never use them. They are as likely to burn fingers as faggots. Was the author of *Appearance and Reality* more burning or more burned? Much use of these words is almost surely a signal of trouble.

Animism is a world theory chiefly inadequate for the indeterminateness of its interpretations and lack of precision; mysticism, chiefly for its lack of scope and its lavish use of "unreality." These two types of inadequacy are plainly visible in these two theories, which will thereby act as models of badness against which to compare the relative goodness of more adequate world hypotheses. If we cannot judge the relative inadequacy of world theories by the comparison with the model adequacy of a perfect theory, we can at least judge relative adequacy by comparison with the model inadequacies of two very inadequate theories. The greater the distance of world hypotheses from the inadequacies of animism and mysticism, the greater their adequacy.

§2. *The animistic world hypothesis, an example of inadequate precision.*—Animism, as a metaphysical hypothesis, is the theory that takes common-sense man, the human being, the person, as its primitive root metaphor. This is the most appealing root metaphor that has ever been selected. Nothing is so interesting to man as man. To take man, everything about him, his body, his shape, his actions, his expressions, his motives, his emotions, and anything else about man that appeals to man's fancy, as the source of explanation of everything in the world: what could be more to man's taste, or seem more natural? Every child is a natural animist, and so (if the secret be known) is every man, not only primitive man, but civilized man as well. This view of the world is the only one in which a man feels completely at home. It is perhaps as well for us to learn early, therefore, that we shall probably never feel completely at home in a world view that is adequate. For the world does not seem to be made after man's own image.

The root metaphor of animism has had its development. The person of man expands very naturally over the universe by the process of personification, not to mention other similar, more vivid, processes such as dreams and illusions. The result has been a certain crystallization of the root metaphor into what may be regarded as its most developed form in the notion of *spirit*. It is characteristic of animism that we can never precisely capture spirit in conceptual terms and list a set of categories that will stand firm. But the following classic summary from E. B. Tylor's *Primitive Culture* may be taken as perhaps as clear a statement of its categorial structure as we are likely to obtain.

To the lower tribes of man [writes Tylor], sun and stars, trees and rivers, winds and clouds, become personal animate creatures, leading lives conformed to human or animal analogies, and performing their special functions in the universe with the aid of limbs like beasts, or of artificial instruments like men; or what men's eyes behold is but the instrument to be used or the material to be shaped, while behind it there stands some prodigious but yet half human creature, who grasps it with his hands or blows it with his breath.[1] [At] its full development, [this view] includes the belief in souls and in a future state, in controlling deities and subordinate spirits.[2] [It culminates in the notion of] the personal soul or spirit.

[This personal soul or spirit] is a thin unsubstantial human image, in its nature a sort of vapour, film or shadow; the cause of life and thought in the individual it animates; independently possessing the personal consciousness and volition of its corporeal owner, past or present; capable of leaving the body far behind, to flash swiftly from place to place; mostly impalpable and invisible, yet also manifesting physical power, and especially appearing to men waking or asleep as a phantasm separate from the body of which it bears the likeness; continuing to exist and

[1] *Primitive Culture* (London: Murray, 1915), Vol. I, p. 285.
[2] *Ibid.*, p. 427.

appear to men after the death of that body; able to enter into, possess, and act in the bodies of other men, of animals, and even things.[3]

The indeterminateness of this notion as an interpretative principle is obvious. What is thunder? It is the angry voice of a great spirit. It is the stamping of the hoofs of the steeds of a great spirit. It is a great spirit clanging his arms. It is the roar of the lightning bolts hurled by a great spirit. It may even be a spirit itself roaring in pursuit of some other spirit to devour. These interpretations are all consonant with the categories of spirit, and there is nothing but the limitations of poetic fancy to put a stop to such interpretations. There is no one precise and determinate interpretation of thunder, nor is there any precise method for finding one, nor is there any hope that more factual observation will ever produce one through these categories. On the contrary, the more details of observation are presented, the more the animistic imagination luxuriates and the more indeterminate the interpretations become—that is, the more mutually contrary and equally consonant interpretations are thrown in our lap.

What means can animism itself suggest for settling upon a determinate interpretation of facts? There are dozens of elaborate animistic mythologies. How can we settle which is right, or even which is the better of any two? The natural animistic theory of cognitive value is the authority of spirit. What a great spirit says is true, and what the greatest spirit says is most true. When the direct word of a spirit cannot be obtained—in his immediate presence, in

[3] *Ibid.*, p. 429.

dreams, in voices, in omens, in prognostications, in sacred traditions, or in holy books—then the word of the most authoritative representative of a spirit must be taken. So we come to the authority of shaman, medicine man, and priest. Animism is the natural metaphysical support of authoritarianism, which inevitably culminates in the dogma of infallible authority. It is ultimately infallible authority that is appealed to for rendering final and determinate the factual interpretation of the animistic world hypothesis.

The unsatisfactoriness of dogmatic authoritarianism we have already seen. A theory that is driven to this extremity to counteract the indeterminateness of its categories and the internal contradictions that develop, automatically confesses its inadequacy. We note, moreover, how quickly this confession appears.

The full maturity of an animistic world theory, then, occurs when the root metaphor of man's personality has developed into the richest conception of spirit, and when a luxuriant mythology has vividly populated the universe with explanatory spirits and has told the world's history in considerable detail from its creation to the day the chronicler was speaking. There are many men in civilized countries today who accept a pretty mature animism. In this country we call them "fundamentalists."

But a fairly reflective civilized man cannot stomach fundamentalism. Accordingly, under the pressure of criticism, mythological interpretations begin to be thinned down. At first they are treated as allegories, then as mere symbols of something higher and finer, and finally the notion of spirit itself is ephemeralized into an emotionally shaded word with a vague direction outward or inward. When this occurs we have an excellent example of that empty abstractionism or hypostatization of which we were speaking at the end of the last chapter. The very emptiness of the concept is used as an argument for its acceptance, and often the claim is made on pseudo-empirical grounds. Since this fallacy appears here more clearly than in better theories, let us notice briefly an example of it, so that we may be on our guard against the fallacy in theories where it is harder to detect.

§3. *An example of empty abstractionism.*—Tolstoy in his *What Is Religion?* provides a good example, especially good because, as a rather reflective civilized man, he is so well aware and so scornful of the luxuriant mature animism which analysis shows is the main source of "facts" for his forthcoming abstract beliefs. Such animistic interpretations as "the absurdities of the Old Testament,"[4] together with the accounts of miracles, the claims of infallibility, and the offices of priesthood, are, he claims, distortions of the "true religion." "True religion," he writes, "is the establishment by man of such a relation to the Infinite Life around him, as, while connecting his life with this Infinitude and directing his conduct, is also in agreement with his reason and with human knowledge."[5] "True religion," we thus see, is something which Tolstoy wishes to be in conformity with "reason and human knowledge."

His means of obtaining this "true religion" in conform-

---

[4] *What Is Religion?* (New York: Crowell, 1902), p. 220.
[5] *Ibid.*, pp. 213–214.

ity with "reason and human knowledge," it soon appears, is to find out what beliefs are held in common by all religions after "distortions" have been cleared away. Such a method is excellently calculated to sterilize the facts. Even if this method were properly used, it is clear the result could not be an induction from the facts concerned, but only from beliefs about the facts. The procedure turns out to be simply a peculiar kind of majority vote, an appeal to authority much diluted, a movement away from the facts rather than toward them.

Take the following passage, in which he summarizes his method and his thesis:

Such a modern religion, common to all men,—not some one particular religion with all its peculiarities and distortions, but a religion consisting of those principles which are the same in all the religions obtaining among men and known to us, professed by more than nine-tenths of the human race,—such a universal religion does exist, and men have not yet become finally brutalized only because the best men of all nations adhere to this religion and profess it, even though unconsciously, and it is only the inculcation of deceit which is practised on men by the aid of the priests and the scientists which hinders them from accepting it consciously.

The principles of this true religion are so natural to men that the moment they are communicated they are accepted as something long familiar and self-evident. For us this true religion is Christianity, in those of its principles in which it coincides, not with the external forms, but with the fundamental principles of Brahmanism, Confucianism, Taoism, Judaism, Buddhism, even Mohammedanism. In the same way, for those who profess Brahmanism, Confucianism, and so on, the true religion will be the one the fundamental principles of which coincide with those of all the other great religions. And these principles are very simple, comprehensible, and not numerous.

They assert that there is a God, the source of all; that in man there is a particle of this divine element which he can either diminish or increase by his life; that to increase this element man must suppress his passions and increase love in himself; and that the practical means to attain this is to act with others as one wishes others to act toward oneself. All these principles are common to Brahmanism and Judaism and Confucianism and Taoism and Buddhism and Christianity and Mohammedanism.[6]

Notice how Tolstoy finds it necessary to interpolate an appeal to self-evidence ("principles so natural that they are accepted as something long familiar and self-evident") to bolster up a cognitive weakness, of which he is partly conscious. He partly knows that his procedure is only pseudo-rational.

Notice also the two sources of the persuasiveness of his procedure—for there is no question that many are persuaded by this and similar arguments: First, the procedure is such as to depersonalize or sterilize the animistic categories and so make them acceptable to a somewhat critical intelligence, which will entertain concepts ("Infinite Life," "God," "source of all," "particle of this divine element") when it would refuse to entertain the images and concrete evidence to which these concepts refer. Second, the procedure does not entirely cut off, though it does greatly constrict and thereby in large part conceal, the evidential channel, which runs from the full and familiar animistic mythology to the acceptable abstractions. The appeal of the abstractions is their animistic source. Such evidence as supports them is there. They would not be entertained for a moment if the source were cut off. But neither would

---

[6] *Ibid.*, pp. 245–246.

they be entertained for a moment by a thinking civilized man if the source were clearly revealed. Tolstoy's "true religion" is a little nest of hypostatizations, concepts subtly claiming cognitive value because of their very emptiness.

Animism thus gives us a good idea of the symptoms of inadequacy through lack of precision. Since the categories lack determinateness, they are unable to control their interpretations, which multiply about the same fact and mutually contradict one another. The situation gets worse rather than better the more information is brought forward. To save the theory there follows a strong tendency to take refuge in abstractions and hypostatizations. On either count the theory convicts itself of inadequacy.

§4. *The mystic world hypothesis, an example of inadequate scope.*—We now turn to mysticism for a view of the opposite sort of inadequacy. Here we begin with a very impressive immediate fact, the mystic experience, a fact that is never lost sight of and never apologized for, a fact that is as certain as a fact can be. But the certainty of this fact is so intense that it undertakes to absorb the whole universe within it. Where it does not plausibly succeed, it denounces the unsubmissive "facts" as unreal; and, since there are many of these, it spreads unreality far and wide. As *the* philosophy of unity and love, it is the most destructive of all world theories in cognition and finally destroys itself by the very intensity of its desire for unity and peace.

Though everyone has heard of mystic experiences and many have had them with various degrees of intensity, we had best begin our criticism by a description of the ex-

perience. I choose from William James' selections in his
The Varieties of Religious Experience a relatively sober
and generalized description by St. John of the Cross:

We receive this mystical knowledge of God clothed in none of
the kinds of images, in none of the sensible representations, which
our mind makes use of in other circumstances. Accordingly in
this knowledge, since the senses and the imagination are not employed, we get neither form nor impression, nor can we give any
account or furnish any likeness, although the mysterious and
sweet-tasting wisdom comes home so clearly to the inmost parts
of our soul. Fancy a man seeing a certain kind of thing for the
first time in his life. He can understand it, use and enjoy it, but
he cannot apply a name to it, nor communicate any idea of it,
even though all the while it be a mere thing of sense. How much
greater will be his powerlessness when it goes beyond the senses!
This is the peculiarity of the divine language. The more infused,
intimate, spiritual, and supersensible it is, the more does it ex-
ceed the senses, both inner and outer, and impose silence upon
them. . . . The soul then feels as if placed in a vast and profound
solitude, to which no created thing has access, in an immense and
boundless desert, desert the more delicious the more solitary it
is. There, in this abyss of wisdom, the soul grows by what it
drinks in from the well-springs of the comprehension of love, . . .
and recognizes, however sublime and learned may be the terms
we employ, how utterly vile, insignificant, and improper they are,
when we seek to discourse of divine things by their means.[7]

From this description we learn that the experience is
felt as (1) supremely cognitive and revelatory ("mystical
knowledge of God"), (2) as immediate and totally un-
interpreted (like "seeing a certain kind of thing for the
first time"), (3) as accordingly certain and indubitable
("wisdom comes home so clearly to the inmost part of the
soul"), (4) as emotionally ecstatic ("sweet-tasting wis-

[7] *The Varieties of Religious Experience* (New York: Longmans, Green,
1928), pp. 407–408.

dom," "from the well-springs of the comprehension of love"), (5) as a unity increasing with the intensity ("the more delicious the more solitary"), (6) as wide and comprehensive ("vast and profound solitude," "immense and boundless desert"), (7) as negating other modes of cognition and other "facts" ("the senses and the imagination are not employed," "we get neither form nor impression," "no created thing has access" in this "desert").

These seven points are a rough statement of the categories of mysticism. For convenience they may be reduced to two: (I) the revelatory, beatific, emotional quality which is the ultimate ground of all evidence (1, 2, 3, and 4), and (II) principles of reduction by means of which all other apparent evidence is reduced to the ultimate ground (5, 6, and 7).

Now, hypothetically, a mystic need not be a metaphysician. He might have and enjoy his experience and make no cognitive claims for it beyond his having had it and enjoyed it. As such, it would be like any intense emotional experience—like being absorbed in a sunset, thrilled with a piece of music, or in love with a girl. In its milder forms, this is perhaps just the way we do take the experience. In fact, these illustrations of emotion just given may be the experience in mild forms. Perhaps any intense, absorbing, sweet emotion is a mild mystic experience. Leuba, for instance, in his study *The Psychology of Religious Mysticism* believes he has evidence that even the most intense mystic experiences are nothing but sublimated sex emotion. So regarded, the enthusiasm for the object of the emotion, and the conviction of its superlative value while the emotion holds, would be smiled at and recognized as simply a curious feature of the emotion to be corrected at a calmer moment so far as it had any cognitive implications. Every lover believes his beloved to be the most perfect and beautiful creature in the world. We expect every lover to have that conviction. We smile at his illusion, wish him his full and happy indulgence of it, make our own cognitive corrections, and expect him to do the same at a soberer time. The feeling of cognitive certainty which normally accompanies the emotion is discounted as cognitive evidence for anything beyond the intensity and sincerity of the emotion. Under these conditions there is no cognitive problem.

But a typical mystic would resent the implications of the previous paragraph. For him, the distinctive characteristic of the mystic experience is that it does make a cognitive claim—a superlative cognitive claim, in fact, which is never rescinded. The mystic himself, of course, does not make the claim. It is not a claim on the grounds of arbitrary authority, or any other authority in the manner of animism. The mystic simply reports the claim which the experience itself reveals. The stronger the experience the stronger the claim, and in the apical form of the experience (which in our terms would be the mature root metaphor of the theory) the claim becomes unique and cancels out all other cognitive claims whatsoever. The revelation of the experience is the truth (or The Truth), and all other cognitive claims are completely or partly false, apparent, and unreal.

This, here, is the stand of the unsystematic metaphysical mystic. He is convinced of the supreme truth of his revelation. He takes his stand on the indubitable certainty of the experience and pays no particular cognitive attention to the other "facts" of the world. In practice he may become a hermit retiring as far as he can from the other "facts" of the world and seeking to be as much immersed as he can in the One Supreme Fact; or he may become a reformer or a poet and like St. Francis or Walt Whitman try to lead as many of his fellow men as he can to a realization of The Truth.

But some mystics, like Plotinus, have had a philosophical bent and have tried to give a systematic account of the world in terms of their insight. These are the systematic metaphysical mystics. These men assume the absolute credibility of the experience. But they have a cognitive curiosity to know how this indubitable experience is connected with the ordinary "facts" of the world. There is, moreover, a practical utility in developing such a world theory as a means of showing common men how they may proceed from common "facts" to the truth.

The immediate temptation here is to deny outright the reality of all "facts" except the one mystic Fact. There is also an aesthetic delight in such wholesale destruction through the possession of an inner secret. So we get a mystical formula for describing this one Reality in terms of everything else which it is not (or, with the opposite twist, which it *really* is), as Emerson in his poem "Brahma," Swinburne in "Hertha," or Dionysius the Areopagite as follows: "The cause of all things is neither soul nor intellect; nor has it imagination, opinion, or reason, or intelligence; nor is it reason or intelligence; nor is it spoken or thought. It is neither number, nor order, nor magnitude, nor littleness, nor equality, nor inequality, nor similarity, nor dissimilarity. It neither stands, nor moves, nor rests. . . . It is neither essence, nor eternity, nor time. Even intellectual contact does not belong to it. It is neither science nor truth. It is not even royalty or wisdom; not one; not unity; not divinity or goodness; nor even spirit as we know it," etc.[8] In the momentum of these negatives this sort of mystic may even end by naming his reality itself "Nothing."

But even a mystic can sometimes see that this is going to ridiculous lengths. A man like Plotinus scrutinizes the nature of the experience more carefully to see if some structure cannot be found in it to provide the theory a little more scope. Plotinus himself was an eclectic, as probably all systematic mystics have been. He filled up the gaps of his theory with some animism and a great deal of Platonic formism, so that he is best known as a Neoplatonist. This in itself is rather enlightening about the theory of the man who is considered the greatest philosophical mystic.

Abstracting the eclectic elements from his theory, we see that the method he used amounts to an application of the generating-substance theory. The revelatory, beatific, emotional quality, our general mystic category I, becomes for Plotinus the source, the end, and the cause of all things, a generating substance. Like the sun it is the light of the universe, and only the light is real. All other "facts" are in outer darkness and are real only so far as they are

---

[8] William James, *The Varieties of Religious Experience*, pp. 416–417.

illuminated by the light of reality which "emanates" (his term) from the intense central reality. This principle of emanation is his principle of change by which facts other than the central generating reality acquire some degree of reality. Since what emanates is some of the reality itself which becomes adulterated in the surrounding darkness of unreality, the outer facts become thus "reduced" to reality and "emanation" is seen as a principle of reduction, our general mystic category II. Such is, we believe, the normal form of the mystic world hypothesis.

So, leaving Plotinus and speaking in less exalted tones, we may venture to describe the typical structure of the mystic world hypothesis as follows: The ordinary common "fact" of the root metaphor is the common emotion of love. This emotion in its most intense sublimated form is taken as the mature root metaphor. The hypothesis states that this emotion is the substance of the universe, and that so far as we differentiate things, these are generated from this substance and are ultimately nothing but this substance. Certain principles of generation or reduction are derived from the observation of the action of emotion upon things. These principles are three: first, degrees of intensity of emotion (the stronger the emotion, the more of it, and the more the reality); second, degrees of fusion (the stronger the emotion, the greater the tendency for things to melt together and unify, and the greater the reality); third, degrees of inclusiveness (the greater the number of things melted together, the greater the reality). The categories of mysticism are thus finally the quality of the emotional substance and these three principles of reduction. The operation of these principles will be recognized as the so-called Mystic Ladder, or the Mystic Way, or the Mystic Symbolism, the "Signature of All Things."

Those "facts" are most real which are most intense in the beatific quality of the emotion of love, most completely fused and unified in that emotion, and most widely comprehensive in the inclusion of fact. By extrapolation, it follows that the most intense, completely fused, beatific, loving feeling of the whole wide world would be an intuitive experience of the whole of reality itself, and would be Truth itself. Such an experience one seems to have in the apical mystic experience, which is, moreover, sealed with the feeling of indubitable certainty. "Facts" are false, and unreal, and apparent in proportion as they fall away from this apical experience. So pain, misery, sorrow, sadness are unreal, as opposed to beatific quality; pleasures, comforts, sensuous delights are false from lack of intensity; intellect, logic, science, analysis, definition, discrimination, differentiation are falsifying as opposed to fusion; selfishness, lust, hate, war are unreal as opposed to comprehension. Appearance and unreality spread wide over the field of "facts."

Such seems to be the hypothesis of mysticism, and such the dogma. On the basis of our previous discussions the criticism is simple and obvious. So far as mysticism trusts to the certainty and indubitability of its intuition, it is dogmatic and untrustworthy. So far as it trusts to its capacity to generate a structural hypothesis, it is almost completely lacking in scope. We notice, furthermore, how quickly it convicts itself of inadequacy by its own logic. For the logic of mysticism is the emotional theory of truth. Having pitched upon an "indubitable" fact as the criterion of truth and reality, inevitably the theory by its own criterion must judge all other facts false and unreal. All we have to do is to accept mysticism's own judgment of its own very great inadequacy.

The only reason the mystics themselves are not convinced by this criticism is that they are dogmatists. A skeptical mystic is a self-contradiction. For as soon as a mystic can entertain doubts about the revelatory powers of his intuition, he will become aware of the absurdities of his denials about pain, pleasure, war, and general common sense. Only while he is intensely certain of his own indubitable fact can he remain beyond the powers of reason and blind to the equal certainties of pain, prose, and separation. Thus mysticism becomes the champion of the dogma of certainty, as animism becomes the champion of infallible authority.[9]

[9] These few paragraphs on mysticism should obviously not be taken as a thorough treatment of the subject. But I do maintain that this is the whole story so far as the evidence for mysticism goes, and the development of a warrantable metaphysics on its basis. If I should write a book on the subject, it would merely be an expansion of the points here condensed, together with direct references to the innumerable exponents and varieties of the doctrine. One classification of varieties of mysticism is the following, suggested by William Savery: I. Self-mysticism, or phenomenological mysticism, II. Cosmic mysticism, the latter divided into (1) pantheistic mysticism (Sankara, or Nagarjuna, or Bradley), (2) emanational mysticism (Plotinus), (3) theistic mysticism (Aquinas). These are different ways of trying to reduce the world to the mystic One, or of trying to give the mystic experience a commanding place in the world. But these varieties, it should be observed, are based on the kinds of eclectic mechanisms employed to produce the reduction. So far as Bradley is a mystic, he mediates his mysticism with organicism, Plotinus with animism and Platonic formism, Aquinas with Aristotelian formism. Spinoza mediates mysticism most amazingly with mechanism. If Bergson may be called a mystic (as some rather

§5. *An example of eclecticism.*—Incidentally, an eclectic combination of animism and mysticism often makes a formidable appearance. Just fill in the empty spirit concept of an emaciated animism with the vivid indubitable mystic emotion, and each theory seems to revive. The mystical lack of scope is lavishly filled out with animistic spiritualism, and the animistic indeterminism is brought up to a supreme determinateness in the mystical intuition. Authoritarianism and certainty appear to join hands to the confusion of skeptics and corroborative reason.

Yet, though this is often a convincing union, it is not a credible one. The mystic intuition still potentially shoves all the multiplicity of spirits into unreality, and the world of spirits still try to raise their Great Spirit upon the throne which the mystic intuition occupies. To the natural internal contradictions of infallibility and indubitability, there is simply added the contradiction of infallibility with indubitability. And historically the ecclesiastics and the mystics have never harmonized very well. Periodically each group has tried to clean the other out—and this may be taken as a typical lesson in eclecticism.

With these examples and preliminaries, we are now prepared to undertake a study of the relatively adequate world theories themselves. From them we trust it will be

---

questionably have done), he mediates it with contextualism. An inadequate view has, in the nature of the case, many more varieties than a relatively adequate view, for there are an infinite number of ways of making errors. When a theory is driven to eclecticism to conceal its inadequacy, there is no end to the number of combinations possible. The summary of the view in the text keeps as close as possible to the mystical experience itself (the root metaphor), and tries to generate the reductive principles directly out of the experience, and tries to avoid all eclectic graftings.

seen that our criticisms and maxims have been justified. For what we have so far said does not prescribe to cognitive practice. On the contrary, it is cognitive practice itself that prescribes these maxims and methods for still better practice.

PART TWO

The Relatively Adequate Hypotheses

Chapter VII : A General View of the Hypotheses

§1. *Comparisons among the four hypotheses.*—There is a certain symmetry about the disposition of the relatively adequate world theories which may itself possess a cognitive significance. Just as in the field of data the table of chemical elements exhibited an order long before the grounds for that order were established by further data and hypothesis, so possibly here in the field of danda.

Four distinct world hypotheses come to view when the various kinds and causes of patent inadequacy have been removed. I am giving these hypotheses slightly unfamiliar names so as to avoid issues over the names themselves. I am calling them formism, mechanism, contextualism, and organicism.

Formism is often called "realism" or "Platonic idealism." It is associated with Plato, Aristotle, the scholastics, neoscholastics, neorealists, modern Cambridge realists. Mechanism is often called "naturalism" or "materialism" and, by some, "realism." It is associated with Democritus, Lucretius, Galileo, Descartes, Hobbes, Locke, Berkeley, Hume, Reichenbach. Contextualism is commonly called "pragmatism." It is associated with Peirce, James, Bergson, Dewey, Mead. There may be a trace of it in the Greek, Protagoras. Organicism is commonly called "absolute (*or*, objective) idealism." It is associated with Schelling,

Hegel, Green, Bradley, Bosanquet, Royce. Many of these men are rather eclectic and some of them develop their views only halfway, as notably Hobbes and Berkeley. These references are given simply to offer some immediate filling of meaning to my names for the four theories. Some of the ascriptions are, no doubt, controversial.

These four hypotheses arrange themselves in two groups of two each. The first two are analytical world theories; the second two, synthetic. Not that the analytical theories do not recognize and interpret synthesis, and the synthetic theories analysis; but the basic facts or danda of the analytical theories are mainly in the nature of elements or factors, so that synthesis becomes a derivative and not a basic fact, while the basic facts or danda of the synthetic theories are complexes or contexts, so that analysis becomes derivative. There is thus a polarity between these two pairs of hypotheses.

There is also a polarity between the members of each pair, and the polarity is of the same sort in each pair. Formism and contextualism are dispersive theories; mechanism and organicism, integrative theories. So, analysis is treated dispersively by formism and integratively by mechanism, and synthesis is treated dispersively by contextualism and integratively by organicism.

That is to say, the categories of formism and contextualism are such that, on the whole, facts are taken one by one from whatever source they come and are interpreted as they come and so are left. The universe has for these theories the general effect of multitudes of facts rather loosely scattered about and not necessarily determining one another to any considerable degree. The cosmos for these theories is not in the end highly systematic—the very word "cosmos" is not exactly appropriate. They regard system as something imposed upon parts of the world by other parts, so that there is an inherent cosmic resistance to determinate order in the world as well as a cosmic trend to impose it. Pure cosmic chance, or unpredictability, is thus a concept consistent with these theories even if not resorted to or emphasized by this or that particular writer.

For the categories of mechanism and organicism, however, a concept of cosmic chance is inherently inconsistent and is veiled or explained away on every occasion that it threatens to emerge. If nothing better can be done with it, it is corraled in certain restricted areas of the world where the unpredictable is declared predictable, possibly in accordance with a *law* of probability. For these two theories the world appears literally as a cosmos where facts occur in a determinate order, and where, if enough were known, they could be predicted, or at least described, as being necessarily just what they are to the minutest detail.

From this parallelism another follows: that the type of inadequacy with which the dispersive theories are chiefly threatened is indeterminateness or lack of precision, whereas the type of inadequacy with which the integrative theories are chiefly threatened is lack of scope.

One rarely hears a contextualist calling anything unreal except in polemical irritation at the danda of some other philosopher (a mode of expostulation which, if not excusable, is easily explainable). Any sort of fact is easily real for a contextualist; and likewise for a formist, though historically many formists have tended to call what they found of determinate order in the world, "real," and what they found of disorder, "unreal." But they need not have been subject to this confusion, and their thinking was often better than their naming. They treated what they called the "unreal" as a cosmic agency, and did so without any categorial inconsistency though with some verbal ambiguity.

But if these dispersive theories have no trouble with scope, they are constantly in difficulty with the number of equally consistent interpretations to which a single "fact" is amenable. In a mild way, they have the same trouble that animism has. The philosophic imagination with them is better controlled, but not sufficiently to produce precision. This trouble is relatively more acute in formism, where, as in animism, it tends unfortunately to increase with added information about a "fact" rather than decrease. With contextualism, the opposite trend seems to hold—the more we know about a "fact" the more determinate the description,—so that this theory has great promise of adequacy. The lack of precision and promise in formism makes this theory appear the least adequate of the four favored ones, and we should be tempted to drop it out of the list altogether were it not for the very strong feeling of certainty which attaches to its root metaphor, namely, the intuition of similarity. No other root metaphor of a favored theory is blessed with nearly so strong a feeling of certainty, which rivals in insistency that of the mystic experience. This feeling may be entirely illusory, but seeing that the formistic categories do have an appreciable degree of adequacy (far in excess of the mystical), and that the interpretations of similarity given by the other favored theories all seem rather strained (in contrast with interpretations of mystical certainty), we believe the feeling should be accepted as evidence of some adequacy and permitted to bolster up the indeterminateness of the formistic categories.

As for mechanism and organicism, these theories are constantly tempted to throw "facts" out into the unreal. Of these two, organicism seems to be definitely the weaker, and the more we study its categories the more convinced we become that the dichotomy of *Appearance and Reality* is intrinsic to them. A wise organicist makes the least he can of "appearance," but even the wisest cannot get entirely away from it. To a less degree the same seems to be true of mechanism. These two theories have, thus, a certain affinity to mysticism. By wishing perhaps too hard to get everything into one determinate order, they have to deny the reality of a good many things. Nevertheless, in contrast to mysticism, it is amazing how much they are able to get into their order. And it is possible on their own showing that actually the entire universe is in a determinate order, and that the dispersive theories are only profiting on human ignorance. To which, of course, the dispersive theories reply that the integrative theories are only profiting on human propensities to rationalization and sublimation.

These elements of symmetry, of which we have been speaking, I summarize (on the next page) in a scheme, for whatever it may be worth in the interest either of cognition or of mere exposition. But it does seem as if the scheme had some cognitive bearing. For the trends of eclecticism in world theories also seem to follow it.

§2. *The trends of eclecticism.*—There is a very strong tendency for formism and mechanism to combine. They fly to each other's arms for mutual support just as ani-

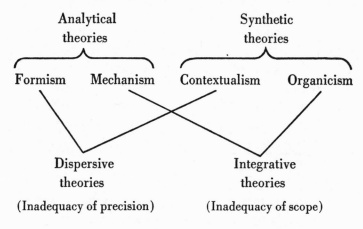

SCHEME OF WORLD HYPOTHESES

mism and mysticism do, and with comparable results. Formism is strong just where mechanism is weak, and both theories are sympathetically analytical, but, once together, the categories of each theory compete for domination. Bertrand Russell has been such an eclectic and his writings record a history of the warring of these two sets of categories in his breast. If ever there were an excuse for eclecticism, it would be here between these two theories; but let anyone try for himself and see if anything is gained by it.

There is also a very strong tendency for mechanism and contextualism to combine. Many pragmatists and some mechanists exhibit this combination in various proportions. The two theories are in many ways complementary. Mechanism gives a basis and a substance to contextualistic analyses, and contextualism gives a life and a reality to mechanistic syntheses. Each is threatened with inadequacy just where the other seems to be strong. Yet, mixed, the two sets of categories do not work happily, and the damage they do to each other's interpretations does not seem to me in any way to compensate for an added richness.

Contextualism and organicism are so nearly allied that they may almost be called the same theory, the one with a dispersive, the other with an integrative plan. Pragmatism has often been called an absolute idealism without an absolute; and, as a first approximate description, this is acceptable. So, a little more emphasis on integration in pragmatism, as Dewey, for instance, shows in his *Art as Experience*, produces a contextualistic-organistic eclecticism; as likewise a little less emphasis on final integration in organicism, as is characteristic of Royce. Royce even called himself somewhere a pragmatic idealist.

These successive pairs in the scheme seem almost to shade into one another. Other pairs of these hypotheses seem to have much less attraction for each other and are much more obviously discordant in eclectic combination. Formism and organicism are especially hostile to each other. There is nothing that an organicist so enjoys as devastating the "linear" or "atomic" logic of the formist, nor anything a formist so enjoys as tearing down and into small pieces the "muddled" and "psychologized" logic of the organicist.

It almost seems as if the four hypotheses drew together and had a tendency to pull cognitively toward the center, as if most cognitive adequacy lay somewhere between mechanism and contextualism. This appearance is strengthened by our previous comments to the effect that formism seems to be the weaker of the analytical theories, and organicism the weaker of the synthetic theories. This leaves mechanism as the stronger analytical and integrative theory, and contextualism as the stronger synthetic and dispersive theory. We are tempted to surmise that whatever system there is in the world is of the mechanistic type, and whatever dynamic vitality, of the contextualistic sort.

But for the present we must let the matter rest as surmise. A combination of mechanism and contextualism reveals all the evils of eclecticism. Besides, formism and organicism cannot yet be neglected for their sins.

And, of course, these statements all come from a wide general survey of the structural hypotheses. When we go down into details, the incompatibilities of the theories become more and more conspicuous, and to sacrifice the insights into fact which any of these theories give would be to sacrifice cognitive values possessing a degree of value which we have no means of estimating. For only the completely adequate world theory could provide that means.

§3. *The approach to the four hypotheses.*—In order not to extend the study of these theories beyond the bounds of a reader's patience, we must deal with them briefly in the pages that follow. To give one a clear idea of how they work is the most that we can try to do. For the detailed expansion of them we must refer to the classics of philosophy and science which exhibit them.

Unfortunately, there are few books that exhibit any of these theories in their purity. Dogmatism and eclecticism permeate the literature of structural hypotheses. But once one has the keys of the root metaphors and their categories in his pocket, he is, I believe, able to unlock the doors of those cognitive closets which constitute the literature of structural hypotheses in philosophy and science. As far as structural refinement in knowledge goes, there will then be no secrets. Some of the closets may be hard to open. It is not always clear how many locks they have, or in what sequence the keys must be used. But I am pretty sure these four keys will open any closet now built that is worth opening. And if one carries about with him the keys of generating substance, animism, mysticism and a few other little keys perhaps of the same sort, he will be able to get into any of the other closets built to date, though he will not find much in them that is worth cognitive scrutiny.

My exposition of these four theories, therefore, will not necessarily follow that of any of the traditional writers. And I shall undoubtedly make mistakes. But my aim is simple. It is to present the root metaphor and the set of categories of each of the four theories in its purest form, and to give some idea of the general appearance of the world as interpreted through each set of categories.

To bring out the divergencies and incompatibilities of the different interpretations in sharp detail in at least one example, I shall take pains to exhibit the theory of truth which each theory generates. This seems particularly appropriate just here, as our interest is focused on cognitive value. The logic of each theory (that is, each theory's own theory of cognitive criticism) follows from its theory of truth. We shall thus incidentally have detailed material for the comparison of truth with adequacy.

Chapter VIII : Formism

§1. *Root metaphor and categories of immanent form-ism.*—The root metaphor of formism is similarity. It has two primitive sources in common sense, differing enough to produce two species of the theory, and it is question-able if the two ever quite completely merge. I shall treat them, however, as if they did. It will simply add a little more to the dispersive character of the theory, and does not quite amount to eclecticism.

The first of these sources is the simple common-sense perception of similar things. The world is full of things that seem to be just alike: blades of grass, leaves on a tree, a set of spoons, newspapers under a newsboy's arm, the sheets of a single ream of paper. On more careful scrutiny, perhaps we find that blades of grass are not exactly alike, nor even the newspapers in one edition or the sheets of a single ream. Our discrimination of differences becomes more acute, but so also does our discrimination of the grounds of similarity. The sheets of paper may have slight differences of texture, or of size, or of color. But the fact that we separate them as a group from other objects is based on their having qualities which the others do not have. These sheets are all yellow, other reams are white or differ in other respects. Let us select two sheets from the yellow ream so closely alike that, if anybody exchanges them one for the other without our following the process, we are unable to tell which is which.

We now have two exactly similar objects before us, both together. We cannot tell them apart except for the fact that we see that there are two—one, let us say, to the right of the other. If it is important to be able to tell such objects apart, we generally put a mark on one of them so as to *make* them different. In other words, they are not different at all unless we *make* them so. This is a common enough experience. Now the mature root metaphor of the sort of formism which we may call "immanent formism" consists in simply describing this experience of two exactly similar objects minutely, and accepting literally the results of the description.

Let us make the description. Here we have together before us the two exactly similar sheets of yellow paper. Let us concentrate our attention on just one of the respects in which the two sheets are similar, their color. We note that the yellow on one sheet is *identical* with the yellow on the other. If there is any question of this, let somebody interchange the two sheets. Since we cannot tell which one was the original right-hand sheet, we must admit that the two sheets have an identical color. There are, moreover, *two* manifestations of the color. We also see that clearly. But we see equally clearly that the color, the yellow, is the identical yellow in both manifestations. There is *one* quality, yellow, in *two* particular manifestations. We see these conditions directly before our eyes, and there is nothing more obvious or certain in the world.

If we accept this intuition at its face value, we have discovered that objects of perception like this have two aspects, particularity and quality, and that these two aspects are absolutely distinct even though we may never experience the one without the other. For we perceive *two* particulars (sheets of paper) with one quality (yellow). To deny these distinct aspects would place us in a contradiction. For if we say there are two yellow qualities, we contradict our intuition of one quality indistinguishable in the two objects. If we say there is only one object, we contradict our intuition of two objects. The only way to avoid contradiction and accept the intuition is to admit the duality of aspects.

This turns out to be a radical duality. Any number of particulars may have a single quality, and any number of qualities may characterize a single particular. There may be a thousand or ten thousand sheets of just the same yellow. And each sheet of paper, besides having the quality yellow, is rectangular, thin, smooth, clean-edged, and so on. Moreover, these qualities can be shuffled about among different particulars in different ways. One particular may be yellow, smooth, thick, and circular; another, white, rough, thin, and rectangular, and so on. As far as particulars in their own right go, they make no demands on qualities, nor vice versa. That is, there is nothing about a particular as a particular to restrain it from having any quality whatever. Nor is there anything about a quality as a quality to restrain it from characterizing any particular. We shall find that qualities do place certain restrictions upon one another. If a particular is yellow, it cannot also be blue. But this has to do with the relation of yellow to blue, not with that of quality to particular. The quality yellow excludes the quality blue from characterizing a particular which the yellow already characterizes, but the particular itself is indifferent and would just as soon have been blue and excluded the yellow.

Sometimes, however, particulars get hitched together in an intimate way. We were just examining a pair of yellow papers, side by side. Let us compare them with another pair of yellow papers, side by side. These *pairs* we now see are exactly alike in respect to side-by-side-ness. This respect in which there is similarity is called a relation. A relation differs from a quality in requiring at least *two* particulars for *one* characterization. One sheet of paper cannot be side by side. For the relation of side-by-side-ness, therefore, two particulars are needed; but so far as the particulars go, any pair of particulars would do.

It is convenient to have a name that will cover both qualities and relations and that will refer to any characterizing entities. The name *character* is commonly used for this purpose.

We thus obtain the following main categories for immanent formism: (1) characters, (2) particulars, and (3) participation. This last is the tie between characters and particulars. It is the particularization of a character, or the characterization of a particular. It has many names, and is often called "attribution" or "predication," referring to the fact that the grammar of our culture is dominated by these categories. "This is yellow" is a sentence epitomizing these three categories. "This" represents the uncharacterized particular; "yellow," the unparticularized character; "is," the participation of each in the other to produce the object.

It should be carefully noticed that "participation" is not a relation, for that would make it a character, and reduce the third category to a part of the second, as a result of which the first two categories could never get together in the production of an object. Such categorial "relations," which cannot be characters, may be called, after Johnson, "ties."[1] There are several other ties, which amount to subcategories of this world hypothesis. For instance, the only characteristic of the basic particulars is difference. Each particular is "other than" any other. All other characteristics which particulars have, come from characters. But this characteristic particulars have in their own right, and must have it, or they would amalgamate into one particular, which would be contrary to the intuition of similarity. Hence, "difference" or "otherness" is not a relation, but a tie. This is the "otherness" of particulars, or numerical difference. There is also an "otherness" of characters which keeps them from amalgamating, and which may be called qualitative difference, and which is also necessarily a tie.

If one asks "Why necessarily?" the answer is, "Because the hypothesis would collapse otherwise, and because the intuition of similarity supports the hypothesis." These ties, however, do have a suspicious look, and formists find it tempting to invent new ones when interpretations become difficult in terms of the fundamental categories. Ties

---

[1] In taking over Johnson's term "tie," I do not wish to be held responsible for his exact uses of the term. The need for such a term indicates a ticklish place in formism, and I have generalized it to cover all categorial "relations" that are not characters. I hold it to Johnson's credit that he realized the need of such a term, and I think I am following the spirit, if not the letter, of his usage.

are relations which are not relations. This sounds very much like a self-contradiction, and seems to indicate a categorial inadequacy. I rather think it is. Nevertheless, the theory contains too many insights for us safely to neglect it, until a much better world theory comes in view.

§2. *The Theory of Types.*—These ties have not restricted their troubles entirely within the field of a single world theory. They have spilled over into the field of data and have occasioned a more than casual threat to the value of all world theories.

The institution of ties is often justified by an instrument called the "Theory of Types." This is a logical conception. It states that the concepts employed in the analysis of other concepts cannot themselves be included among the concepts analyzed. It is pictorially confirmed by the image of the eye that cannot see itself, or the telescope that cannot be focused on itself. If the principle could be established beyond question, it would constitute a definite prescription upon world hypotheses. For it states that some items in the universe cannot be included in a theory about the universe (namely, the analyzing concepts themselves), whence it follows that descriptions of the universe as a whole are meaningless—a typical dogma of the modern positivists. The question, of course, is what certifies to such a sweeping validity of the Theory of Types.

The answer of those positivists who make the allegation of the meaninglessness of world hypotheses is that the efficiency of symbolic logic and the refined multiplicative corroboration of logical data provide the certification. These evidences certify with a maximum of refinement

concerning what does or does not have cognitive meaning.
These accordingly prescribe the limits of cognitive mean-
ingfulness—or, specifically in this context, noncontradiction. Accordingly, world hypotheses, which by definition
violate the Theory of Types, are meaningless, self-contradictory, and cognitively impossible.

This allegation is not lightly to be set aside, coming as
it does from one of the ultimate achievements of cognitive
refinement. At the very least it exemplifies the cognitive
strain that exists between multiplicative and structural corroboration. For it seems pretty obvious that philosophers
are not going to stop making world hypotheses because
logicians say these are impossible.

As a beginning, it may be noticed that the images of the
eye and the telescope are not serious obstacles even pictorially. For an eye can indirectly see itself in a mirror,
and one telescope can be focused upon another of the same
make, so that eyes and telescopes do know themselves, so
to speak. Moreover, as a matter of common-sense fact we
do seem to know our analytical tools as well as what we
analyze by them. And lastly, as our preliminary study of
cognition seems to show, structural corroboration does not
give way to multiplicative corroboration except with regard to the reliability of data themselves. Where multiplicative corroboration begins to trespass upon the domain
of structural corroboration and to make prescriptions
about hypotheses, there structural corroboration ceases to
be respectful.

Such appears to be the present situation. Structural corroboration raises no question about the logical data, or the

validity of the transitions in the development of a logical system, say, *Principia Mathematica*. But as to the cognitive status of the system as a whole, that is different. If this system begins to prescribe to knowledge in general, then it exceeds the claims of multiplicative corroboration and sets itself up as a hypothesis concerning the nature of knowledge; and the grounds for that claim come under the scrutiny of structural corroboration.

Now a logical system such as that of *Principia Mathematica* is not simply a collection of logical transitions. It is based on a set of postulates and primitive ideas. These are not necessarily refined data at all. Where did they come from?

Remembering that symbolic logic originated in the intention of giving a mathematical formulation to the concepts of the traditional formal logic which came down through the formistic scholastics, and which owed its origin to Aristotle and Plato, who were the great original formists, we suspect that the primitive ideas of symbolic logic are in large part derived from the categories of formism. We suspect, therefore, that the Theory of Types is nothing more than a systematization of the categorial distinctions in formism between relations and ties, and that it presupposes the very world theory and the very difficulties of that theory which it is proposed to resolve. We fear that it is a subtle hypostatization. It does not, therefore, solve the problem of ties. It only gives a name to it, and tells what concepts we are to exclude from an analysis in formistic terms if we wish to avoid trouble. It probably represents an irremediable inadequacy within the formistic world theory, and points to a region where the theory in terms of its own logic confesses its inadequacy.

If this suggestion is correct, there is a particular irony in the prescription of modern positivists upon the development of world hypotheses. For it was a self-confessed inadequacy of a world hypothesis which supplied the ground for the prescription.

§3. *Classes.*—Returning from this important digression, we come upon a powerful cognitive instrument which is generated by the participation of characters in particulars, namely, the concept of *class*. A class is a collection of particulars which participate in one or more characters. Thus all the particulars which are blue—the sky today, and the water, the bluejay, the larkspur, the book on the table, the jar on the mantel, these and all other blue things—constitute the class of blue things. This class exists, of course, whether we name it or not. But if we wish to name it, we might call it the class of bluethums. If we add the character thick, we should obtain the class of thickbluethums, which obviously contains a much smaller collection of particulars. If to "blue" and "thick" we should add a considerable number of other carefully selected characters, we would obtain the class bluejay, which contains a still smaller collection of particulars.

This mode of selecting characters suggests that classes themselves are organized. An organization of classes is called a classification. Normally a classification proceeds from the more general to the less general, that is, from the classes with the smallest number of characters and largest number of particulars to those with the largest number of

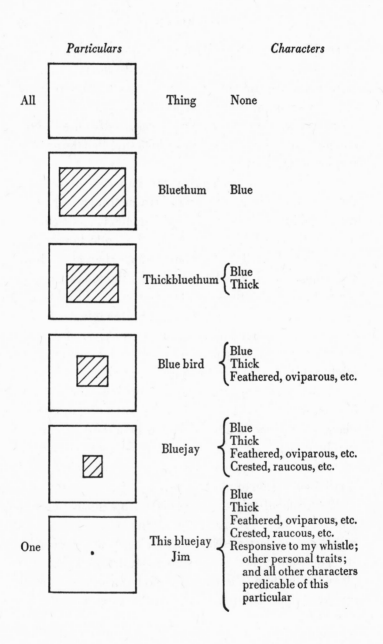

characters and the smallest number of particulars. This may be represented as in the diagram on the opposite page. It is not a very illuminating classification. But that is all the better, since it indicates the catholicity of classes.

We notice that the lowest item in the classification, "this bluejay," is not, strictly speaking, a class. "This bluejay" is a particular bluejay, and if we are familiar with him we give him a "proper name," such as Jim. If a classification is carried down to the limit, it always comes upon particular things like Jim.

We notice also that the highest item, "thing," which I inserted in order to bring out its peculiarity, is not, strictly speaking, a class either. It is simply the category of all particulars. It possesses no character by definition—or, rather, by analysis of the intuition of similarity. Some formists try to give it the character of particularity. But this is clearly a mistake (or a hypostatization), for the character of having no character is a self-contradiction. Or if we try to say that the character of particulars is numerical difference, we are involved in the confusion of a character (relation) with a tie.

Sometimes formists put the name "entity" above "thing" and say that "entity" is the class defined by the character "being," which has the two subclasses, "character" defined by qualitative difference, and "thing" defined by numerical difference. But this also must be a mistake. For character, like thing, is a category, not a class; and "entity" and "being" are simply names for the categories indiscriminately. To make them classes or characters is again to confuse ties with relations. The formistic hypoth-

esis will not work at all unless this distinction is persist-
ently held.

We notice also that a class is itself neither a character,
nor a particular, nor a participation, nor a separate category. It is simply the actual working of the three categories
in the world. We simply observe that a character or a
group of characters normally participates in a number
of different particulars. We give a name to that observed
fact and call it "class." Class is simply a name for a specific operation of the three immanent categories, an operation completely analyzable into the functioning of those
categories. A class is, accordingly, a thoroughly real thing,
but what is real is the functioning of the categories.

Having thus learned what character, particular, participation, and class are in immanent formism, and having
noted that all are derived from the root metaphor of strict
similarity, we shall now turn to the categories of transcendent formism.

§4. *Root metaphor and categories of transcendent formism.*—The common-sense or primitive root metaphor of
transcendent formism comes from two closely allied
sources: the work of the artisan in making different objects on the same plan or for the same reason (as a shoemaker making shoes, or a carpenter making beds), and
the observation of natural objects appearing or growing
according to the same plan (as crystals, oak trees, sheep).
Plato stressed the artisan, Aristotle the natural growths,
but the categories achieved along this route are the same.
Consider the making of stout shoes for a man. Here is a
set of natural conditions dictating an ideal plan for such

a pair of shoes. And here is the available leather as matter to be shaped into that plan. The plan appears as a norm which the shoes fulfill according to the skill of the artisan and the limitations of the available material. The norm may rarely be fulfilled. Deficiencies in the leather and in the skill of the artisan lead to variations in the shoes and discrepancies from the norm. The shoes made by the same plan come out more or less similar, and their similarity is due to the identity of plan, but the norm is usually not completely revealed in the shoes, but transcends them.

It is much the same with an oak tree. There is no artisan here. The dynamics of creation comes out of the acorn and tree itself. But there are evidences of a uniform plan which all oak trees apparently seek to approximate. Oak trees vary because of variations in their conditions of growth, because of unsuitability of soil, water, neighboring growths, or inheritance. So, few oak trees are permitted to grow normally and to exhibit the full potentiality of the oak. In one way or another they are distorted, and the norm of the oak transcends them.

This root metaphor of plan and material also develops three categories which closely parallel those of immanent formism. The categories of transcendent formism are: (1) norms, (2) matter for the exemplification of the norms, (3) and a principle of exemplification which materializes the norms.

The only important difference between the immanent and the transcendent categories lies in the first category. Both sets recognize a category of (1) forms, a category of (2) the appearance of these forms in nature, and a category of (3) the connection between the first and second categories. Can these two sets be amalgamated?

Let us compare norms with characters. A norm is a complex set of characters. The norm of an oak tree is roughly the botanist's description of it. The idea then suggests itself that a norm is a misnomer for a class. But the two are quite different. A class, we saw, is not a form (not an instance of the first category), but a discrimination of the specific functioning of the immanent formistic categories. A norm, contrariwise, is a form, an instance of the first category. Moreover, a class implies the immanent and *full* appearance of the characters concerned in any particular thing which has them. The blue of a bluethum is fully present in every blue thing. It is not a matter of approximation. But with norms it is different. The norm of the oak is rarely or never fully present in any particular oak. Particular oaks merely approximate the norm. Thus the character or characters of a class draw a circle, so to speak, about the particular objects which fully participate in them. But a norm is a center of a rather vague extensity, claiming as exemplifications objects which closely approximate it and making lesser and lesser claims toward the periphery and scarcely claiming at all so-called sports or freaks. So, a norm is definitely not a class.

The next idea perhaps is that there may be no adequate evidence for norms and that we can better employ merely the immanent formistic categories, and regard norms as fictions. Possibly. What evidence is there for norms?

Of course, we were just giving the common-sense evidence in describing the root metaphor. There is the shoemaker's norm of a good pair of shoes, the nature lover's norm of an oak tree. But further than these is evidence that norms seem to be used or presupposed in much of the basic work of empirical scientists. The specimen of flower, or bird, or insect sought after by a biologist is not *any* member of the *class*, but the "good specimen" or *norm* of the species. The biologist seems to have a pretty definite idea of the *normal* habits and the *normal* appearance of his species, and even if what he offers as a description of the species is simply the average, this average is not a class, but a norm. A species seems to represent, at least often, a state of biological equilibrium in nature, a structural point of balance and stability, and as such it would be not a class, but a norm. Similarly with the forms of matter—molecules, atoms, electrons. These seem to be, at least often, treated by empirical scientists as norms of physical structure. It is often assumed that matter must take these forms. There are the ninety-two atomic elements. Matter in the atomic stage is expected to appear in one of these forms and not otherwise. In the atomic stratum of nature, observation seems to exclude the anticipation of gradation between the different species of matter, such as biologists are accustomed to expect between biological species.

Incidentally, the hypothesis of norms as categorial structures has nothing essential to do with the doctrine of the fixity of species, with which a famous debate has associated it. There is no reason why, in a world in which norms constituted a basic type of order, there should not be an order of evolution among the norms. If there is good evidence that the ancient ancestors of men were fish, that does not in any way disturb the structural differences between men and fish. Lead is no less lead today when we find it may be derived from uranium. During the nineteenth century, scientists, on the evidence before them, believed in the fixity of atomic species in the constitution of matter, though they had come to believe in the evolution of plant and animal species in life. Today, of course, the evidence supports an evolution of atomic species, and the doctrine of the fixity of species descends to the subatomic level, where it still survives.

The obvious interpretation of all such facts is that there are norms in nature, just as Aristotle observed. If this interpretation is not often openly accepted today, the avoidance of it in favor of less obvious interpretations is due to other causes than the direct observations themselves. There seems to be plenty of apparently direct inductive evidence for norms exemplified in nature.

In fact, every law of science may be so interpreted. Persons who accept the theory that there are laws of nature, and that the aim of science is to discover these laws, which nature "follows," seem (if their words do not belie them) to imply that these laws are norms which regulate (literally render regular) the occurrences of nature. On this view, the inductive method is a method of collecting observations for the discovery of the regularities or laws which "hold" in nature. Any actual induction may be in error, but its aim is to approximate to the law exemplified in natural phenomena. Whether any or all laws of nature are fully exemplified in nature is itself a matter of inductive inquiry. The most obvious interpretation of the regularities found in nature is that they are genuine norms and that they are literally found there. So, there is no scarcity of evidence for natural norms.

§5. *Amalgamation of the immanent and the transcendent categories of formism.*—How, then, can norms be amalgamated with characters? It can be done if characters can participate in norms, and if norms can be regarded as particulars of a second degree, distinct from the basic particulars of immanent formism. It can be done if, so to speak, the transcendent categories can be superimposed upon the immanent categories.

To explain this amalgamation, it will now be convenient to use the two terms *existence* and *subsistence*, which are used by many contemporary formists. By "existence" we shall mean primarily the field of basic particulars (the collection of all elements of the second immanent category), and secondarily such particulars with any characters they may participate in. The field of existence, then, is primarily the field of bare particulars, and secondarily the field of all basically particularized characters. A bare particular (that is, a particular with no characters at all) may be a sheer abstraction. It could not possibly be observed. Whether there is any evidence for the existence of bare particulars, is an issue that need not concern us. But it is convenient to define the field of existence as primarily that of bare particulars, even if this is a sheer abstraction, in order to avoid possible ambiguities. Concrete objects such as we perceive and handle are all in the field of existence as secondarily considered. That is, they are all basic particulars with characters. We might call the field of existence thus secondarily considered the *field of concrete existence.*

By *subsistence* we shall mean the field of characters and norms so far as these are *not* considered as participating or being exemplified in basic particulars. Whether in fact there are any characters or norms which are not particularized in basic particulars, is another issue with which we shall not concern ourselves; though this is a serious issue and is the ground for the split between the so-called Platonists and the Aristotelians. The Platonists hold that subsistent entities have a being independent of basic particulars. The Aristotelians hold that subsistent entities are an abstraction from concrete particulars, and that the ascription of independent being to them is a hypostatization. It is highly questionable if a character or norm can be directly known except as it appears in a concrete existent object or event (that is, as basically particularized), though many Platonists have believed that these can be directly intuited in pure subsistence. However that may be, there is no question that, in terms of the formistic categories, characters and norms may be *considered* in abstraction from basic particulars, and the "relations" they have to one another may be studied.

All these "relations" are, of course, ties of various sorts. And here is where it is possible to amalgamate norms with characters. Norms, as we pointed out, are complex in character and are definitely subsistent forms. A norm, therefore, such as a shoe or an oak must participate in characters—in shape, color, and so on. A norm, therefore, is a sort of particular. But it is not a basic particular, because it may not be fully particularized. It is a subsistent or second-degree particular. It is a subsistent entity which, as subsistent, participates in certain subsistent characters. Such participation is, of course, also a second-degree participation, and does not constitute concrete existence.

It is thus possible to classify norms in "thought" independently of consideration of their concrete exemplification. Frequently, through our reflection on their "logical" connections, new norms come to light which sometimes are later discovered to have concrete exemplifications in existence apart from the activity of thinking them. Such are mathematical systems discovered in thought and subsequently, like non-Euclidean geometry, found exemplified in nature. Such evidences are the ground for Platonists' belief in the being of subsistent entities independent of concrete existence. There is some strength in the argument, though we must not forget that the act of thinking is always itself a concrete existence.

Not only norms participate in characters, but characters themselves seem to participate in other characters. We thus have complex characters or patterns (*Gestalts*) which are not analyzable completely into elementary characters, though they participate in them. Thus the pattern, square, is a character which participates four times in a straight line of given length, four times in right angularity, and once in a spatial spread of surface. It cannot be "reduced" to four lines, four angles, and a surface, unless we wish to affirm that a square is just a *name*, and that things never resemble each other because they are *square*, but only because they participate in lines, angles, numbers, and surfaces. Since, however, the basic root metaphor is the intuition of similarity, and we do seem to intuit the similarity of squares as square, it seems wiser to accept the intuition at its face value and admit complex characters which are secondary particulars participating at a second degree in other characters.

Then there are the "relations" between what have been called determinates and determinables, between scarlet, red, and color, for instance. These are easily accounted for in terms of second-degree participations, though otherwise quite puzzling formistically. In terms of second-degree participation, scarlet participates in red, red in color, and all three are genuine characters. When we see a scarlet object we see it also as red and colored. But we may with weakened discrimination see it only as red and not scarlet. The more highly discriminated character in the sequence is called the relative determinate, and the less highly discriminated, the relative determinable. Both are equally genuine characters, and what character in the sequence (what determinate in a determinable sequence) will be selected by concrete perception is a matter to be discovered through experience.

The immanent and transcendent categories can then be merged as follows: (1) forms consisting of characters and norms which may have second-degree participations with one another, (2) basic particulars, and (3) first-degree participations or exemplifications.

§6. *Concrete existence.*—We can now examine how these categories work out in nature and in consciousness.

The first fact that strikes us is that in concrete existence no characters ever seem to appear except in the form of time or in the forms of space and time. It would be rash to state that there are no concrete existences free from time and space, but there seem to be no very reliable evidences of them. Santayana, indeed (on his formistic side), makes much of the "intuition of essence." It is not quite clear whether he intends this as an intuition of a *particular essence,* or as a *particular intuition* of an essence. The former would suggest some special mode of insight into forms freed from concrete existence. It would suggest that the "intuition" was not a basically particularized act, but a release from existence bringing the mind into the direct presence of some secondarily particular essence. This seems to me a very dubious doctrine, especially as it introduces the notion of mind, or "spirit," as Santayana calls it, which is neither existent particular nor subsistent form, and which has an odor of animism about it. But this latter issue is beside our present point.

If, however, Santayana means that there may be a *particular intuition* of an essence (any essence), this doctrine, if substantiated, would often appear to give us a concrete existence free from temporal or spatial form. Thus, the intuition of a musical chord as an isolated form— say, the three related pitches, do-mi-sol—might be a concrete existent free from temporal or spatial form. A still more plausible instance would be the intuition of the complex essence, $5 + 7 = 12$. But we note, in point of fact, that the tones of the chord must have some duration to be perceived, and that the arithmetical equation must be written out or in some other way temporally symbolized in order to be comprehended. It is not that a pitch or an arithmetical relationship necessarily participates in the form of time, but that in fact we note that all basically particularized pitches and mathematical forms are accompanied by temporal durations. Probably Santayana would not wish to deny this.

But he might wish to deny something else which rapidly grows out of this. It is soon discovered that the durations which all the concrete existents seem to have can be fitted together into successions and simultaneities and so dated within an extensive form which is often called "physical time." Now, physical time is in the nature of a law, and there seems to be a great amount of empirical evidence suggesting that every concrete existent participates in this law. It is on the basis of this law that we speak about the future and the past so confidently. What the future may "hold in store," we do not know, but we are very confident that there will be a future and we will even date it off indefinitely—A.D. 3000, A.D. 10,000, A.D. 90,000, etc.

It is much the same with physical space, though there we must introduce a qualification. Though there seems to be no very reliable evidence of concrete existences without durations, we are all of us familiar with concrete existences without spatial extensions. Every time we are well absorbed in abstract thinking or in a piece of music, so that we "forget" where we are sitting or where the music comes from, we are apparently experiencing events with temporal characters but without any spatial characters. For sounds have no spatial attributes (or so, at least, many

agree), nor has thought when carried on in auditory or
kinaesthetic symbols. Visual symbols, of course, are
always accompanied by spatial extensities.

But experienced spatial extensities soon get organized
into a form of physical space, just as durations into the
form of physical time. And the form of physical space
appears, in fact, to be a law regulating concrete existences
almost as universally as the form of physical time. It is
observed to regulate concrete existences so nearly universally that the question arises whether it does not entirely
do so; and it comes to be suggested that physical space
regulates, out of sight, even those concrete existences in
which it is not experienced. On this hypothesis, when, as
we say, we "forget" where we are sitting at a musical con-
cert, we almost literally are forgetting. The location of our
hearing is actually characterizing the event, but it has
slipped our attention. The event which seems to be characterized only with auditory and temporal characters is
really also characterized by spatial relations, namely, the
relations of our seat to the stage, the walls of the room,
and the like.

The evidence for this is rather strong in view of the fact
that the laws explanatory of the intensity, timbre, pitch,
and the sequence of the sounds we hear seem to involve
ineradicably spatial measurements. That is, empirical evidence seems to show that the intensity of the sound we hear
is of just that intensity because it participates in a certain
acoustical law of sound transmission and reflection, a law
which itself participates in the law of physical space.
Hence, so far as this acoustical law is true, we must be

hearing the sound in a certain place even though we are not aware of it as a character of our auditory event.

On this basis, it would seem probable that all concrete existences participate in the laws of physical time and space, whatever other forms they may also participate in. It is possible also that the laws of physical time and space should be distinguished from sensuous duration and sensuous extensity even though these latter are evidences for the former, as if the latter were qualities and the former relations. However that may, the possible ubiquity of the physical laws of time and space easily lead many formists to identify them with basic particulars. In other words, many formists identify the second formistic category with physical time and space.

This identification seems to me unjustified by the root metaphor, and a source of unnecessary categorial confusion. For then the relational structures of time and space must be converted into ties among particulars, which unnecessarily aggravates the problem of ties, and threatens, moreover, to plunge formism into mechanism and thereby wreck the whole categorial structure of formism. There is nothing gained for formism by converting the structures of time and space into the category of particularity, and much is endangered. All the formist needs to observe (if he does observe it) is that as an empirical fact all concrete existences do participate in the physical laws of time and space, so that every concrete existent object or event is to be located at a date and at a place.

Now this seems to be what Santayana on another interpretation of his "intuition of essence" would deny. He

seems to identify belief in existence with reference to date
and place, and to say that this reference may easily be
abstracted from any given conscious event and its validity
doubted, whereupon any other forms present in the event
are intuited directly without reference to time and space.
And he also points to certain events of the absorbed and
contemplative type in which the forms of physical time and
place are not explicitly present. So far as this is what he
does, he is arguing for the fact of there being concrete existences which do not participate in time and space forms.
Certainly, there is no categorial reason in formism why
there should not be such concrete particular existences.
The only question is whether a careful sifting of the evidence shows that in fact there are.

It looks, however, as if all empirical laws (except possibly those of introspective psychology) did in fact participate in the forms of both physical time and space. These
constitute accordingly a basic restriction upon what characters can and cannot appear in concrete existence, and
upon the order of their appearance. And still further restrictions are placed upon the order of concrete existences
by natural laws. We come, in a word, upon *causality*.

It follows, then, that a concrete existent that was not
characterized by a law participating in time or space relations would be a spontaneous appearance quite free from
physical or any other kind of causality. It would be a fact
of pure chance. In formism, this is possible.

But how does causality work in formism? It is the result
of the participation of patterns, norms, or laws in basic
particulars through the forms of time and space. Consider

the law of gravitation operating upon a lead ball dropped from a height to the surface of the earth. Consider the law as it was conceived in the nineteenth century as a law distinct from the structural laws of time and space.

We have then as concrete existences the masses of the earth and the lead ball. These are also characterized by their spatial relation to each other, their distance apart. They are also characterized by a temporal relation, the date at which the lead ball is dropped. Now all masses participate in the law of gravity. According to this law, these masses are, as we say, attracted to each other, which means that the law necessitates, in this case, the motion of the ball at a specified acceleration in a straight line to the earth. The law thus regulates the appearance of new characters of time and space relationships—new dates, distances, and velocities—which are given to the ball at each stage of its descent. These *changes* are determined by the law which applies to the ball as a concrete existent on account of its character, mass.

The *causal* structure of a series of events is thus as follows: first, a basic particular (or set of basic particulars) having certain characters; second, the participation of these characters in a law, which itself participates in time and space characters; third, the determination, by the law, of other basic particulars as having certain dates or positions and as having certain characters the same as those possessed by the first basic particulars, or different from them. Causality is the determination of the characters of certain basic particulars by a law which is set in motion by the characters of other basic particulars which participate in that law. A law, in other words, is a bridge from one set of basic particulars to another set, determining the characters of one set by those of the other.

These laws are, of course, real natural structures. Events are genuinely similar to one another because they genuinely participate in the same law. But the law must not be identified with any one of its particular exemplifications, nor with any collection of particular exemplifications. A law is not a basic particular, nor a concrete existent particular (i.e., a single exemplification of the law), nor a collection of concrete existent particulars (i.e., a class). *A law is a form,* and its status is that of an entity of the first category.

According to a Platonist, a law *subsists* even though it were never exemplified in concrete existence. An Aristotelian would be less bold, would agree that a law subsists by the definition of form as opposed to particular, but would declare that a law has no being outside its exemplifications. It is, however, very important to notice that in formism a law is not to be identified with a concrete existent structure. Whether Platonist or Aristotelian, for a formist a law is a form. This is one of the fundamental distinctions between formism and mechanism. These two world views contradict each other on this issue. And the question is whether an Aristotelian is not hedging so as to avoid the full import of this contradiction. If one wishes to get the sense of formism in clearest relief, he does better to take the view in bold Platonic terms. Later he can consider whether an Aristotelian can hold his more moderate position without self-contradiction.

A law, then, participates in existence by virtue of particularized characters, like mass, which themselves participate in the law. What, then, about a mass that is restrained from following its law, such as the lead ball held in the hand before it is dropped? As far as the formist is concerned, this law is still acting and shows itself as weight or pressure downward, but it is being interfered with by another law in which this particular lead ball also participates. This lead ball is a solid and thereby participates in a law of impact which holds in the relationship between the solid ball and the tensions of muscle and bone in the hand that holds it.

These interferences of laws with one another as a result of the participation of basic particulars in characters which themselves participate in laws, which frequently conflict, constitute so marked a feature of formism that they deserve further illustration. Take the orbit of a planet about the sun. Here we have the gravitational law which would take the planet at an accelerated velocity in a straight line to the sun, and an inertial law which would take the planet at a constant velocity in a straight line off into space. Both these laws participate in the mass of the planet and this mass participates in a basic particular at a date and place. The result is a conflict between these two laws, and a distortion of both of them out of their straight lines into an ellipse, the character of which is determined by the numerical relationships of the two laws themselves, that is, the character of the ellipse is a *resultant* of the forces of inertia and gravitation exerted upon the mass of the planet.

Now, let us go quite a way from physics and consider ·
an oak tree. There is evidence, we saw, for the norm of an
oak tree. A botanist or horticulturist could tell us in great
detail what is the *normal* growth and appearance of any
particular variety of oak. Give the oak suitable soil, water,
sun, fertilization, and freedom from other vegetation,
from insects, and the like, and the normal oak will be exemplified. The law of the oak will exhibit itself in concrete
existence just as the law of gravitating mass exhibited
itself in the dropped ball. But plant the oak in poor soil
or on a windswept hill, or in a thick forest, and it will be
distorted from its normal growth just as the planet was
from the normal gravitational path. This distortion will
be a resultant of the forces of other laws in which the characters of the oak participate in conjunction with the normal law of growth of the oak.

The same distortions occur for the same reasons in the
norms of animals, of men, and of human societies. These
last, of course, are the basis for formistic ethics. Human
and social norms are ethical standards of value. In concrete existence, especially among the more complex forms
of existence, these norms seem to exhibit states of human
and social equilibrium, and serious distortions are accompanied with discomfort and pain. Hence Plato's search for
the perfect State, Aristotle's for the several types of social
structure, exhibiting a golden mean, and the search of
many modern men for the life cycle of a normal culture, or
for the life cycles of the several normal types of culture,
or for the normal stages of transition of culture toward
the perfect social structure. All such social studies presup-

pose formistic categories. For no other world hypothesis supports the reality of norms as laws determining (even though not always without interference) the concrete course of existence.

§7. *Truth in formism.*—The theory of truth which grows out of the formistic categories is the correspondence theory. Truth consists in a similarity or correspondence between two or more things one of which is said to be true of the others. In the extreme, truth might be ascribed to any one of a lot of similar concrete objects, as when we say of one apple taken out of a box that it is a true sample of the whole lot. But ordinarily the term is reserved for such objects as pictures, maps, diagrams, sentences, formulas, and mental images. These are all concrete existents and the objects they are said to be true of are not exactly similar to them, but only in respect to the form under consideration or in accordance with certain conventions. We speak of a portrait as being a true likeness when all it possesses that is identical with the sitter (supposing it to be a small picture in black and white) is certain relations of light and shade and certain two-dimensional proportions.

Let us call these objects which are said to be true, "descriptive objects" or just "descriptions," and let us call the objects they are said to be true of, the "objects of reference." It appears that men are not particularly anxious to have their descriptive objects correspond in all respects with the objects of reference, but prefer a partial correspondence if the descriptions can be made handier thereby. The handiest of all descriptive objects for men have turned out to be combinations of verbal or of mathematical symbols. That is how it happens, says the formist, that the normal descriptive objects employed for knowledge are so different from the objects of reference. What one wants for a description is the handiest thing one can get because most of the objects we want to know through our descriptions are very unhandy things. Nevertheless, says the formist, one must not think that a verbal description does not exemplify the form of its object of reference just as much as a map or a picture. One must be able to read off the conventions of a map or picture to grasp their resemblance to the object represented. So, only to a much greater degree, with a sentence or mathematical formula. At least so some formists say. If the reader balks at this, if he will admit that a drawn circle resembles the shape of a ball but will not admit that the algebraic equation for a circle does, he will only slightly embarrass the formist, for the drawn circle can always be substituted for the equation. The embarrassment simply consists in the fact that an equation, a formula, or sentence cannot then be said to be literally a description and so cannot be true or false, but must be regarded as some sort of convenient symbolic substitute for a genuine description such as a diagram, sketch, or mental image.

With these preliminaries in mind, we may very simply define truth as the degree of similarity which a description has to its object of reference. It follows that a true description actually possesses the form of its object—within the limitations prescribed by the conventions of the description. Within the limitations of size and black and white, a charcoal portrait actually participates in the form of the sitter; within those limitations that form is there as much as in the sitter. This rather remarkable consequence is guaranteed, of course, by the formistic analysis of similarity and its category of subsistence.

As a further consequence, we find that there are two kinds of truth in formism, depending upon the categorial status of the objects of reference: historical truth, and scientific truth. The first refers to existence and consists in descriptions of the qualities and relations of particular events. The second refers to subsistence and consists in descriptions of norms and laws.

There is no necessity in historical truths. The historian describes events as they have occurred. If he finds that they are causally related, he describes the causal relations as part of the existential events. But his interest is primarily in the character of the events that occurred, not in the laws which they may exemplify.

The scientist, on the other hand, is primarily interested in the laws of nature, and attends to actual events only because they exemplify the laws. Scientific induction is a method of studying particular events in such a way that they will reveal the laws which they exemplify. The formist recognizes two types of inductions: (1) those yielding descriptions of empirical uniformities, and (2) those yielding descriptions of natural laws. The first are simply statements of observed correlations in concrete existence, and contain no reasons why these regularities should occur. The second are statements of genuine laws of nature, which are regarded as necessary and therefore as explanatory of the reasons why certain regularities occur.

As examples of empirical uniformities are such observations as that day follows night, that the moon passes through monthly phases from crescent to full moon, that the tides rise twice a day. These are very reliable uniformities and we can make predictions about them without knowing why they hold. But when we have discovered the laws of gravitation and inertia and the laws of the propagation and reflection of light, then we realize the necessity of those regularities. The regularities are explained as exemplifications of fundamental physical laws.

Descriptions of empirical uniformities thus lie midway between historical statements and scientific statements properly so called. They are statements of facts observed in concrete existence and, so far, are historical in nature. But as generalizations of regularities observed in these facts they have a scientific bearing. Yet as failing to exhibit the necessity for these regularities they are not completely scientific.

From the point of view of a formist, statements of empirical uniformities are only half truths. Full truths are descriptions which accurately correspond with facts that have occurred or with laws that necessarily hold. Descriptions of empirical uniformities are simply rungs in the ladder from contingent fact to necessary law. They are signs of human ignorance. For if we knew the whole truth about them, we should know the law or the combination of laws which made their regularity necessary, or we should know that they were not necessary but were mere historical coincidences which have been mistakenly generalized and which cannot be relied upon for scientific predictions.

If most of what we call scientific knowledge is, we suspect, merely description of empirical uniformities, and therefore liable to error, that does not alter the situation, according to the formist. He points to the fact that descriptions of regularities in nature do seem to become more and more reliable as science progresses, and seem to be successively approximating to a complete reliability which would be natural necessity. According to the formist, the principle of successive approximation noted by Lenzen as characteristic of scientific method is a series of descriptions of regularities of nature successively approximating to the actual necessary laws of nature which subsist. The formist refers to the history of science as evidence for the correctness of his analysis of truth.

§8. *The transition to mechanism.*—There is another possibility, however. The laws of nature may not be so discrete, so separate from one another, as the formist assumes. The laws of temporal and spatial structure, of gravitation, and of inertia are not now regarded as separate laws, but as the structure of a cosmic field. If all laws were amalgamated in this way into the structural skeleton of a universe, then what scientific descriptions would successively approximate would not be a number of separate subsistent forms, but the single concrete existential structure of the universe. There would be no subsistence left. This is the mechanistic interpretation. The integration of scientific laws into a single system is thus a constant threat to the validity of formism. As long as that integration is not complete, formism has a case. But if one believes that the trend of evidence is in the direction of such an integration, then he will wish to turn his attention to mechanism. For the weakness of formism (at least as it now presents itself) is its looseness of categorial structure and consequent lack of determinateness. Just what constitutes one particular, or one character, or one norm or law? How many particulars are there in a sheet of paper? How many in the flight of an airplane? How can we definitely tell a tie from a relation? We are put off for answers to these questions. We are told that the answers lie in the future, when there will be enough evidence to fill in the details. It may be so. But meantime there is much vagueness, vacillation, and indefiniteness. Add to this, signs in the evidence itself that nature is intrinsically more organized than the formistic categories suggest, and we feel that the very indeterminateness of formism hands us over into the firmer categories of mechanism.

Chapter IX : Mechanism

§1. *Two poles of mechanism.*—The root metaphor of mechanism is a machine. It may be a machine like a watch or a machine like a dynamo. Species of mechanisms develop on the basis of the type of machine that is regarded as fundamental. A recent revolution in physics consisted largely in a shift from what is called a mechanical theory of matter to an electrical theory. This is really a shift from a lever to an electromagnetic field as the ultimate model of physical description. Many details are altered by this shift, but, since the basic categories are the same, the general theoretical attitude is not changed. The term "mechanism," which we are using for this type of world theory, must not, therefore, be identified with the so-called "mechanical theory of matter." The electromagnetic theory of matter is also in our terms a mechanism, provided it is accepted as a basic mode of description of fact and not interpreted in formistic or operational or other terms. The possible ambiguity of this name is unfortunate, but it seems to involve less potential misunderstanding than such names as materialism, naturalism, or realism. Let the name signify precisely that theory which is determined by the categories to be listed, and there will then be no ambiguity.

The shift in mechanism from a lever to an electromagnetic field as a material model was nevertheless no trifling shift. It corresponds to a polarity contained in the world theory itself, a polarity between what may be called a discrete and a consolidated mechanism. The most influential historical example of a discrete mechanism is the atomic materialism of Lucretius, which came down through Epicurus from Democritus. Previous to the field theories of the present, the best example of a consolidated mechanism is the world view of Spinoza mechanistically interpreted as many interpret it. The discrete and consolidated species of mechanism seem to repel each other. Yet unless they keep some contact with each other they tend to be projected quite out of mechanism, the one into dispersive formism and the other into synthetic operational contextualism. We shall have to direct attention to some of the details of this internal tension in the exposition of the theory, for the inconsistencies involved seem to constitute a permeating inadequacy of the theory. For many reasons it is best to begin our study with the older and better-known root metaphor of the lever or the push-and-pull machine which stresses action by contact; and then notice how this involves, and more or less leads into, a field conception which at the present day dominates in terms of the root metaphor of the electromagnetic field which stresses action at a distance.

§2. *The mechanistic root metaphor.*—Let us examine a single lever consisting of a bar resting on a fulcrum. By means of this machine we can push down on one end of a bar and pull up a weight on the other. The lever specifies and magnifies the push-and-pull efficacy of nature, or efficient causal structure. A simpler example would in a way be a direct bodily push or a bodily pull on a block of wood or a boulder. But the lever conveniently combines the push with the pull and very clearly exemplifies the system by which molar bodies affect one another through contact. It is a pretty simple form of the mechanistic root metaphor, but amazingly fruitful in its literal implications. The basic categories of mechanism come immediately to light in a description of the main features of this machine.

Let us imagine a lever, then, set up before us. Let it consist of a rather long bar resting on the edge of a triangular block which serves as a fulcrum. Let the object to be pulled up or lifted be the stump of a tree, and let the force to exert the push on the bar be the arm of a man (my arm, for instance).

Now these features will do for a very rough description of a lever—bar, fulcrum, pressure of an arm, and pull on a tree stump,—but more detail must be given if we are to know the lever as an effective machine. So far as the present description goes, there are many conditions under which this combination of features will not act as a machine at all. It is especially important to know where the fulcrum is placed, where the weight, and where the pressure.

A little experimenting brings out a law for the arrangement of these parts of the lever. I find that if the weight is put at one end of the bar, and the pressure of my arm at the other, then the nearer the fulcrum is placed to my end of the bar the harder it is to lift the weight, while the nearer it is placed to the stump's end of the bar the easier it is. This is a rough statement of the principle of the lever. But can we make this description more precise?

We can, if we can find an exact quantitative way of expressing the relations of the parts of the lever to one another. As far as the positions on the bar are concerned, these can be precisely found by means of a meter stick or some equivalent. Suppose the bar is three meters long, we can then precisely determine the positions of the push, pull, and fulcrum by locating the first two at opposite ends of the bar and then stating in centimeters the distances of the location of the fulcrum from one and the other end of the bar.

But what about a quantitative description of the tree stump to be lifted? Some experimenting shows that the only characteristic of the stump that is pertinent to the efficacy of the machine is what we commonly call its weight. We find, for instance, that the feeling of muscular effort exerted at the arm end of the bar for any set position of the fulcrum is not altered if, in place of the tree stump, there is hung a basket with a certain number of bricks all of the same size which may be called kilograms. Suppose the basket which is found equivalent to the pull of the stump contains fifty kilogram bricks. Then we may substitute the fifty kilogram bricks for the tree stump so far as the pull on the lever is concerned. Thus fifty kilograms may be regarded as the more precise description of the part of the machine situated at the stump end of the bar—that is, so far as this part has any bearing on the efficacy of the machine.

But what about the pressure of the arm? Is there any way of describing this more precisely? Yes, we discover a very interesting fact. And that is, that if a basket of bricks is substituted for the pressure of the arm at the arm end

of the bar it will lift the tree stump (or the equivalent basket of kilogram bricks) at the stump end of the bar. A
human arm is not necessary. All that is required is a sufficiently large number of kilogram bricks. Accordingly,
since we found that we could substitute kilogram bricks
for the tree stump and so increase the precision of our description of the machine for that end of the bar, it follows
that we can do the same for the pressure of the arm at the
arm end of the bar.

If we have any doubts about this substitution we are confirmed in our procedure by a further fact. If the fulcrum
is placed exactly in the middle of the bar and fifty kilograms of weight is put at one end, exactly fifty kilograms
lifts the fifty kilograms at the other end. This is the fact of
balance. It is important because it exhibits the equivalence
of push and pull. The kilogram bricks for the tree stump
and the arm are now seen to be just equal and just alike.
We might have thought of the stump as a passive pull and
of the arm as an active push. We now see that push and
pull can be substituted for each other. With exactly the
same weight at either end, either end could represent the
push or the pull, the arm or the stump. So in describing the
effectiveness of the machine it is fair enough to put kilogram bricks in place of both the arm push and the stump
pull. These kilograms are all we need to know concerning
these features of the machine.

And now we are able to give a rather precise description
of the action of a lever as a machine in terms of just the
amount of weight at one end necessary to lift and balance
the weight at the other end for any position of the fulcrum

along the bar. This description can be given as an equation, as follows:

$$\frac{\text{Kilograms at stump end of bar}}{\text{Kilograms at arm end of bar}} = \frac{\text{centimeters from fulcrum to arm end}}{\text{centimeters from fulcrum to stump end}}$$

or, generalizing,

$$\frac{\text{X kilograms}}{\text{Y kilograms}} = \frac{\text{centimeters from fulcrum to Y}}{\text{centimeters from fulcrum to X}}$$

Still further precision is possible. But we have carried the description of the lever far enough to exhibit the mechanistic categories that lie embedded in it. This description of a machine is the root metaphor of mechanism; or rather, a fair sample of the root metaphor, for a description of any machine carried about this far would exhibit the general categories of mechanism.

§3. *The mechanistic categories.*—There are six important points to notice about the foregoing description of a lever.

First, the lever is a configuration of parts having specified *locations*. The bar, we said, is three meters or three hundred centimeters long. We locate the arm push at one end, or at 0 centimeters, and the stump pull at the other end, or at 300 centimeters. If the fulcrum is two-thirds the way down the bar, we locate that at 200 centimeters. We have here a specification of the precise locations of the parts of the machine. These locations determine the mode of functioning of the machine, and until these are specified there is no way of getting an exact description of the machine.

Second, we notice that the parts of the machine are all ultimately expressed in exact quantitative terms quite different from the objects as viewed in their common-sense guise. The rough old tree stump is taken only as a weight of kilograms, and so also is the exertion of my arm. So far as relevancy to the efficacy of the machine goes, the kilograms of these two parts are all that is needed. Such quantities as alone are relevant to the description of the efficient functions of a machine are historically called *primary qualities*.

Third, we find that there is an effective relationship or *law* which holds among the parts of the machine, and which we have described in the form of a functional equation. This equation exhibits the interrelation of the various parts of the machine in its action. For instance, the equation shows that if the parts of the lever have the configuration just suggested, the fulcrum being at the point 200 centimeters from the arm, then the pressure of the arm would need to be only 25 kilograms to raise and balance the tree stump of 50 kilograms. The equation, in short, describes an efficient law of action inherent in the structure of the machine.

But, fourth, we also notice that this mode of describing the machine in terms of centimeters and kilograms does not dispose of the qualities of the parts apparently irrelevant to the efficacy of the machine. The colors and textures and smells of the old tree stump, as well as the pleasantnesses and unpleasantnesses of these, still remain, as also my vivid feeling of exertion in my arm at my end of the lever and the pleasantness or unpleasantness there. These feelings and qualities in these parts of the lever have not disappeared. They are as vivid as ever and, even though not essential or even relevant to the effective action of the machine, are not to be forgotten, for they are still in some way attached to the machine. Such qualities, which are observed in parts of a machine but are not directly relevant to its action, have been called *secondary qualities.*

Fifth, though these secondary qualities do not seem to have any effective bearing on the machine, they seem nevertheless to stick around it by some *principle,* and if we were to make a complete description of the machine we should want to find out and describe just what that principle was which kept certain secondary qualities attached to certain parts of the machine.

Sixth, just as the primary qualities have laws among themselves, which we noticed under the third heading above, it is possible that the secondary qualities might have some *secondary laws* among themselves also. A man conscientiously describing all the characteristics of a machine, the ineffective ones as well as the effective, would wish to note any regularities that held among the secondary qualities as secondarily relevant to the description of a machine.

Now the generalization of the six foregoing features of a machine into cosmic structural features develops the categories of mechanism. These are:

Primary
categories
1. Field of location
2. Primary qualities
3. Laws holding for configurations of primary qualities in the field (primary laws)

Secondary
categories
$\left\{\begin{array}{l}\text{4. Secondary qualities}\\ \text{5. A principle for connecting the secondary qualities}\\ \quad\text{with the first three primary or effective categories}\\ \text{6. Laws, if any, for regularities among secondary}\\ \quad\text{qualities (secondary laws)}\end{array}\right.$

The first three categories may be called the primary or effective categories of mechanism, the last three the secondary or ineffective categories. The two sets of categories seem to be rather loosely attached, and sometimes in the development of world hypotheses they drift apart. A materialist might be defined as a mechanist who ignored or denied the last three categories. Hobbes sometimes comes near to doing this; for instance, when he says that color or sound is nothing but the motions of matter. And a subjective idealist might be defined as a mechanist who ignores or denies the first three categories. Berkeley attempts to do this. Either of these attempts is bound to be unnecessarily unsuccessful. Detailed criticism of such views has abundantly shown their shortcomings. But when we have seen the origin of these two sets of categories in the root metaphor of the machine, we do not need to scrutinize much farther. Either set without the other is bound to be miserably lacking in scope.

We shall find it convenient in our exposition of mechanism to separate these two sets of categories and to consider the primary categories in isolation first. We shall consider this set of categories first in their discrete development and then in their consolidated development. Then we shall consider the secondary categories in their connection with both the discrete and the consolidated developments of mechanism.

We must bear constantly in mind, however, not only that the two sets of categories (the primary and the secondary) need each other if they are to furnish the scope required of an adequate world theory; they need each other more directly still. It turns out that, ultimately, our cognitive evidence for the structure and details of the cosmic machine described through the primary categories comes entirely from materials within the secondary categories. The more detailed the development of the primary categories the more obvious this fact becomes. And, on the other side, it turns out that the very conception of the secondary categories depends upon their contrast with the primary categories, so that any attempt to develop the former without the latter defeats itself, that is, implies what it denies. This last dilemma cannot so clearly be shown within the limits of the exposition contemplated, but a review of the derivation of the secondary categories from the root metaphor, as just presented in this section, will pretty surely convince one that these last three categories come to light only as a result of the prior discovery of the first three categories. Subjective idealism, phenomenalism, and solipsism, as historically developed, are all mechanisms trying to get on without the primary categories. They can all be easily refuted (contrary to a widespread superstition) by simply examining their categorial presuppositions. For what is a mechanism without a machine!

§4. *Discrete mechanism.*—The assumption of discrete mechanism is that many of the structural features of nature are loosely, or, as the technical expression goes, externally related. So space is distinct from time, the primary qualities are distinct from the field of locations, each primary quality is perhaps distinct from every other, certainly every atom (i.e., localized group of primary qualities) is distinct from every other atom, has an independence of its own, and every natural law (such as the law of inertia, or the law of action and reaction) is distinct from every other law, and distinct, moreover, from the field of locations and from the atoms distributed over the field.

The idea is that time can be truly described or designated without any reference to space; a point or locus of space, without any reference to any other point; the shape, texture, mass of an atom, without any reference to date or place; one atom, without reference to any other atom; and a law of nature, without reference to the atoms that obey it, and vice versa. It is absolute mechanism. In such a universe almost anything might have been different, because almost everything is independent of almost everything else. If this atom had happened to be somewhere else at another time (and there is no necessary reason why it might not have been), then it would not have been hit by that atom; or if instead of the law of inertia for unaffected bodies there were a law of acceleration or deceleration (which might well have been), then also this collision would not have occurred. But since this atom did *happen* to be at this place at this time and had been obeying the law of inertia, it was *inevitable* that the collision should have occurred. There is this strange polarity of accident and necessity in discrete mechanism, which is understandable as soon as it is realized that the accidental comes from the conception of the independence of the details, and the necessary from the inevitability of the event's being just what it is since there is no reason to be found for its being anything different. But there is also a tendency in discrete mechanism for the accidental to be pushed farther and farther back into the basic structure of the universe, which is looked upon as purely and utterly irrational, and then to admit or asseverate the necessity and inevitability of almost everything that follows. This tendency clearly leads the way toward a consolidated mechanism in which the details are seen so to involve and determine one another that the accidental almost completely disappears within the folds of the inevitable.

Now let us consider the three primary categories one by one in the manner of discrete mechanism, making the independence of each detail as great as possible but proceeding with our analysis far enough to show the reason for the trend toward consolidation.

i) *The field of locations.*—This is the fundamental category of mechanism, for this is the category that defines existence and determines reality for this theory. Whatever can be located is real, and is real by virtue of a location. What cannot be located has an ambiguous reality until its place is found. Hamlet is a mystery until we can locate him in Shakespeare's brain. Then Hamlet is seen to be an idea or reaction of Shakespeare's and, having a local habitation, acquires the reality the locality endows it with. This does not mean that the reality of a thing is simply its location. There are the other five categories and all their derivative details. But it does mean that nothing will be accredited as being which does not have a location.

This categorial requirement marks off mechanism from formism. For in formism there is the reality of the forms apart from, or at least distinct from, the reality of the particulars. In mechanism, as its proponents are fond of reiterating, "only particulars exist." Moreover, these particulars of mechanism are not the bare or basic particulars of formism, but the structural particulars of space and time loci. Spatial and temporal structure define the nature of existence and the limitations of reality. That is why mechanism can be safely defined, as it frequently is, as the theory which makes space and time fundamental. And that is why formism is in danger of dissolving into mechanism when it identifies its category of existence with space and time.

In the earlier stages of mechanism the field of locations was identified with space, or even with the ambiguous term "emptiness" or "void." Space was thought of as a cubical room infinitely expanded in all directions. In this infinite or absolute space were absolute locations. And it was the particularization of a thing in one of these locations or in a line, or path, or volume of these locations that certified its reality. The determination of the absolute locations of objects might be difficult. We might at first think that the objects at rest in this room were all maintaining a single absolute location. Further observation, however, such as the relation of the earth to the sun, convinces us that these objects are only apparently or relatively at rest and are really in motion, which means that they are occupying

paths of locations, not single locations over a stretch of
time. The nature of this error, however, must not be exaggerated. We made a mistake about the successive locations
of the objects in this room, but not about the objects' having locations. An object is *where* it is, says the mechanist.

At first the system of possible places where an object
might be was conceived as an infinite three-dimensional
manifold—the absolute space of Newton. Moreover, the
principle of external relations which, it was thought, hold
in the relation of an object to its locations signified that
the location of an object made no intrinsic difference to
it, and seemed to signify further that the locations themselves made no intrinsic differences to one another. Inconceivable though it were, if some thousands of cubic miles
of locations went out of being somewhere in the universe,
no other locations in the universe would be affected. The
loss could only conceivably be suspected by the fact that
nothing ever appeared there.

To this absolute space of externally related locations
was gradually added an absolute time similarly conceived
as an infinite one-dimensional manifold of externally related dates. The dimension of time was not even at first
amalgamated with the three dimensions of space. Space
was rather conceived as traveling intact like a freight car
along the track of time. Thus one could have the identical
space location at different times. Space, in other words,
was external. It was changeless though it did move bodily
from date to date.

But even while this conception was being described, a
more reasonable conception was being used, in which time

was treated as a fourth dimension of the field of locations. All this latter conception means is that a location is not regarded as established unless you know not only the three determining spatial measurements, but also the date or time at which these measurements are made. Nevertheless, this shift of conception was very important, for it amounted to an amalgamation of time with space. The existential particular then became the space-time particular (the *here-and-now*), and not the mere spatial particular (the mere *here*).

But this shift of conception was also a consolidation, for it meant that a spatial location could not be regarded as independent of (or externally related to) time. In fact, it becomes so dependent that a spatial location shifted to another time becomes a brand new particular, another location entirely. And then perhaps it dawns on us that spatial locations themselves were not so independent of one another as had been supposed. For on the analogy of the independence of time to space, as formerly held, each dimension of space should have been independent of every other. Then a point on a plane should have been regarded as that identical location when extended as a line into other dimensions. The end of the room, for instance, should have been regarded as *one* particular location, determined as the end of the left side of the room but extended in the width dimension, just as the volume of the room was supposed to remain identically that volume as it extended through time. If the center of the room is regarded as a single particular location, whatever the time, so the end of the room should be regarded as a single particular location, whatever the width of the room. But, on the contrary, every point in the end wall of the room was regarded as a particular spatial point in its own right. Therefore, by the same insight, every point-date must be regarded as a particular of the field of locations in its own right. But that means that the determination of any one location whatever depends upon *all* the dimensions of the field, which in turn means that the field of locations has a highly consolidated structure and that no locus escapes from that structure. In other words, the field of locations has a determinate field structure. Thus the field of locations was impliedly consolidated even before the advent of relativity theory. The Michelson-Morley experiment simply emphasized the need of consolidation and specified certain details of field structure different from those of the Newtonian field.

ii) *Primary qualities.*—The traditional discrete mechanism is the theory of the atoms and the void, or, as the view develops, the theory of elementary particles distributed in space and time. The particles are regarded as elementary because they are the smallest pieces of matter into which bodies can be broken up. The argument for the reality of these particles is stated in the language of contemporary science by Reichenbach as follows:

... Do atoms have reality in the same sense as the things about us, which can be grasped?

Precisely this reality of the atoms was contested by the investigators named [Mach, Ostwald, Berthelot]. They were very ready to admit that the atomic theory furnished an extremely simple and fertile instrument for describing the phenomena of natural science; but they wished to restrict the concept of the atom to the

rank of a "working hypothesis," and not admit that this useful-
ness gave it any claim to the character of reality. However cor-
dially we must welcome the reduction of the rôle of speculation
in natural science to a minimum, we can, nevertheless, not agree
with the argumentation cited in the case of atoms. For natural
science must necessarily go a certain way beyond the content of
what is immediately given; indeed, the real process of research,
the progress to new and deeper-lying phenomena, consists in such
extension. When this extension is accompanied by so many facts
of experience as in the case of the atomic theory, when the most
diverse computations lead to numerical agreement on the same
values for size and number of atoms, when predicted laws are
confirmed to such a high degree as in the framework of the atomic
theory, then we have a right to characterize the theory as scientific truth. Between these two sources of knowledge there is no
third; thought has no tool which does research such good service
without at the same time corresponding to reality. If matter filled
space continuously, it would be quite unthinkable that a theory
which starts from the discontinuous, granular structure of matter should arrive at such quantitatively satisfactory results. Assertions about small-scale structure simply cannot forgo indirect
reasoning, because they must, in the end, be brought into connection with the world of moderate dimensions in which we have
our sense experiences; if, nevertheless, one should contest the
validity, for reality, of conceptions won by such reasoning, this
would, therefore, amount to saying that physical reality ends
when a certain degree of smallness has been reached. But this is
obviously nonsense. When we saw a piece of wood, the particles
of sawdust are quite as real as the large piece of wood from which
they came; if the sawdust is then further pulverized, we come to
particles which can only be distinguished with the aid of a microscope. If the continuation of this process of division results in
particles which even the microscope cannot reveal, these particles
can, nevertheless, not be said to be less real than the larger ones
which could still be observed. This fact is not altered when the
demonstration of their reality, because of their smallness, requires
more complicated methods. All attempts to degrade the atomic
hypothesis to a mere fiction, to a technical instrument of scientific

thought without real meaning, rest on a complete failure to recognize the mode of thought used in investigations of natural science.[1]

In the older theories, it was assumed that the atoms, or ultimate particles of physical analysis, were indestructible and therefore eternal, and therefore described continuous paths in time from the infinite past to the infinite future. This assumption, however, is not essential to mechanism— that is, the categories do not require it—though it greatly simplifies analysis if it can be assumed. Some recent electronic theories find it necessary to postulate the discontinuity of the paths of ultimate particles. Electrons are described as skipping from one orbit to another about a nucleus without traversing the intermediate spatial locations. There appears to be no skipping of any *temporal* locations, however, and the intrinsic characters of the electron are regarded as unaffected by the skip. This minor aberration from age-long assumptions in mechanism indicates that much greater liberties can be taken with the histories of ultimate physical particles without straining the categorial framework of the theory. It is even possible to conceive of atoms popping in and out of existence all over the field, so long as their popping should conform to the structure of the field. That would, after all, be the fully discrete treatment of atoms in the field. The fact that we instinctively reject the idea indicates that a fully discrete mechanism has never been seriously contemplated.

Now atoms, or elementary physical particles, are qualitative differentiations of the field of locations. Without

---

[1] Hans Reichenbach, *Atom and Cosmos*, trans. E. S. Allen (New York: Macmillan, 1933), pp. 194–196.

such differentiations the field would be utterly undifferentiated. Every location would be like every other—or, as we
should commonly say, empty. Nothing, as we should say,
would be going on in the universe. There would be no
spatiotemporal paths or configurations. Reciprocally, if
there were only the characters of matter, and no field in
which these characters could be deployed, there could be
no configurations. Field and matter are, therefore, complementary concepts—and very nearly relative to one another, so that the postulation of the one almost commits one
to the other, but not quite, for that would deny the possibility of their discreteness on the one hand, and of their
complete consolidation on the other. It is the underlying
pressure of the root metaphor and the relevant facts that at
once separates them and joins them together as factual but
not logical correlatives. So we need differentiating characters in the field to render the cosmic machine descriptive
and explanatory of the actual world in which we live. The
ultimate differentiating characters of the ultimate physical
particles are the primary qualities. Or, more precisely, the
ultimate particles are the spatiotemporal volumes differentiated by the primary qualities. The atoms are determinate sets of qualities characterizing specific locations
of the field.

The traditional primary qualities are size, shape, motion, solidity, mass (or more often weight), number. These
come down from Democritus through Lucretius to Galileo
and thence into the stream of Renaissance and modern
science and naturalistic philosophy. These were traditionally supposed to inhere in spatial volumes and to

continue unaltered through time except for changes of position in the field according to certain basic physical laws (our third category). It is noteworthy that the shift from the mechanical to the electrical theory of matter has merely the effect of substituting electrical charge for mass (or adding it), with whatever modifications follow in the detailed application of the other primary qualities. These modifications are far-reaching and go a long way toward hastening the trend toward mechanistic consolidations, but they put no fundamental strain upon the categories. The shift had simply to do with the choice of one of the primary qualities—the pivotal one, as it proved, but still just one.

Now, a little scrutiny of the traditional list of primary qualities reveals a peculiar thing. All of them except mass (or weight) are configurational properties, that is, properties that have to do with localization in the spatiotemporal field. Size means the spatial volume of the differentiated locations, shape the boundaries of these, motion their temporal path, solidity the absence of undifferentiated interior locations, number the means of specifying distinct locations. All of these properties are structural relations of the field in relation to the one and only truly differentiating quality, mass. They are, in other words, not technically qualities at all, but field *relations* in *relation* to the one genuine quality, mass. The discrete conception of them, therefore, as simple qualities inhering in a spatiotemporal volume of locations breaks down. They consolidate into structural relations of the field constellated about the one truly differentiating quality, mass.

It is evident that the same situation holds when electrical charge is substituted for or added to mass, and would hold however extended the list of primary qualities. Some of the primary qualities (so called) would be field relations specifying the locations of differentiating qualities, and some would be truly differentiating qualities. It is a matter of detail, having to do with the application of the mechanistic framework to the observed facts, how many qualities, and which ones, will be chosen for the list of primary qualities. But what we have just shown makes it evident that this list will normally contain two sets of "qualities": (1) properties of location in the field, and (2) differentiating properties.

The first are obviously highly consolidating properties, being actual field properties. Can the discreteness of the second be maintained? So far as we can see from our study up to this point, they can. Mass and charge, or any comparable differentiating properties, seem to be discrete qualities inhering in spatiotemporal volumes. An atom seems to be a certain chunk of mass with possibly other unanalyzable properties such as "affinities" and "valencies," and these properties are in no way intrinsic to their locations in the field, but just *happen* to have the locations they have. These differentiating properties are not structural characteristics of the field like volumes, not consolidated with the field. Similarly with electrons and their charges. An electrical charge and its positive or negative properties seem to be discrete from the structural properties of the field of locations, though as present in the field these charges naturally submit to the relational properties of the spatiotemporal field.

We have here a semidiscrete mechanism. Can this degree of discreteness be maintained when we come to consider the third category?

iii) *Laws holding among the primary qualities in the field.*—A mechanism without any laws is abstractly conceivable, but it would be like a mechanism without any differentiating primary qualities. It would not describe the facts of the world and it would have lost contact with its root metaphor. The law of the lever is as much a feature of the machine as its configuration of parts. It is, in fact, that efficient action described by the law which brought the machine so vividly to our attention and suggested its suitability as a cosmic root metaphor.

A mechanism without any laws has, so far as I know, never been suggested. The opposite conception, however, of a complete and rigid determination of configurations in the spatiotemporal field, is common in mechanism, especially in recent times. It is perhaps one of the chief attractions of the theory. It has probably had much to do with its attractiveness to scientists, and as a faith on their part that there is a law for everything that happens in the physical world it had undoubtedly had much to do as a stimulus toward the discovery of such laws. Formism affords no such faith. And, strangely enough, neither does mechanism except as one becomes aware of the trend within it toward consolidation. A completely consolidated mechanism would be a completely mechanized and internally determined universe. This does indeed seem to be the drive of the mechanistic categories; and as we shall see, there is a reason for it. Yet superficially the drive seems unnecessary. What is there in the root metaphor or its derivative categories to require that the filling of every spatiotemporal location in the universe shall be strictly determined? Why may not sheer chance and real chaos go on in some parts of space or time? The early mechanists thought just such a chaos did exist in the earliest cosmic times, and that order and law came out of chaos by a sort of chance.

Or, not to go so far as that, why could not some ultimate natural laws be flexible, permitting indefeasible alternatives? Why not ultimate statistical laws? Superficially, there seems to be no reason why the ultimate laws of the mechanistic universe should not be statistical or only partly determinative. But basically we should find some difficulties, which will explain why mechanistic physicists and philosophers have instinctively staked their faith on precisely determinative laws.

No one has so startlingly propounded the completely deterministic universe as Laplace. If we knew the configuration of matter in the whole universe at any one time, he said, and the precise laws of matter, or if we knew the configurations of matter at two times, so that we could deduce the laws which led from one configuration to the other, then we could deduce the configurations of matter for any other times whatsoever. At the beginning of the third book of his *Système du monde* he writes,

In the midst of the infinite variety of phenomena which succeed one another continuously in the heavens and on the earth, one is led to recognize the small number of general laws which matter follows in its movements. Everything in nature obeys them; everything is derived from them as necessarily as the return of the seasons; and the curve described by the dust particle which the winds seem to carry by chance, is ruled in as certain a manner as the orbits of the planets.

I think no one can fail to feel that there is something mechanistically satisfying in this complete systematization of the universe, this rendering of the world a cosmos in truth. It feels right, and anything less than this feels mechanistically like a failure or a frustration. This feeling, I believe, has categorial justification.

Let us take, as typical suggestions for ultimate cosmic laws, Newton's three laws of motion and the refined formulation of his law of gravitation, and try to see what they signify in mechanistic terms. These are all laws that operate upon mass, and are the very laws to which Laplace was referring.

Laws of motion:

I. Every body continues in its state of rest, or of uniform motion in a right line, unless it is compelled to change that state by forces impressed upon it.

II. The change of motion is proportional to the motive forces impressed; and is made in the direction of the right line in which that force is impressed.

III. To every action there is always opposed an equal reaction; or, the mutual actions of two bodies upon each other are always equal, and directed to contrary parts.[2]

Law of gravitation:

$$G = k \frac{mm'}{r^2}$$

The gravitational attraction of two bodies is directly proportional to their masses and inversely proportional to the square of their distance apart, multiplied by the constant of gravitation.

[2] Isaac Newton, *Mathematical Principles*, ed. Florian Cajori (Berkeley: University of California Press, 1934), p. 13.

These laws, it will be seen (exactly these laws for Laplace, these or similar laws for other mechanists) constitute the dynamic element in the mechanistic universe. The field itself is static and undifferentiated. Even when the field is dotted with masses, it still lacks efficacy. The dynamic structure of nature comes from the laws which connect the masses together and guide them from one configuration to another.

Now, there is an important point to notice in the Laplacean conception. He says, Let me know the configuration of masses in the spatial field at any one time, and the laws which operate upon these masses, and I will describe the configuration of the field at any other time past or present. What is the status of these laws? He speaks of them as if they were discrete and separable from the masses in the field, or as if they operated upon the field but were not of it—as if, in a word, they were *forms* which are repeatedly exemplified in the field.

But this is formism and not mechanism. The status of subsistence is implied. And if we allow this status to appear here in the laws, it will spread into the primary qualities, and eventually into the field itself. For if the laws are conceived as repeating themselves identically over the spatiotemporal field, so will the sizes, shapes, and masses, and so perhaps even the locations. For are not all locations just alike, discretely considered? Thus mechanism dissolves into formism, and all its categories vanish to be reinterpreted in terms of the categories of formism. This, as we have earlier hinted, is the constant threat in the rear of mechanism.

The only way of avoiding this mechanistic catastrophe is to imbed the primary qualities and the laws firmly in the spatiotemporal field. Things are real only if they have a time and a place. *Only particulars exist.* This principle must never be abandoned, for the penalty is the dissolution of mechanism. If this implication is realized, one sees at once that in a mechanistic nature there can be no alternatives, and that for mechanism statistical laws are not laws of nature in any ultimate sense, but only human constructions symbolizing to some *approximation* the actual interrelations of nature. The mechanists' instinctive belief in the complete determinateness and determination of nature is hereby justified. Laplace had the right idea in terms of the implications of his presuppositions.

Discrete mechanism is thus internally contradictory. It implies strict similarity and, consequently, the formistic categories. Indeed, not only are laws threatened with the status of forms, but also the atoms. The typical mechanistic way of handling similarity is in terms of the similarity of the basic constituents and configurations of things perceived as similar. Drops of water are similar because they are composed of similar atoms of hydrogen and oxygen which have a similar configuration in the proportions of two to one. The similarity of drops of water is thus reduced to the similarity of atoms and the configurations of atoms. But what about the similarity of the atoms and the configurations? The intention is to reduce similarities to configurations of ultimate differentiations of the spatiotemporal field—to draw nature completely and solidly into that field. The mechanist is scornful of abstractions and forms. He wants his feet on the ground, and the ground is the field of time and space, and he does not want to believe in anything that is not also on the ground. To achieve this end, however, he must consolidate his categories. The primary qualities and the laws must become structural features of the spatiotemporal field as intimately involved in it as the dimensions of space with one another. Similarity can then be relegated to the structure of that field and kept from flying into subsistent forms.

§5. *Consolidated mechanism.* — Discrete mechanism thus leads to consolidated mechanism. The customary mechanistic picture of the world as groups of planetary systems, or as particles pushed up and down and back and forth in the production of apparent waves, or as particles in random motion in a box, gives way to a picture more in the nature of a crystal or gelatin with an intricately involved internal structure. In place of the discrete particle is the spatiotemporal path, and in place of the discrete laws of mechanics is a geometry, or, better, a geography. The purpose of this cosmic geometry is simply to describe to us the unique structure of the spatiotemporal whole.

What gives us grounds for a rather high degree of credence in this type of mechanism is that scientific observation and thought has been moving rather steadily in this direction. The official theory for scientists in the eighteenth and nineteenth centuries was discrete mechanism. Today it seems to be something vaguely centered in consolidated mechanism with borrowings in one direction from discrete mechanism and in the other from operational contextualism.

The chief modern impetus for consolidation comes, of course, from relativity theory, for this has to do with the details of the spatiotemporal field. The special theory of relativity breaks down the clean-cut traditional separation between space and time. Within certain limits, space and time are ambiguous until one establishes a reference system; just as vertical and horizontal are ambiguous until one has a system of spatial reference. Time is thereby drawn right into space and the field is unquestionably consolidated.

But the most important evidence is the general theory of relativity, which amalgamates the gravitational field with the spatiotemporal field. For gravitation is a phenomenon of mass, which is a primary quality, a pivotal differentiating quality. But more important still, this gravitational mass is interpreted in terms of a gravitational field, which has the effect of amalgamating the law of gravitation into the first category, so that the field is no longer just the spatiotemporal field but the spatiotemporal-gravitational field. The importance of this amalgamation for mechanism is that the program for a consolidated mechanism is lifted out of the relatively speculative status it would otherwise have had, and is given the authority of the most advanced theoretical work in physics.

Still further evidence—or, better, encouragement—for the program of a consolidated mechanism is the use of the electromagnetic field, which has obviously close analogies with the gravitational field as the basic conception of matter. The qualities of electric charge and of magnetic attraction are absorbed in the electromagnetic field laws, and these laws operate directly in the spatiotemporal field. That is to say, an electromagnetic field is nothing more nor less than electromagnetic forces acting in a spatiotemporal field. There have been serious, though so far unsuccessful, attempts to carry the amalgamation still farther and resolve the electromagnetic laws into the geometry of the basic field itself just as was done with the gravitational law.

Consolidated mechanism is not a dream, but is the most plausible theory of the nature of the world so far as physical evidence goes. Electrons, positrons, neutrons, and the like must not, however, be conceived of in terms of particles like Lucretian atoms, but as structural modifications of the spatiotemporal field, the paths of which can be mapped out and expressed in that symbolic shorthand which we call descriptive laws. Strictly speaking, there are no laws in consolidated mechanism; there are just structural modifications of the spatiotemporal field. And no primary qualities, either, for these are resolved into field laws, which are themselves resolved into the structure of the field.

So now, at last, *only particulars exist*, or, more truly still, *only a particular exists*, namely, the consolidated spatiotemporal-gravitational-electromagnetic field, which, by the way, may not be infinite entirely, but may be bounded in some or all dimensions. This is (one cannot see how it can be otherwise) a fully determined field. The Laplacean ideal applies to it more fully than it ever applied to Laplace's world. For there might have been a slip between Laplace's configuration of masses and his laws, but in this world the laws and the masses *are* the structure of the field itself, which is just the structure that it is. There is obviously no place in this world for statistical laws except as convenient symbolic instruments for prediction in place of the actual knowledge of field structures. The structure of the field is just what it is at whatever spatiotemporal point (or "interval") we take it, and in a certain sense that structure is laid down now in the geometry of the universe even though we who are thinking about it may be at a very distant date-place from that point. For if we as mechanists do not accept consolidation, we must accept discreteness, and we have seen where that leads. Now we see where consolidation leads. We must not start back at it because of its uncompromising finality. We gain nothing by diluting it with eclectic filters. It is the most nearly adequate form of mechanism, and, all in all, surprisingly adequate.

What it appears to lack is scope. How far can the secondary categories fill up the gaps?

§6. *Secondary categories.*—On the efficient structural base of the primary categories are erected the secondary categories. The first of these is the secondary qualities themselves. These comprise all the irreducible characters of the world which are not identifiable with the primary categories. What these are is a matter of empirical observation. But among them are probably *all* the characters of human perception.

The farther mechanism is carried the more obvious it becomes that the effective underlying cosmic machine is quite out of sight in all its workings. The extension and duration of ordinary perceptions are not the spatiotemporal structures of the cosmic field. Those have constantly to be corrected by measurements of rule and clock and further corrected by mathematical formulas for probable error, the final result not even then being a precise description of the cosmic field structure, but only a statistical approximation. It is likewise, and even more patently, with other qualities such as weight, mass, charge, and the like. What we experience are secondary qualities only, from which as evidences we infer the mechanical efficient structure of the universe.

The connection between these primary structures and the secondary qualities is described by the second of the secondary categories. In recent literature this category has received a great deal of attention under the term "emergence." There have been traditionally three main theories of the connection between the secondary and the primary qualities, namely, identity, causation, and correlation. The first of these we can rule out at once, even though it is still not uncommonly resorted to. Color and sound, for instance, are not literally electromagnetic or air vibrations, nor even neural activities. They are irreducible qualities. Causation can also be ruled out, if by causation is meant any of the efficient features of the primary categories, and something of this sort is what is generally intended by the suggestion. The laws of motion, in the electromagnetic-field laws, describe masses and charges and have no application to such qualities as colors and sounds. Some sort of correlation is all that is left, that is, the observation that upon the occurrence of certain configurations of matter certain qualities appear which are not reducible to the characters of matter or the characters of the configurations. The term emergence signalizes such correlated appearances.

How far secondary qualities extend in nature it is difficult to ascertain, but possibly they extend very far. The theories of levels of emergence testify to such a belief. The gap between such secondary qualities as our sensations of color or sound and the configurations of matter among primary qualities seems to be so great as to suggest many intervening levels of successively emerging secondary qualities. Thus we pass from the elementary and primary electrons, positrons, neutrons, and so forth, to atoms, molecules, crystals, amino acids, cells, tissues, organisms. At each level new properties seem to emerge which are not reducible to, or predictable from, the properties of the configurations at the lower levels. But whatever question there may be respecting whether these properties are emergent or not, there is no question of the emergent nature of sense qualities that appear on the level of human organisms and are apparently correlated with certain neural configurations.

The problem of the relation of these sensory emergents to the cosmic machine has been one of the principal concerns of philosophers during the last three centuries, when physicists, chemists, and physiologists were building up the details of the cosmic machine. This is the redoubtable mind-body problem. What is to be done with these sensory qualities, which appear so superfluous to the great machine? The obvious answer is: "Nothing; just note them

and the physical configurations with which they are correlated. If these configurations can be precisely determined
and the secondary qualities correlated with them noted,
then it is possible thereafter to predict the emergence of
the correlated qualities. What else could be desired?"
Nevertheless, there is a difficulty involved here which
mechanists have instinctively felt, just as they have instinctively felt that mechanism somehow involved determinism.
It is the same problem of an unresolved discreteness.

In this brief sketch we shall not concern ourselves with
any of the emergents other than these immediately sensed
qualities. What is done with these is a sample of what can
be done with all. The sensed qualities are the introspective
materials of what we commonly call mind or consciousness. We are apparently aware of them only as they per-
tain to our own individual organisms. The immediate
evidence for them seems to be private, though we have
abundant indirect evidence through communication that
all human organisms have them also. We infer that other
animals also have them, and possibly even plants.

Restricting ourselves to human psychology, we find that
mechanistic psychology also has its discrete and consolidated treatment. In the discrete treatment complex mental
states are regarded as analyzable without residue into
mental elements of a relatively small number of kinds:
sensations of color, sound, taste, smell, various sorts of
tactile sensations, feelings such as pleasantness and unpleasantness, and possibly a few other elements. These
are conceived of very much on the analogy of the chemical
elements, so that this sort of psychology is sometimes

dubbed "mental chemistry." It is sometimes suggested that the laws of association are distinctively mental laws operating upon those elements to produce the more complex mental states. If so, these laws would be the filling of the sixth mechanistic category earlier mentioned. Often, however, the laws of association are regarded as simply the introspective manifestations of physiological laws, which may be regarded as complex operations of mechanical laws, so that the efficient side of the secondary qualities is referred outward into the physical world, into the primary categories of the cosmic machine. This psychology of discrete mental elements is the neatest and, in that respect, the most intellectually satisfying psychology that has been developed. It almost works, and has been very widely accepted from its first extensive systematization by Locke to its complete development in Titchener.

There are some facts, however, which this atomic psychology has great difficulty in handling, and through all these mechanistic decades there has been a good deal of grumbling about it, chiefly by philosophers and psychologists who were not mechanists. Recently a revolt has occurred among psychologists, some of whom may be regarded as mechanists themselves. Many of the men in the so-called *Gestalt* school of psychology are quite clearly mechanists. Kohler may be regarded as typical of these. He insists that mental facts are configurations, patterns, *Gestalts* which cannot be legitimately analyzed into mental elements. The conception of the *Gestalt* itself in mechanistic terms is rather vague except (illuminatingly enough) as it is correlated with somewhat imaginary electromag-

netic fields, which are considered as the physiological correlates of these mental states. Thus mechanistic *Gestalt*
psychology becomes the analogy in terms of the secondary
categories of consolidated-field physics in terms of the
primary categories.

On this issue of consolidation, however, one outstanding
fact obstinately remains, namely, that the secondary categories themselves cannot be consolidated with the primary
categories. And this obstinate discreteness threatens mechanism again with formism. The formistic threat to mechanism of a catalogue of elementary mental atoms which
are identically repeated in multitudes of complex mental
states is obvious enough. What are these atoms but the
very immanent forms which formism is built up from?
Even *Gestalts* mechanistically conceived seem to be re-
peatable and to call for a category of subsistence. The
difficulty can be avoided only by conceiving of the great
machine as a highly structured field that never literally
repeats itself in any details and that here, there, and elsewhere exhibits emergent qualities which also are never
repeated in detail. But if emergent qualities are never repeated, they can never be predicted, and consequently
cannot be said to be correlated with configurations of the
machine in any ordinary sense of the word correlated.
This predicament is serious, because it is apparently only
by such correlations that we are able to make inferences
outside our conscious states to the cosmic machine which
supposedly suggests them. If there is no reliable correlation between physical structures and mental states, then
not only can we not predict or infer the mental states from

the physical structures, but, worse, we cannot infer the physical structures from the mental states. And this is very bad, because our only human knowledge of the physical structures is on the evidence of our mental states.

The mechanist's dread of the mind-body problem is well founded. It is a threat to the integrity of the mechanistic categories.

§7. *Mechanistic theory of truth.*—Now for a brief statement of the mechanistic theory of truth, for this brings out another curious side of the difficulties of mechanism. As we noticed in the foregoing section, all immediate evidence seems to be of the nature of secondary qualities (all ultimate primary qualities such as the properties of electrons and the cosmic field being far from the range of immediate perceptions); moreover, this evidence seems to be correlated with the activities of organisms, specifically with each individual organism that is said to be immediately aware of the evidence. All immediate evidence is, therefore, private to each individual organism. It follows that knowledge of the external world must be symbolic and inferential. How is the truth of that knowledge established?

In the older mechanistic theories an attempt was made to solve this problem in terms of a correspondence theory of truth. This, as we saw, is the theory of truth proper to formism, and we anticipate at once that it will not amalgamate satisfactorily with the categories of mechanism. For the correspondence theory presupposes the formistic analysis of similarity and the presence of an identity of form in different particulars. The attraction for the correspondence theory among the older, and even some more recent, mechanists arises in part from a scholastic inheritance, in part from the character of discrete mechanism which cannot dispense with ultimate identities of form in the mechanistic field, and in part from an inability to conceive any other hypothesis for the nature of truth.

In the older mechanistic theories truth was conceived quite naïvely as a correspondence between visual images and external facts. The mental image or idea was thought to be like a mirror image or a portrait or possibly a map which reproduces exactly or in some proportion the features of the object represented. The idea was true in proportion as it reproduced the object represented.

This theory works well enough where both the idea and the object are the immediate mental states of an individual organism. I personally test the truth of a portrait by comparing my immediate perception of the picture with my immediate perception of the sitter, or, in the absence of the perception of the sitter, with my image of the sitter. The same may be said, though in a more complicated way, of my method of testing the truth of a map.

But what the early mechanists did not clearly see was that in all such cases both the object and the idea which are being directly compared for their correspondences are private awarenesses of the individual organism making the comparison. We get no assurance from such correspondences about the truth of our ideas concerning the external world. For, if it is true, as we were just saying, that all our ideas and perceptions are of the nature of secondary qualities emerging from neural configurations of an organism, these ideas and perceptions are entirely within the boundaries of each organism and accordingly confined within those boundaries and literally private. This situation has been aptly called the egocentric predicament. It appears that both the idea and the object are always within the organism wherever direct comparison can be made. For if the object is outside the organism, the organism cannot be aware of it, since, as we seemed to find, all immediate experiences are emergents from neural configurations inside the organism. If the object of knowledge, then, happens to be outside the organism, it would seem that its truth can never be known, since it can never be reached for direct comparison with an idea that is within the organism. Knowledge of the external world thus appears to be impossible.

Berkeley was the first philosopher to be fully impressed with this consequence of the mechanistic hypothesis, and he did his best to accept it uncompromisingly. He denied the existence of the external world in the typical mechanistic sense of a world of primary qualities, that is, of basic and unperceivable configurations of matter in a spatio-temporal field. He denied the cosmic machine. He asserted virtually that only the secondary categories exist, that is, that only minds and mental contents exist. And he attempted to account for the hypothesis of an external world in terms of a supreme mind or God whose ideas had a permanence which the ideas of mortal minds have not. Such a theory is known as "subjective idealism." It is, as we said earlier, a truncated mechanism. The force of the theory comes from the fact, which seems to be quite correct in mechanistic terms, that *all* data, whether of common sense or science, are private. All evidence is of the nature of secondary qualities, so that in a mature mechanism (and the maturer the plainer) the primary qualities and all the primary categories are not evidence but inference, or, if you will, speculation.

The argument is very persuasive. If all data are private and mental, and if the matter of the mechanists is never anyone's datum, and if truth is the correspondence of an idea with its object, then clearly it would seem that the truth of the idea of matter can never be established, and that the idea of matter is nonsense and should be given up.

What this argument omits, however, is its own presuppositions (the categorial framework on which it itself rests). How did the hypothesis develop that all ideas, evidence, data were private? Only on the discrimination of organisms as configurations of matter in the spatio-temporal field separated from one another as bounded volumes. The privacy of data as mental contents within insulated minds presupposes the material configuration of space which can insulate the minds within organisms. Mind in Berkeley's sense presupposes matter in the mechanistic sense. Or, more broadly, the secondary categories presuppose the primary categories, even though all ultimate evidence turns out to be located among the secondary categories. Berkeley's argument is, therefore, utterly untenable.

It is clear that the relations between idea and object must be conceived in some other way. The naïve pictorial theory of correspondence was accordingly rejected by the more critical mechanists, and numerous attempts have been made to deal with the problem in terms of a symbolic theory of correspondence. Let the idea be a group of symbols in a sentence or scientific formula. Then if these symbols correspond with features of the object, and the symbolized relations among the symbols with the relations among the objects, the sentence or formula is true. But still the question remains, how to compare the symbols which we are aware of as secondary qualities with the features of material objects which are in terms of primary qualities and of which we cannot be aware.

The hypothesis of symbolic correspondence, however, creates a transition which has led many recent mechanists to suggest that it is not correspondence that is important in the truth of a sentence or formula, but the predictive power of these to produce expected results. The truth of a formula is its workability. This, however, is the operational theory of truth characteristic of contextualism, and, as we shall see in the next chapter, involves an interpretation of symbolic reference which, followed to its ultimate implications, would cause a revision of the mechanistic categories and convert mechanism into contextualism.

It is noticeable that the tendency among modern mechanists to accept an operational theory of truth is simultaneous with the trend to consolidation in mechanism. Thus discrete mechanism gravitates toward a correspondence or formistic theory of truth, while consolidated mechanism gravitates toward an operational or contextualistic theory of truth. That instability in the theory which we have already noticed comes again to view.

There does lie in mechanism, however, a principle which suggests a theory of truth proper to it. Mechanists have always been known as nominalists. The nominalistic theory of abstract and general terms was the regular mechanistic means of combating the arguments of the formists for the reality of forms and the category of subsistence. Says the traditional mechanist, a form such as blueness or bluejay is nothing but a word which stands for a number of objects. There is no form of bluejay, but there is the word which we have conventionally learned to use in reference to a number of physical objects. Bluejays are grouped into a class simply by virtue of the fact that they are all called by that name.

In this naïve formulation nominalism does not carry much conviction. For we are at once prompted to ask how it comes about that this name happens to have been applied to just those physical objects and no others. Is not the reason precisely that those objects do in fact have the common properties of blueness, featheredness, and so on? If we push nominalism no farther, there does not seem to be any adequate answer, and the formists carry the field.

But suppose the mechanist accepts the challenge and asks in terms of his own categories how indeed it does happen that certain names get applied to certain configurations of matter. What, now, is a name? It is a specific response made by an organism on the stimulus of specific environmental configurations. In principle it is exactly the sort of thing that happens when an organism reacts positively to food stimuli and negatively to prick stimuli. It is simply specificity of response in an organism carried to a higher degree of refinement. Instead of stepping on a nail and negatively reacting to the direct prick, an organism learns to react negatively to the visual stimulus of the nail associated with an original direct prick, and then learns to react negatively to the word "nail" associated with the visual stimulus which is associated with the original prick. All this is simply a complicated chain of physiological reactions, the whole sequence being explicable in physiological terms. And what is explicable in physiological terms is, as we have seen, theoretically explicable in physicochemical terms and can be amalgamated with the spatiotemporal field and the primary categories generally.

Now, a sentence or scientific formula physiologically interpreted is nothing but a combination of such reactions or conditioned reflexes. The whole thing can be causally interpreted. Suppose my organism on the stimulus of light rays impinging on the retina of my eye responds with the articulate words, "That is a sharp nail." Suppose I wanted to find out whether that was a true response. What would I do? I would work back to the original reaction which conditioned the whole train of reactions of which the foregoing sentence is the last term. In other words, I would tentatively step on the nail, and if I reacted negatively I would say that the sentence was true; if not, I would say that it was false and look about for the causes which had produced the illusion.

We have hereby developed a causal theory of truth. Nothing is implied about an identity of form between the sentence and the nail. Nor, as we shall see, is this an operational theory in just the contextualistic sense. In this mature nominalism what is implied is a system of causal connections which holds between an environmental stimulus and the response of an organism. What makes error possible is itself causally explained. An organism develops a set of attitudes, or physiological sets, on the basis of certain physical stimuli. These attitudes often lack specificity, so that they may be set off by stimuli which usually support the attitude by subsequent stimuli but on this occasion do not. The nail turns out to be a twig that looked like a nail. The mistake can be easily explained, and is the basis for making the attitude still more specific, so that these mistakes will be rarer.

Truth thus becomes a name for physiological attitudes which are in adjustment with the environment of the organism. One mechanistic writer, Prall, calls it "the aptness of the body." Error arises from lack of adjustment, or inaptness of the body.

How does this theory, which we may call the causal-adjustment theory, meet the problem of the gap in mechanism between the evidence which is private and in terms of the secondary categories and the basic facts of mechanism which are outside and in terms of the primary categories? In this way: The secondary qualities are correlated with the physiological configurations which are the effective structures of the attitudes mentioned. These physiological configurations are in the effective spatiotemporal-gravitational-electromagnetic field. They are part of this cosmic field and therefore reflect its structure directly. The effects of this field structure are immediately reflected

in terms of the secondary qualities correlated with the
physiological configurations. We thus learn about the
structure of the great machine by a sort of detective work.
We note the changes among our private secondary qualities, infer their correlations with the physiological configurations which are in our organism, and thence infer
the structural characters of the surrounding field from its
effects upon the configuration of our organism.

Suppose we want to know if there are any red-winged
blackbirds. We construct the image in our minds or write
out our description in words. Whichever we do, we are
aware of a pattern of secondary qualities. We infer that
these are correlated with effective and specific physiological configurations within our organism. We then
propel our organism about the environment to find out
whether there are any configurations in the world that will
directly stimulate this physiological attitude, and so bring
up the correlated words in our sentence, or the correlated shapes and colors in our perception. If this happens,
we call our sentence or idea true; if not, and if we think
we have sufficient evidence to believe that this attitude
will never be externally stimulated, we call our sentence
or idea false. The construction and verification of a hypothesis about the structure of the hydrogen atom is no
different in principle.

Does this causal-adjustment theory of truth in terms of
mechanical causal connections succeed in avoiding the
threats from the two neighbors, that of correspondence on
the one side and operationalism on the other? Do not these
physiological attitudes with their inferences to configura-

tions in the environment presuppose a correspondence between the attitudes and the environmental configurations?
I think not necessarily. It would in a discrete mechanism,
but in a consolidated mechanism the adaptation would be
simply one of causal or geometrical fitting together with
no implication of repetition.

But a difficulty does arise between the physiological
attitudes and their supposedly correlated secondary qualities. What sense can be given to correlation in mechanism,
or what evidence can be found for it, that does not involve
repetition? We are back to the difficulty we reached at the
end of the last section. In order to make inferences across
the gap, we have to set up some sort of connection between
the two sides. Since in mechanism the causal connection
is excluded, correlation seems to be all that is left and this
seems to imply similarity in the formistic sense.

The causal-adjustment theory of truth does seem to get
one successfully across the gap, but it does not seem to
be able to dispense with the implication of formistic similarity that lies in the notion of correlation as the connecting link between the primary and secondary categories.

One other suggestion comes to mind. Suppose instead
of correlations we take the symbolic reference involved in
the concept of nominalism, namely, the reference which a
name has for its object. But no sooner do we consider this
suggestion than we drop it. For the whole point of nominalism is to account for symbolic reference in terms of mechanistic causation, and causation is categorially excluded
as a bridge across the gap. Moreover, if a more immediate
sense of symbolic reference were used—namely, the in-

tuited sense of reference, which when followed leads one from the awareness of a symbol to the awareness of a perception symbolized,—not only would that recourse deprive nominalism of most of its virtue for mechanism as a way of solving the truth problem, since it would confine this problem to the sphere of the secondary categories, but it would actually carry mechanism right over into contextualism.

So the gap between the primary and the secondary categories still remains the center of inadequacy for mechanism.

Chapter X : Contextualism

§1. *The contextualistic root metaphor.*—When we come to contextualism, we pass from an analytical into a synthetic type of theory. It is characteristic of the synthetic theories that their root metaphors cannot satisfactorily be denoted even to a first approximation by well-known common-sense concepts such as similarity, the artifact, or the machine. We are too likely to be misunderstood at the start, even though the basic synthetic concepts do originate in common sense or are, at least, discoverable there. The best term out of common sense to suggest the point of origin of contextualism is probably the historic event. And this we shall accordingly call the root metaphor of this theory.

By historic event, however, the contextualist does not mean primarily a past event, one that is, so to speak, dead and has to be exhumed. He means the event alive in its present. What we ordinarily mean by history, he says, is an attempt to *re-present* events, to make them in some way alive again. The real historic event, the event in its actuality, is when it is going on *now*, the dynamic dramatic active event. We may call it an "act," if we like, and if we take care of our use of the term. But it is not an act conceived as alone or cut off that we mean; it is an act in and with its setting, an act in its context.

To give instances of this root metaphor in our language with the minimum risk of misunderstanding, we should use only verbs. It is doing, and enduring, and enjoying:

making a boat, running a race, laughing at a joke, per-
suading an assembly, unraveling a mystery, solving a
problem, removing an obstacle, exploring a country, com-
municating with a friend, creating a poem, re-creating a
poem. These acts or events are all intrinsically complex,
composed of interconnected activities with continuously
changing patterns. They are like incidents in the plot of a
novel or drama. They are literally the incidents of life.

The contextualist finds that everything in the world consists of such incidents. When we catch the idea, it seems
very obvious. For this reason, it is sometimes easy to confuse the historic event of contextualism with common-
sense fact, and some contextualists have encouraged the
confusion. But there are lots of things in common sense
that are not events. Common sense is full of animistic,
formistic, and mechanistic substances. But contextualism
holds tight to the changing present event. This event itself,
once we note it, is obvious enough, but the tightness of the
contextualists' hold upon it is not usual. It is this hold
that makes contextualism a distinctive philosophic attitude and a world theory. For the tightness of this grip is
obtained through the set of categories derivative from the
historic event as a root metaphor.

§2. *Derivation of the contextualistic categories.*—The
contextualistic categories are derived from what we may
call the total given event. Since any event is a rich concrete
thing, in which features interpenetrate, there is a degree
of arbitrariness in selecting one feature rather than another, or so much of one feature against so little of another. To complicate matters, novelty is a not uncommon

feature of these events, so that many virtually categorial features are not universal. The principle that nothing can come from nothing is not accepted by contextualism, so that one given event may have predominant and permeating structural features that another lacks.

How far one will carry a set of categories into detail is a more arbitrary matter here than in any other relatively adequate world theory. In other theories one can pretty clearly distinguish categories (the basic universal structural features of nature) from subcategories, which are clearly derivative from the former and lead down into the minor detailed structures of limited portions of nature. There is an orderliness about such theories. Even formism has it, dispersive as it is in categorial structure. But, so to speak, disorder is a categorial feature of contextualism, and so radically so that it must not even exclude order. That is, the categories must be so framed as not to exclude from the world any degree of order it may be found to have, nor to deny that this order may have come out of disorder and may return into disorder again—order being defined in any way you please, *so long as it does not deny the possibility of disorder or another order in nature also.* This italicized restriction is the forcible one in contextualism, and amounts to the assertion that change is categorial and not derivative in any degree at all.

Change in this radical sense is denied by all other world theories. If such radical change is not a feature of the world, if there are unchangeable structures in nature like the forms of formism or the space-time structure of mechanism, then contextualism is false. Contextualism is constantly threatened with evidences for permanent structures in nature. It is constantly on the verge of falling back upon underlying mechanistic structures, or of resolving into the overarching implicit integrations of organicism. Its recourse in these emergencies is always to hurry back to the given event, and to emphasize the change and novelty that is immediately felt there, so that sometimes it seems to be headed for an utter skepticism. But it avoids this impasse by vigorously asserting the reality of the structure of the given event, the historic event as it actually goes on. The whole universe, it asserts, is such as this event is, whatever this is.

The ineradicable contextualistic categories may thus be said to be *change* and *novelty*. When these, however, are further specified in terms of given events of the sort with which we are acquainted in the present epoch of our universe, these ineradicable categories are exhibited as details within other categories which it is convenient to place first. I shall call these other categories *quality* and *texture*. Every given event in our present epoch has quality and texture. Whether events of other epochs will lack these categories we cannot say, but if they do they will have *changed* into something *novel* we know not of. We can describe only the events we have and know, and for these quality and texture are basic.

Our procedure in developing the categories of contextualism will be as follows: First, to point out that in this theory nothing shall be construed as denying that anything may happen in the world. Thus *change* and *novelty* accepted in the most radical sense will be regarded as the fundamental presuppositions of this theory. But, second, to note that we have to deal with the world as we meet it, and we meet it only in the events of the epoch in which we are living. The events of our epoch seem to exhibit a structure which may be regarded as relatively uniform, and the basic concepts for this structure may be taken as *quality* and *texture*. We shall therefore regard quality and texture as the basic categories of contextualism for our epoch. That is, they will be regarded as the basic categories subject to the general proviso above mentioned regarding change and novelty.

Third, we shall elaborate what is meant by quality and texture by means of a number of subheadings under each. Under quality we shall consider (1) the *spread* of an event, or its so-called specious present, (2) its *change*, and (3) its degrees of *fusion*. Under texture we shall consider (1) the *strands* of a texture, (2) its *context*, and (3) its *references*. Among these references we shall further note the following sorts: (*a*) linear, (*b*) convergent, (*c*) blocked, and (*d*) instrumental. This system of concepts may be regarded as a set of working categories for handling the events of our epoch. This system may be differently framed. Some contextualists (those who call themselves instrumentalists) are particularly interested in the instrumental references and subordinate all the other categories to these. This is possible. There are many ways of framing a set of working categories for contextualism. I do not claim any other virtue for this set except its balance and clarity for the purpose of our present rapid exposition.

It is worth noticing that the different emphases provided by different arrangements of concepts governing events contextualistically viewed do not ordinarily produce different world theories. Moreover, there is no definite number of concepts that must be named. The relations involved in a historic event are inexhaustible, and a set of contextualistic categories does not so much determine the nature of our world as lead one to appreciate fair samples of the world's events.

Then, fourth, having spread out the categories, we shall show how they thicken up in the production of continuous and individual objects, and how science and hypothesis in general are related to the control of these.

We begin, then, with quality as the first basic category of events in our epoch.

§3. *Quality.*—We cannot appreciate quality without contrasting it with texture. We shall start, then, by exhibiting these two categories and showing their close relation to each other. This will be actually a showing. They cannot be explained, since they are categorial. They can only be pointed at. We need for this an illustration, some present given event. Let us take one out of what we are doing. I am writing sentences. Let my writing of the next sentence be our illustration. *A period will be placed at the end of this sentence.* This is my illustration. Let yours be your writing this sentence. Reading it would be the same sort of thing, but writing it makes the event a little more intimate, more temporal, and active, and less likely to be interpreted in other than contextualistic ways. We might equally well have taken a trip downtown for a loaf of bread. Then we should have had a succession of acts in pursuit of the bread. Here we are in pursuit of a period. Such events make actual history as truly as Alexander's pursuit of an empire, or Caesar's conquest of Gaul. There is a certain object lesson in seeing if we cannot enter our universe through so trivial a thing as a trivial sentence.

Now what is quality and what texture in this event? Its quality is roughly its total meaning, its texture roughly the words and grammatical relations making it up. Generalizing, the quality of a given event is its intuited wholeness or total character; the texture is the details and relations which make up that character or quality.

The two are not separable, though in different events one or the other may be the more prominent. We may now pay more attention to the total meaning, now to the words. The events in the two cases are different events, but in each case both the total character or the quality and the details making up the quality or the texture are present. There is no such thing as a textureless quality or a qualityless texture. It follows that contextualism denies that these are absolute elements. It denies that a whole is nothing but the sum of its parts. It even denies that a whole is a sort of added part like a clamp that holds together a number of blocks. A whole is something immanent in an event and is so intuited, intuited as the quality of that very event.

We intuit the character of a face as Jim's, Mary's, Eliza's, and later discriminate the features. We intuit the character of a melody as "Old Black Joe," "Tipperary," "Drink to Me Only with Thine Eyes," and afterward discriminate the tones and intervals. We intuit the familiar character of home as we drive up to our door, and only occasionally ask ourselves what features distinguish this from the hundreds of other houses we drive up to. We intuit objects as chairs, cups, cats, tulips, oaks, linnets, and only rarely wonder how we know these so quickly and surely. These intuitions are of the qualities of these textures, and the textures are rarely noticed except when we do notice intently, and then it is the qualities that are not noticed. Qualities are most commonly in the focus of our attention but never (except for philosophic or aesthetic purposes) in the focus of analysis. That is why they are so easily neglected in analysis, and why, says the contextualist, the discrete mechanist is so plausible when he explains them away in terms of the elements of a texture. Those elements, details, features, components are there and constitute the texture, but the texture has also its intuited quality, which is not reducible to these though it is precisely the wholeness of these.

If now we are aware of what quality is, we can study it more closely and examine what we may call its subcategories.

i) *Spread.*—The quality of a given event has a *spread*, or, as it is sometimes called, a *specious present*. As I am writing, *A period will be placed at the* . . . , my act is rather thick in its duration and spreads, as we say, forward and back. I lift my pen at "the" and am just about to put down "end." The word "end" is not yet down, but it is being reached for and its meaning is already largely taken up in what has preceded. This forward reach in the quality of an event is the feeling of futurity.

There is a corresponding feeling of pastness which draws into the quality all the preceding words of the sentence. Even if I am saying the sentence and not writing it, so that I have not the assistance of the spatial line of words, still the word "period" is drawn from the past as I utter "the." That is to say, the word "period" is active now in the quality of this event, even though it is mathematically past.

The word "end," though not yet written, is already active in the quality of the event, and the word "period," though previously written, is still active in the event at the moment that I am writing the word "the." Moreover, the contributions to the quality of the event made by "end" and "period" are obviously much greater than that made by the "the," even though "the" is the word being written.

Now, this is what is meant by the *spread* of an event, or, as it has been paradoxically called, the *specious present*. For a contextualist there is nothing specious about it. It is part of the basic structure of all fact. What is present in an event is whatever contributes directly to its quality. Since "period" and "end" so contribute, they are present in the event, even though one comes quite a little after the other and neither happens to be the word I am writing.

The paradox of the situation arises only if one tries to impose a linear scheme of "time" on the intuited event. For the contextualist, the dimensional "time" of mechanism is a conceptual scheme useful for the control and ordering of events, but not categorial or, in that sense, real. The scheme is useful in this event to describe the order of the words. "Period" is the second word, "end" the eighth,

and "the" the seventh. Taking the word I am writing as
the schematic present, then "period" is quite a little past
and "end" is in the immediate future. But if a mechanist
goes on to argue that accordingly the only word actually
existing in the present is the word I am writing, "the," the
contextualist flatly contradicts him with his intuition of
the spread of the present quality of the event.

If it is objected that this is equivocating in the word
"present," the contextualist declares that he has as much
right to the word as the mechanist. In common sense the
word is ambiguous. On refinement we discover that it may
mean either the event actually going on or a point in a
dimensional scheme. Call the one the "qualitative present"
and the other the "schematic present," and the equivoca-
tion and much of the paradox is resolved.

But the basic issue will not be resolved, because it is a
categorial issue between mechanism and contextualism.
Mechanistically inclined people, like Broad describing
the specious present in his *Scientific Thought*, will continue to try to "clarify" the fact by reducing the intuited
spread to the terms of a dimensional scheme. They will
try to show that the qualitative present is nothing but a
confused way of saying something that is much more
clearly expressed in terms of schematic points or slices
along a line. There is no denying the clarity of schematic
time. According to the contextualist, its clarity is the reason for its invention. But this particular mode of clarity,
he insists, distorts the qualitative fact, and is no substitute
for the fact. And since the issue respecting whether or
not there is such a distortion is a categorial issue, it can-

not be settled by a simple confrontation of fact. It takes something more than the clarity of an expression to convince the contextualist that his intuition of the qualitative spread of a present event is fictitious.

So, the contextualist is careful to distinguish between qualitative time (often called "duration") and schematic time. For him the former is categorial and the latter derivative. He does not deny the utility of the latter, but he denies its adequacy to reveal the nature of an actual event. In an actual event the present is the whole texture which directly contributes to the quality of the event. The present therefore spreads over the whole texture of the quality, and for any given event can only be determined by intuiting the quality of that event.

Beyond the intuited present quality we have evidence for events that are past and for events to come. The great function of schematic time is to order these nonactual events. But actual time is the forward-and-back spread of the quality of an event. It is the tensional spread of that quality.

ii) *Change.*—If we write out our sentence again, we shall see that its quality is continuously changing. As I write "the," the focus of the quality balances (for me, of course) between the schematically past "period" and the coming "end." As soon as I have written "end," this word occupies the focus of the quality, and "period" takes on a modifying role, and the immanence of the last phrase is acquiring prominence. With the writing of each word the tensions of the previous words are redistributed, the configuration of the total meaning is altered, and the quality is accordingly changed. This change goes on continuously and never stops. It is a categorial feature of all events; and, since on this world theory all the world is events, all the world is continuously changing in this manner. Absolute permanence or immutability in any sense is, on this theory, a fiction, and its appearance is interpreted in terms of historical continuities which are not changeless.

iii) *Fusion.*—Quality always exhibits some degree of fusion of the details of its texture. This feature is perhaps most clearly perceived in savors and musical chords. William James's lemonade has become famous in this regard. Lemon, sugar, and water are the ingredients or details of the taste, but the quality of lemonade is such a persistent fusion of these that it is very difficult to analyze out its components. A simple musical chord is perhaps a still better illustration because most people can voluntarily take it as either fused or unfused. The tonic triad C-E-G has a distinctive character. Most of us hear it strongly fused and recognize it at once for its distinctive quality just as we recognize lemonade. Flat the E, and another chord is felt which has another highly distinctive quality. But with a shift of attitude the C-E-G chord can be perceived relatively unfused, that is, as the simultaneous combination of these three tones at certain intervals apart.

The event quality in the two perceptions is quite different. Where fusion occurs, the qualities of the details are completely merged in the quality of the whole. Where fusion is relaxed, the details take on qualities of their own, which may in turn be fusions of details lying within these latter qualities. Fusion, in other words, is an agency of qualitative simplification and organization. It is the qualitative sign, and probably the ultimate cosmic determinator of a unit. Wherever a quality is had, there is a unit, and the tighter the fusion the greater the unification. Every given event, as we have seen, has its quality. That is thereby the first unit. And the unity of the event, as we have also seen, is actually defined and determined by that quality. As far as the event quality extends, so far does the event extend, so far does the actual present extend. Occasionally such an event is completely fused, as in a mystic experience or an aesthetic seizure. But generally there is some *degree* of qualitative integration in an event, in which case the fusion of the event quality is relaxed and the qualities of the details of the texture begin to be felt in their own right though still as within the quality of the event. Such qualitative integration may pass through several levels in a single event with varying degrees of fusions at the different levels.

Returning to our sentence, and taking it this time as completed, we may find that the event of writing it was almost completely fused. This will be the result if our attention was completely concentrated on the meaning, which would entail that the writing was entirely mechanical and that the separate words were not separately noticed. The words and the writing of them and whatever else was involved would then have been completely fused in the quality of the total meaning. This is not an uncommon experience. It is our commonest way of reading. We tend not to notice the experience, however, because when we begin to notice it we begin to analyze and to break down fusion. As soon as individual words are noticed, the event quality of the sentence becomes integrated into the qualities of the details, which are more or less fused into the total event quality. But some fusion must remain in the quality of the event; otherwise the event would break apart and we should have not a single event, but two quite unconnected events.

Contextualism is the only theory that takes fusion seriously. In other theories it is interpreted away as vagueness, confusion, failure to discriminate, muddledness. Here it has cosmic dignity. And it takes a certain revenge on the indignity to which it is subjected by other theories, by interpreting all cosmic simplicities as instances of fusion. Is a sensation of yellow a simple sensation? Then, if there is such an occurrence, it is a fusion of details which have not been discriminated—specifically, a fusion of dozens of relations schematized in the color pyramid. Is "good" a simple quality, like yellow? Then, if G. E. Moore is reporting truly, he has had a highly fused experience of a complex texture of social relations. All supposed elements are such fusions, says the contextualist, so far as anyone claims immediate experience with them. (As to inferred entities like electrons, he says these are only schematic concepts.) Whatever is simple and unified in experience, therefore, is the result of fusion. It is not a mere psychological affair. It reflects the active structures of textures, and we may infer that qualities and fusions are as extensive as the events of our cosmic epoch.

But the analysis and practical control of events goes on in terms of the categories of texture. It becomes easy, there-

fore, to forget the categories of quality. But, without qualities, textures would be as empty as sentences the words of
which had no meaning. As will be seen, the categories of
texture are inexplicable except on the assumption of the
categories of quality—as is equally true conversely.

§4. *Strands and context of texture.*—The first two categories of texture, namely, strand and context, are so interlocked with texture that the three can only be taken up as
a group. A texture is made up of strands and it lies in a
context. There is, moreover, no very sharp line between
strands and context, because it is the connections of the
strands which determine the context, and in large proportion the context determines the qualities of the strands.
But by way of definition we may say that whatever directly
contributes to the quality of a texture may be regarded as
a strand, whereas whatever indirectly contributes to it will
be regarded as context.

Let us write out our sentence once more: *A period will
be placed at the end of this sentence.* Let us keep the event
quality somewhat diffused so that the articulations of the
sentence into phrases and words will be felt. Then let us
take the phrase "at the end" for consideration. This phrase
with the other three ("A period," "will be placed," "of
this sentence") are details of the total sentence with integrated meanings or relatively fused qualities of their
own and as such are textures in their own right. They are
textures defined by the fused meanings of the phrases.

Now, with the phrase "at the end" taken as a texture,
we may roughly say that its strands are "at," "the," and
"end," and that its context is the other three phrases of

the sentence. The meanings of "at," "the," and "end" contribute directly to the total meaning of the phrase. But the
total meaning of the phrase depends also on the connections of these strands with outlying words and phrases
which indirectly enter into the meaning of the phrase and
constitute its context. The particular meaning of "end,"
for instance, in this phrase is determined by connections,
partly grammatical and partly of other sorts, with the
already written "period" on the one side and the about-
to-be-written "sentence" on the other. These contextual
connections are gathered up into the word "end," which
contributes them as a group to the meaning of the whole
phrase. Even the little word "the" has a strong forward
reference to a definite point in the near future, a point
which reciprocally has a backward reference as part of
the context to the meaning of the total phrase. Change
"the" to "some" and notice what happens to the meaning
of the phrase. It implies that *this* sentence may not have
a period. It demands that the coming "this" in the phrase
"of this sentence" should also be changed to "some,"
showing up a close connection between "the" and "this."
It threatens to change the quality of the meaning of the
phrase from what we call sense into what we call nonsense.

This sort of experimentation shows the sort of thing a
strand is. It is a contributing detail in a texture, but it also
reaches out into a context and brings some of the quality
of the context into the texture. It shows that too sharp a line
cannot be drawn between texture, strand, and context. It
constitutes incidentally a running demonstrative criticism
of the method of element analysis, and of the analytical

theories generally. For contextualism, element analysis is intrinsically distortive.

We see also, what has come out in another way earlier, that context, texture, and strand are relative to one another. If the phrase "at the end" is taken as a texture, the surrounding phrases are context and the included words are strands. But if the whole sentence is taken as a texture, then the still wider references become context and the phrases of the sentence become strands. If a single word like "the" becomes a texture, then the words "at" and "end" become its context and its letters and phonetic and grammatical constituents become its strands. And so on.

What is the actual structure of an event, however, is ultimately determined by its qualitative structure. If the quality of the event of writing the sentence is taken up in the meanings of the sentence as a whole and the articulated meanings of its phrases, which seems to have been the case when I last wrote it, then in that given event a single word would not function as a texture at all, and the word's potential alphabetical and phonetic constituents would function only as context. This point has important analytical consequences, which we shall immediately consider. Here I am merely indicating that the relativity of context, texture, and strand is itself relative to the actual qualitative structure of a given event. The qualitative structure of an event is for that event final, whatever potentialities for the qualities of other events it may have within it.

Let us proceed, now, to the important analytical consequences of the things we have just been saying. The implications here are revolutionary from the standpoint of the analytical theories, formism and mechanism. In these theories it is assumed that any object or event can be analyzed completely and finally into its constituents. There is disagreement respecting what the constituents are, but none respecting the aim or the theoretical possibility of achieving that aim. Water, it is assumed, can be completely analyzed into atoms; or, if not into atoms, into electrical elements; or, if not into these, into other elements. But that there is an ultimate and final and complete analytical constitution of water is assumed. This assumption is categorially denied by contextualism; for according to its categories there is no final or complete analysis of anything. The reason for this is that what is analyzed is categorially an event, and the analysis of an event consists in the exhibition of its texture, and the exhibition of its texture is the discrimination of its strands, and the full discrimination of its strands is the exhibition of other textures in the context of the one being analyzed—textures from which the strands of the texture being analyzed gain part of their quality. In the extended analysis of any event we presently find ourselves in the context of that event, and so on from event to event as long as we wish to go, which would be forever or until we got tired. The quality of an event is the fused qualities of its strands, and the qualities of its strands come partly out of its context, and there we are outside the event. All contextualistic analysis has this sheering effect. As we work down into the constituents of a texture, we presently find ourselves in textures quite different from the one from which we started, and somewhere in its context.

We start to analyze our sentence, and we exhibit the articulation of its phrases; and then we analyze the words into their sounds and letters; then the sounds into their timbre constituents; then their timbre constituents into vibration correlates; then vibrations into the characters of waves; then waves into mathematical coördinate systems. And so on. Each of these steps does have a bearing on our original sentence. But long ago our analysis has come out from under the immediate texture of the original event and even from under the textures of its immediate context. And so with the analysis of any event. As we analyze a texture, we move down into a structure of strands and at the same time sheer out into its context. A bottom is thus never reached. For the support of every texture lies in its context. This support is as extensive as you wish, but you never reach the end of it.

It follows, moreover, that there are many equally revealing ways of analyzing an event, depending simply on what strands you follow from the event into its context. At each stage of your analysis (that is, in each new texture into which you have been led), this choice of what strand to follow comes up again, and every strand is more or less relevant. Hence, the contextualist rather disparages analysis for analysis' sake. What is the good of it, except as the mere fun of paddling about in the ocean of things? Serious analysis for him is always either directly or indirectly practical (whence the term "pragmatism"). If from one texture you wish to get to another, then analysis has an end, and a direction, and some strands have relevancy to this end and others not, and the selections of strands to follow are determined from stage to stage, and the enterprise becomes important in reference to the end. But there is no importance in analysis just for analysis.

Contextualism is accordingly sometimes said to have a horizontal cosmology in contrast to other views, which have a vertical cosmology. There is no top nor bottom to the contextualistic world. In formism or mechanism or organicism one has only to analyze in certain specified ways and one is bound, so it is believed, ultimately to get to the bottom of things or to the top of things. Contextualism justifies no such faith. There is no cosmological mode of analysis that guarantees the whole truth or an arrival at the ultimate nature of things. On the other hand, one does not need to hunt for a distant cosmological truth, since every present event gives it as fully as it can be given. All one has to do to get at the sort of thing the world is, is to realize, intuit, get the quality of whatever happens to be going on. The quality of blowing your nose is just as cosmic and ultimate as Newton's writing down his gravitational formula. The fact that his formula is much more useful to many more people doesn't make it any more real.

For the contextualist, therefore, even an attempt to name different sorts of references among strands, as we are about to do, has no significance in itself. Its significance lies in some purpose we are pursuing. This purpose determines why we classify strands rather than artichokes or buttons. And this purpose does arise from the circumstance that we are philosophers and not wholesale dealers in groceries and drygoods. But the philosophers' classificatory scheme is no more real than the wholesale dealers'. It simply has a wider potential range of application, though, paradoxically, it will probably never be so widely used.

The contextualist, therefore, does not make any exceptions to his analysis of analysis, not even for that analysis itself. All analysis, including his own world theory when he is driven to admit its presuppositions, is a tracing out of strands and has this sheering character. If you ask him, "Then how do you know that your analysis of experience is true of all experience?" he replies, "I don't." If you ask further, "Then you admit that your analysis is false?" he replies, "Catch me if you can."

But now we are getting off into his theory of truth, which I wish to reserve until later. Here I merely want to indicate the extreme implications and consequences of the contextualistic theory of analysis, and the way in which the contextualistic theory does not consider itself under any necessity of making an exception even of itself.

§5. *References of strands.*—So now we come to the third category of texture, references. These references consist simply of the strands more intimately considered.

i) The simplest and basic reference may be called *linear*. All the references of strands so far talked about have been of this sort. A linear reference has a point of *initiation*, a transitive *direction*, and achieves an ending or *satisfaction*. Every word in our sentence is a bundle of such references. We have already followed out some of these in the words "end" and "the." For instance, one of these linear references initiated by "end" (in "at the end of this sentence") reached forward and achieved satisfaction in "sentence." It was the reference answering to the implied question, "End of what?" With the completion of "sentence," we knew "of what" and the reference was satisfied, and that strand terminated. And note the transitive direction with the implied doubleheadedness or before-and-afterness of the reference. From "end" this reference pointed forward to a satisfaction, from "sentence" backward to an initiation, but at any intervening stage such as the writing of the word "this" it pointed both ways.

Some pragmatists have overstressed the forward and neglected the equally important backward reference in the transitive direction of linear reference. This has involved them in many unnecessary difficulties and misunderstandings. The linear reference is intrinsically a forward-and-back, future-and-past, initiation-and-satisfaction activity. This doubleheadedness is contained in the very category of the specious present, for it is just this polarity that affords the spread of texture, just this that spreads immediacy. Let the backward reference go, and a texture shrinks to a mere cross section and threatens to disappear in a temporal slice that is not even clearly definable. No pragmatist with his eye on the active present event, which is his root metaphor, ever intended such a denouement. Yet many pragmatists have said things that encouraged this notion, and have given justification for a set of stock criticisms of the theory, which no relevant factual evidence substantiates. A linear reference is a transition from an initiation to a satisfaction with a continuous intervening spread pointing both forward and back.

ii) A *convergent* reference is a complex linear reference in which there are either several initiations converging upon one satisfaction or several satisfactions derived from one initiation. This is the contextualists' description of the common experience of similarity.

Return to our sentence. The letter "e" was there repeated seven times. We probably had not noticed it. If now we notice it, we shall see that these seven letters stand out and gather together. They may do so in two ways. If we are looking for them, we have an initiated reference from which we derive seven satisfactions. But if they spontaneously impress us with their identity, then we have seven initiations converging upon one satisfaction.

The important thing to notice is that for the contextualist these letters are not intrinsically identical or similar, but only as they are made so, or become so, through the activity of convergent reference. When they were not noticed, they were not similar because no convergent action (presumably) was present. If we have written the sentence longhand and now look at the shapes of the seven letters more carefully, we shall see that they cease to be similar because their shapes vary so. If we are asked to count *all* the letters in the sentence, then not only do these seven letters become similar again, but they become similar to all the other letters in the sentence, for all the letters then converge upon a reaction which all can satisfy.

Similarities emerge only when convergent references occur. In the absence of the convergent references there are no similarities. No two things in the world are, in other words, inherently similar, but only become so when they initiate convergent references. Such references may, indeed, be predicted, but the objects are literally similar only when the strands converge. Before the convergence, they can only be said to be potentially similar. Two five-pound lead weights are not inherently similar, but when they react upon scales to produce the identical reading they are similar. And, of course, a five-pound bag of feathers is exactly similar to the weights under these conditions. But what makes all of these similar is their convergence of action on a single effect.

Since what we call physical properties are all of them convergent references of this sort—weights, dimensions, temperature changes—it follows that for the contextualist none of these is a permanent inherent property of natural objects. Physical properties are simply predictable convergences of references in physical textures.

iii) The subcategory of *blocking* is not, strictly speaking, a reference, but the breaking of a reference. Linear and convergent references are sometimes initiated but fail to reach satisfactions. It might be argued that the end of a reference must be the end of it, however it comes about. But the contextualist denies this and reminds one it is a categorial fact that a reference involves a satisfaction. Blocking is the concept for the irreducible fact that strands do not always run smoothly from their initiations to their satisfactions. Smooth-running strands constitute the contextualistic interpretation of what we generally mean by order. Blocking is accordingly a fact of disorder, and it inevitably involves some degree of novelty. For, concerning the strand blocked, the blocking is not expected or included in the reference of the strand. An unexpected turn in a road, for instance, is a partial blocking of a strand of reference, and a novelty. But if the curve is expected, it is incorporated in the reference of the strand and contains no novelty and involves no blocking.

Ordinarily the blocking of a strand can be analyzed as due to another strand which cuts across the one blocked. "Cutting across," like "strand," is of course a metaphorical technical term here. The reader must try to pass right through these terms to what is referred to. When one strand cuts across another, it simply means that an action has been unexpectedly held up by a conflicting action. When the intrusive strand or action has its own past history, we call this sort of novelty an intrusive novelty. The novelty is relative to the strand intruded upon. It is not, so to speak, an absolute novelty. After the conflict or blockage has occurred, it is theoretically possible to account for it in terms of the past history of each strand and show how their references led to a conflict.

It is possible that all textural novelties are intrusive novelties and are, accordingly, explicable as strands entering a texture from some distant context. But such explanation in contextualism is never to be assumed, but only to be discovered. It is always possible that a strand should be initiated or blocked absolutely and without explanation. Such occurrences we may call "emergent novelties."

As to the qualitative side of an event, nothing is more empirically obvious to a contextualist than the emergence of a new quality in every event. He notes the fact immediately, for one thing. I look out of the window and there is the quality of that event; I look back into the room and a totally different quality emerges. But, for another thing, he reasons to the same result from the very nature of a texture. As we have seen, a texture, through its strands, is constantly involved in its context, and the two together are so complex and so constantly changing that the nature of a total texture could hardly be expected ever to be duplicated. Since quality is the immediate character of the texture as a whole, a new quality must emerge from event to event. Emergent qualitative novelty is, therefore, unquestionably present in contextualism.

This admission or requirement respecting the qualitative side of an event gives a certain encouragement to the idea that there are emergent novelties on the textural side. This is amply justified. We speak of a strand as being initiated. What is initiated, as follows from our examination of the relation of strands to textures, is an integration of substrands. For if a strand is taken as a texture, it is itself composed of strands with references into the context. So, when we say that a strand is initiated, we find this means that a set of references is integrated. The integration is accordingly an emergent novelty, and is effective in a manner in which the unintegrated strands are not.

We are thus justified in admitting the existence of textural novelties resulting from an integration of strands which become fused into a texture that appears qualitatively as a novel strand. Such textural novelties are, however, analyzable into the strands which are integrated and fused, and these strands, like those of intrusive novelties, find their initiations similarly in other contexts.

Besides intrusive novelties, emergent qualitative novelties, and emergent textural novelties, are there any others of a still more radical sort? There appear superficially to be absolute endings, as when a blocked strand is not carried through. Yet most of these endings seem to be analyzable, and what is destroyed in a complete blocking seems to be an integration. The constituent strands are disintegrated, but seem to be traceable into future contexts. Like an army in defeat, the men are all dead or scattered, but they can all be identified somehow, somewhere. It is only the army that is gone. The texture, the integration, the fusion, the quality is gone, and that is something utterly lost to the universe, just as an emergent textural novelty is something utterly new and added, but both integrations and disintegrations are still analyzable in terms of constituent strands which pass into other contexts. Are there still more radical novelties and endings where a whole texture or strand utterly disappears without trace or appears without any premonition? We may call these "naïve novelties" or endings. Is there evidence for these?

There is evidence that these would be easily missed. As C. I. Lewis in his *Mind and the World Order* repeatedly shows, our practical and intellectual attention is inevitably attracted and concentrated upon the schemes and regularities and continuities of experience which can be relied upon for prediction and analysis. Naïve novelties and endings would not, ordinarily, even be named. Certainly not naïve endings, for a genuine name that refers to and means its texture is a strand of that texture, and while meaning survives in that strand, so long and so much of that texture survives. That texture is still denotable, though no doubt very indirectly. A naïve ending by definition signifies that a strand has ceased to have any causal connection even the most indirect with any actual present, and consequently any future, events. An utterly meaningless name might be evidence for such an ending, provided we had reason to think that the name once had meaning and that what it meant had left no other trace in nature. Conversely with respect to the evidence for a naïve novelty, we must find evidence for the likelihood that no previous event ever referred to this strand, that its initiation was absolute and not an integration and fusion of other strands.

As we said, there is a powerful practical and intellectual bias against noticing such strands, should they emerge in our textures, and even against admitting their possibility; but there is nothing in the nature of things (that is, in the contextualistic categories) to exclude their existence. In any specific occurrence, the evidence must necessarily be the presence of something like a blocking or a surprise with a total lack of evidence of any source for it. When we cannot find a source, we generally assume that the references are merely blocked off, that they are traceable but that *we* have not been able to trace them. Moreover, we have so often been able to trace what we thought were untraceable references that we have acquired great confidence in our assumption of universal traceability. But, as Lewis suggests, in the whole extent of experience our successes are only as a few square miles to the area of a continent and these few square miles may have been rather carefully chosen for their suitability for cultivation. There may be plenty of naïve novelties. They may enter into all our textures. And yet, when every allowance is made, the absence of any evidence to the contrary is never very good evidence to the affirmative.

An integrative novelty, however, is almost as novel in action as a naïve novelty would be. It does institute a new strand through fusion, and it has new causal potentialities. It is analyzable and understandable in retrospect, but not predictable in its nature, nor in all its effects. The contextualist doubts if the properties of water could have been predicted from those of oxygen and hydrogen, or the effects of the corporate organization of industry from individual psychology and economic needs.

iv) From blocking references we are soon led to *instrumental references*. Those who call themselves instrumentalists among contextualists give these references a dominant position among the categories. As we have said, it does not make much difference in contextualism what traits are emphasized first; the others will all come in sooner or later. But beginning, as we have, with quality and texture, we come upon instrumental references as a certain type of integration of the preceding kinds of references.

An instrumental action is one undertaken as a means to a desired end and as a result of some obstacle that intervenes between the beginning of the action and its end or satisfaction. Instrumental action accordingly implies a linear reference that has been blocked, and a secondary action which removes or circumvents the blocking. The instrument proper is the secondary action that neutralizes

the blocking. And the references involved in this secondary action are the instrumental references.

The result is often a texture of very extended and complicated integration. What holds it together is a linear reference that persists from lack of satisfaction. This is the
positive dynamic factor in the integration. The negative
factor is the blocking in the form of an intrusive novelty.
Such a blocking sometimes effectively brings the linear
reference to an end without satisfaction. But at other times
it initiates one or more subsidiary references or instruments, which in their turn either effectively block off the
intrusive reference or switch the action around it or actually integrate it into a more complicated texture that
carries through the original linear reference to its satisfaction.

An instrumental reference, therefore, involves three
factors: (1) First, it is a linear reference in its own right,
with its own initiation and satisfaction. But (2) this satisfaction is dependent upon the satisfaction of the original
reference which it serves, this dependency or service being
the instrumental factor proper, the reference which connects the instrumental strand with the terminal strand.
And (3) it is a reference to the blocking strand. An instrumental action is thus a texture in its own right with its own
satisfaction, but it is guided on the one side by the super-
vening terminal action which it serves and on the other by
the blocking action which it neutralizes. These two latter
actions are in the context of the instrumental action, but
so closely connected with it as to constitute much of its
structure because of the number of strands or references

that pass directly from these actions of the context into the instrumental texture. So close are these connections that, when an instrumental action is thoroughly integrated with its end and its obstacle, all three work together as one total texture. The obstacle no longer appears as an obstacle, nor the instrument as an interpolated action, but all as simply articulations of a total complex action.

For example, a hunter starts from his cabin to a meadow where he believes that deer abound. His path is obstructed by a stream. The strand of his purpose is thereby blocked. He may give up. But, if he persists, he finds perhaps a log and a pole, and pushes himself across. The activity of pushing himself across has its own initiation as he steps off one bank of the stream, and its satisfaction as he steps up on the other bank. It is set in motion, however, by the obstacle of the stream, and is directed by the meadow he is aiming for. At this stage the action is clearly an interpolation and distinct from the main action of walking to the meadow. But when he returns, he knows just what to do, and the separateness of this action at the stream is scarcely felt. And if thereafter he often goes to the meadow, he will think no more of the ferry across the stream than of any turn or dip in the trail. The ferry across the stream is just one articulation of a total integral act like the other landmarks of the trail. What was originally an obstacle turns into a stimulus for reference that leads right over to the next stage of the journey.

In this way instrumental reference tends gradually to turn into articulated linear reference. Contextualists often make a great deal of this fact, especially in ethical theory, pointing out the dangers of conceiving the distinction of means and end as absolute. An instrumental activity enters right into the texture of a terminal activity, and the structure of any complicated terminal activity is largely instrumental.

This becomes still more striking when we consider the immediate quality of such acts. At the early stages of an instrumental act, when the obstacle is vividly felt, the instrumental activities are qualitatively taken as rather separate events, but as they become integrated with the terminal texture they fuse into the quality of one total texture. At the beginning we are aware of each separate act in running an automobile. Later, running an automobile becomes a total texture with a quality of its own, quite distinct, for instance, from the act of riding a bicycle.

If now we return to our basic illustration of the sentence we shall see that it is full of articulations which function as instrumental activities. If we are writing the sentence with the foregoing considerations in mind, we soon see that every word is a means for the expression of what we call the thought. Like the hunter, we start out for a certain end, which for us in writing this sentence is the period. If, as we write along, we become stumped for a word—have forgotten, for instance, the word for "placed" (an occurrence frequent enough in a foreign language, if not in our own),—what happens to us is just what happened to the hunter when he came to the stream. Then we realize, with some measure of surprise perhaps, that every word in the sentence has an instrumental reference. And it will perhaps further dawn on us that any highly articulated texture is an integration of instrumental references which ordinarily are fused in the total quality of the event.

We also see that any considerable instrumental texture is more than the texture of a given event and extends beyond the range of the specious present. If the thought is a long one, its exposition extends beyond phrases and sentences into paragraphs, chapters, and books. Many given events are connected in such a texture, and we become aware of continuities of texture that outreach the actual contextualistic present.

It is still convenient to speak of these as textures, but in order to differentiate them from the textures of given events let us call them individual textures. The texture of a given event is defined and determined by the extent of its qualitative fusion. But an instrumental integration, as we have seen, extends far beyond the limits of a given event. I may take in a whole sentence in one present fused act, but not a whole page or chapter. The integrations of experience extend beyond the present of any given event. They are not completely actual in any one present, but they become actualized through successive actual presents and hold experience structurally together, and render the course of history orderly and predictable.

In coming upon individual textures we are thus stepping out of the immediacy of present given events into the evidence for a widely extended universe in which myriads of given events are interlocked and march forward arm in arm into the future with great strides.

§6. *Individual textures.*—Individual textures are not a category, but are derivative, as we have seen, from the categories of contextualism through the subcategory of instrumental references. One of the strong arguing points for contextualism is that all its categories are derived from the immediacy of any given present event, and that the public world about us is directly derived from these and does not need to be inferred or assumed in the manner of mechanism. The contextualist insists that a study of any private event carries of itself into a public world. The context of a private texture is already some other texture, and the two textures are thus mutually conjoined and interpenetrating, and so on as far as we wish, out into any epoch.

This interpenetration of textures in any act of social coöperation is clear enough from the contextualistic categories. But the same is true in any act of ordinary perception. When I perceive a table, there is, according to the contextualist, an interlocking of two or more continuous textures. There is a good deal of evidence for an individual textural continuity which we call the physical table in constant causal interaction with its environment. We would hardly assume that a table which burst upon our vision was a naïve novelty. We have even better evidence of a textural continuity which I call my physical organism and which is ever in the context of my given events. In what we analyze as certain conditions of light and spatial proximity, references are set up between these two physical continuities fusing into a given texture of considerable complexity. The qualities of this texture include what we call color and shape. As these are perceived, they are textural and qualitative emergents. That is, previous to the interlocking of the strands of the continuous textures of table and organism there were no such colors or shapes in existence (at least, not there in the texture of the perception). These are emergent qualitative and integrative novelties arising from a texture of strands partly derived from the so-called physical table and partly from the so-called physical body of me. If I look away, that perceptual texture is disintegrated and its qualities, of course, disappear. If I look back, it is reintegrated and the qualities emerge once more. But the important point to note is that the qualities arise in the integration of the texture and belong neither to me alone nor to the table alone, but to the common texture. In seeing a table I am interacting with my environment and am so far out in it.

If now it be asked what is the status of the physical table when not interacting in perceptions, the contextualist answers that it is some sort of individual continuous texture with appropriate qualities, but that our knowledge of it apart from perception is entirely relational. As a texture a physical continuant has its complex quality just as the texture of a sentence or a melody or a continuously sounding chord of an organ has its quality. What this quality outside of perception is we naturally cannot know, since we intuit a physical continuant only in perception, but we infer that in other contexts where the strands of the texture of an organism do not mingle with those of a physical continuant in perception the physical continuant has other qualities. But though we cannot intuit the qualities of a physical continuant independent of perception, we can make inferences about its texture or relational structure outside of perception.

What is the nature of this relational knowledge we have of textures we cannot intuit? It consists in the relations or strands of *schemes* which satisfy predictions. These schemes, such as maps, diagrams, formulas, functional equations, and symbolic systems, are themselves continuants and are instruments of prediction. These have been developed on the basis of past social experience, and their status is a good deal like that of a social institution. Just as the American Constitution is an instrument for governing social affairs, both a summary of past social experience and a guide to future experience, so, with certain modifications, with these schemes. They constitute what is called "the science" of a period, and change from period to period. Some pragmatists have exaggerated the significance of this change in schemes and speak as though the structure of physical nature changed from age to age because "the science" of an age changes. Physical nature may well change in different epochs, but there is no reason in contextualism to identify the structure of nature at a period with "the science" of that period, any more than we must identify the evolution of tree forms with the evolution of saws and axes.

The structure of physical events is not literally the structure of the schemes which control them. But we do with some legitimacy impute to a physical texture the relational structure of a hypothesis which controls it. That does not mean that the structure of a gasoline engine can be literally identified with the structure of the diagram which controlled its manufacture or which successfully indicated to students the disposition of its parts and mode of working. But the diagram does contain a system of references which when followed enter without blocking into the texture of the engine—that is, if the diagram is verified and found true.

§7. *Operational theory of truth.*—Thus we come to the contextualistic theory of truth. It was with a theory of truth that contextualism came to birth. The early contextualists like Peirce and James insisted that no world theory was involved in this conception of truth. Pragmatism (or pragmaticism, or whatever they chose to call it) was, they said, simply a method. It presupposed and implied nothing. It was purely empirical, purely a noting of what men actually did when they came to conclusions which they called true. The contemporary name for this method is *operationalism,* and many present-day operationalists share the opinion of the early pragmatists that this theory of truth has no presuppositions.

The history of the theory, even so brief as the history is, has not supported this idea. The method has thickened into a doctrine and thence into a world theory. Our exposition has accordingly been in reverse order from the history of contextualism. We come out where contextualism began. The course of this exposition, especially in the company of the expositions of other world hypotheses with their special-truth theories, shows pretty clearly why the operational theory of truth is also only a special-truth theory. It is truth in terms of action, of actual events having references which lead to satisfactions in other actual events.

The general statement of the theory is pretty obvious against the background of our previous exposition. The question of truth arises when a strand is blocked. This strand then seeks satisfaction in the context of the blocking. In colloquial terms, a problem arises and we seek a solution of the problem. We proceed then to analyze the situation in search of a hypothesis which will lead us to a solution of the problem. This analysis consists in following out the strands of the blocking conditions in the context of the blocked strand. If the problem is of any complexity, this analysis leads us into various relational schemes. The relations (i.e., the strands) of these schemes are studied in their relation to the blocked strand. A tentative hypothesis is constructed, this hypothesis being in the nature of an instrumental texture with definite references for action. These references are followed out, and this activity is the act of verifying the hypothesis. If the hypothesis is blocked, and accordingly the original blocked strand (the problem) is not satisfied, then the operation is said to be false and the whole process of analysis, construction of hypothesis, and verification starts over again. If, however, the following of the hypothesis leads to the satisfaction of the blocked strand and to the solution of the problem, then the operation is said to be true. Truth is thus the result of an instrumental texture which removes a blocking and integrates a terminal texture.

Such is the general statement of the operational theory of truth. It is, however, an ambiguous statement. Three distinct specifications of the theory can be brought out. Roughly they indicate steps in the development of pragmatism. The first is the narrowest and the one the enemies of pragmatism try to associate with it; the last is the broadest, but comes dangerously near to overstepping the categorial limits of contextualism. The first two have been named by C. W. Morris "successful working" and "verified hypothesis"; the third may be called "qualitative confirmation."

i) *Successful working.*—In order to have specific details, let us return to our illustration of the hunter. He came to the stream. He found his way to the meadow blocked. He looked over the situation, brought his memories and concepts to bear upon it, and framed a verbal hypothesis or an equivalent, which consisted of a texture of references that passed into a succession of activities (picking up a pole, stepping on the log, pushing with the pole), which brought him to the other bank, whence he went on.

The "successful working" theory states that the hunter's arriving at the other bank and proceeding on his way constituted the truth of the activity. Truth is utility or successful functioning, and that is the end of it. When a rat in a maze tries a number of blind alleys, and is unsuccessful in reaching its goal, its actions are *errors,* but when it is successful in reaching its goal, it finds the *true* path. The successful action is the true one, the unsuccessful actions are false; and similarly with the hunter's acts. The only difference between the rat and the hunter is that the hunter is more skillful in making his errors in tentative or symbolic terms, that is, he thinks out his alternatives rather than acts them out.

Two objections are raised to this statement of the operational theory. First, it is asserted that this does not define truth and error; it merely points out existent facts.

Some actions are successful and reach their goals and some are not. So, also, some actions are swift and some are slow; some are delightful and some are painful; some are socially approved and some socially disapproved. James came very near equating truth with these last two. " 'The true,' " he said, "is only the expedient in the way of our thinking. . . . We have to live today by what truth we can get today, and be ready tomorrow to call it false-hood. Ptolemaic astronomy, euclidian space, aristotelian logic, scholastic metaphysics, were expedient for cen-turies, but human experience boiled over those limits, and we now call these things only relatively true, or true within those borders of experience."[1] James spoke somewhat vaguely, but some of his followers took the equation of truth as "the expedient in the way of our thinking" quite literally. So Ptolemaic astronomy was true while it worked, while it was socially approved, and while it satisfied peo-ple to believe in it. This is certainly carrying the term "truth" rather far from common-sense usage, and these pragmatists have been butts of much hilarity for the sug-gestion. Nevertheless, they would have been quite justified in this extension of the term if only a matter of usage was concerned. If the "successful working" of an idea were the closest equivalent in contextualism to the common-sense term "truth," then for contextualism that would be the proper meaning of "truth" with whatever restriction or extension it entailed.

This, however, is not the case. The second objection brings this out and goes to the heart of the matter. This

---

[1] *Pragmatism* (New York: Longmans, Green, 1922), pp. 222–223.

objection asks what happens to the "hypothesis" in the "successful working" theory. Taken literally, this theory asserts that the hypothesis is neither true nor false when it is framed, since as yet it is not either successful or unsuccessful. For how can you know how it works before it is carried into operation? But after it is carried into operation and success has been attained, the hypothesis cannot be called true, because it is past and gone. So, a hypothesis can never be successful when it is framed, nor can success ever be hypothetical when it comes.

The "successful working" theory excludes hypotheses from truth, yet hypotheses are prominent textures in contextualism, and they are the very textures to which usage applies truth and falsity. A contextualistic theory of truth that leaves hypotheses out of the theory is not fitting common-sense truth as closely as possible into the contextualistic categories. In fact, the "successful working" theory is only a halfhearted contextualistic theory. It leaves out not only the function of hypotheses, but also the still more important function of references without which the operations could not ensue from the hypotheses. When hypotheses and references are incorporated into the operational theory, then we have the "verified hypothesis" theory.

ii) *Verified hypothesis.*—The slogan of this type of operationalism is that truth is verification. According to this formulation, it is not the successful act that is true, but the hypothesis that leads to the successful act. When there is no hypothesis there is neither truth nor falsity, but just successful or unsuccessful activity. The operations of following out the references of the hypothesis retroactively render the hypothesis true if the result is successful, false if it is unsuccessful. Successful working on this view does not constitute truth, but it is the final factor in the constitution of truth. Truth on this view is a much more complex activity than on the "successful working" view. Truth is not the quality of an act as successful or unsuccessful, but a relation between a hypothesis and its eventuality. It entails a wager of success on the part of a hypothesis. It involves a texture of symbols with references toward a definite total satisfaction. If the satisfaction is achieved, the symbolic texture is true.

In the total act of verification there are at least three articulations: the formulation of a symbolic texture (the hypothesis, which may be telescoped into a mere attitude, but which, when fully expanded, appears as a verbal statement), a following out of the symbolic references (the operations), and a satisfaction or blocking of these references (the verification proper). The "successful working" theory attributes truth to the last articulation and renders the previous articulations otiose or nearly so. The "verified hypothesis" theory attributes truth to the first articulation if satisfaction is achieved in the last.

Trial-and-error behavior, for instance, would produce true and false judgments according to the "successful working" theory, but not according to the "verified hypothesis" theory. A rat that tried one alley after another in random fashion would have unsuccessful and successful acts. These would be false and true acts according to the "successful working" theory, but not according to the "verified hypothesis" theory. But if the rats showed evidence of anticipatory attitudes which their acts proceeded to verify, then an unsuccessful act would show the falsity of the attitude, and a successful act its truth. This interpretation is more closely in conformity with the common-sense meaning of the term and with what other world theories mean by it, and carries one much farther into the structure and spirit of contextualism. Most of the paradoxes of the pragmatic or operational theory of truth vanish on this interpretation.

It is, for instance, now possible to speak of the truth of a hypothesis that has not been verified. The hypothesis is potentially true or false, and indirect evidence may be brought out to increase or decrease the probability of satisfaction in direct verification. For instance, the hunter was so sure that the hypothesis that he could not walk across the river was true that he did not even try to verify it. As for that river, the evidence was all indirect—based on previous experiences with water. We should all agree with him that his hypothesis was true; but it was only very probably true, true on excellent credit only, for it had not been verified. Much of our scientific knowledge is, of course, of this sort, and a good deal of it is unverifiable. There is nothing involved in the "verified hypothesis" theory that does not give high credit to an unverifiable hypothesis for which there is good indirect evidence. But the theory does clearly exhibit the danger of such hypotheses, especially if they are piled one on top of another like the pyramiding of credits in holding companies.

This theory still stresses one pragmatic paradox, however, and that is that a true hypothesis gives no insight into the qualities of nature. It insists that a symbolic statement or a map or a model is no more than a tool for the control of nature. It does not mirror nature in the way supposed by the correspondence theory, nor is it a genuine partial integration of nature in the way supposed by the coherence theory of organicism. Therefore, says the exponent of the "verified hypothesis" theory, one gets no insight or intuition of the quality of nature out of an operational hypothesis. The texture of the hypothesis is one thing, the successful act which verifies it is another, and the references between simply link the two operationally together. This seems to me an unnecessarily stern if not perverse interpretation. As a reaction against the traditional insight theories of correspondence and coherence it is understandable. But the contextualistic categories which imply this theory and are empirically implied by it do not substantiate this radical severance of the qualities of a true hypothesis from the qualities of the event it is true of. Just as a clarification of the "successful working" theory turns into the "verified hypothesis" theory, so, I believe, a clarification of this latter (now orthodox) contextualistic theory leads into the "qualitative confirmation" theory.

iii) *Qualitative confirmation.*—This theory simply stresses the basic contextualistic principles that the meaning of a symbol is found in the quality it leads to and that the quality of a strand takes up the qualities of its context. On the basis of our earliest discussions in this chapter, it is inevitable that the quality of a texture which carries through to a total satisfaction should be qualitatively premonitory of the quality of the satisfaction. In fact, by our examination of the texture of perception we see that the texture of the verifying act (which is a perception) must be partly made up of the strands carried into it by the activities of the perceiver. When these activities are the operations of verifying a hypothesis, these operations are precisely the agent's contribution to the verifying texture. They are accordingly found qualitatively present in the successful act of verification. (They are, of course, blocked off and not found in an unsuccessful act of verification.) The referential structure of a true hypothesis therefore does carry through a set of operations and enter into the structure of the event referred to by the hypothesis as its successful verification.

Suppose the hunter, on looking over the situation, should make the explicit statement: "If I take up that pole, and step on that log, and push myself off from this bank, I can push myself up to the other bank." As a meaningful sentence this is already an articulated texture of references. These references are the beginnings of the operations themselves already qualitatively appearing in what we call images. These incipient references or images fill out and actualize themselves in the operations of picking up the pole and stepping on the log, balancing there, and placing the pole firmly against the bank, and so on. But these acts now are the very acts of perceptual verification of the hypothesis. The qualities the hunter is now experiencing are the very qualities of the event referred to as verifying the verbal statement. But these qualities are also the very qualities of the texture of the verbal references thickened out by the environmental contributions of the river, air, roughness of the pole, rollingness of the log, and so on. The structure of the verifying event is an integration of contributions coming partly from the operations of the hunter and partly from continuous physical textures among which these operations are carried on. The qualities intuited are those of this integrated texture. This texture actually fulfills the hunter's expectations, actually incorporates the structure of references initiated in the verbal statement. The structure of that sentence as a set of incipient references finds actual realization in the event referred to. The intuition of that structure is, therefore, a partial or premonitory intuition of the structure of the event it refers to. A true hypothesis, accordingly, does in its texture and quality give some insight into the texture and quality of the event it refers to for verification.

Thus, in a certain sense, a true hypothesis corresponds with the event that verifies it, for the references carry through continuously into the verifying event. In a certain sense a true hypothesis coheres with the event that verifies it, for its references are not blocked, but are integrated there. Such, says the contextualist, is the modicum of truth in these theories of truth. But, he adds, the first goes wrong in thinking that events can correspond without an active operational juncture of one with the other, and the second in thinking that there is integration in any sense prior to the act of integrating there. Both theories are wrong in implying that truth is a relation independent of the act of verifying.

The operational theory seems thus to culminate in the "qualitative confirmation" theory, which suggests that the body of hypotheses possessed by science and philosophy gives us a considerable amount of insight into the structure of nature. Where these hypotheses are directly verifiable we have insight not only into the texture, but also into the qualities of the events referred to. Where hypotheses are not directly verifiable we may be said to know something about the texture or relational structure of the events referred to, may be pretty sure there are such events, but we can have no glimmering of their qualities, though we may be as sure that they have qualities as we are of anything not directly verifiable. Contextualism works from the present event outward. It is very definite about the present event and the premonitions it gives of neighboring events, but less and less definite about the wider structure of the world. It is willing to make more or less speculative wagers about the wider structures of the world. But if anyone pushes a contextualist hard, he retires into his given event and the direct verification he makes from it.

But cannot a contextualist be forced, on his own principles, to admit that events have certain structures independent of his acts of verification? Are not hypotheses true or false of contemporary events which cannot be directly verified? Do not his very categories indicate a correspondence or an immanent integration between his hypothetical textures and other textures of the world? In short, would not a still further clarification of the operational theory of truth lead inevitably into a correspondence or causal-adjustment or coherence theory of truth which would commit a contextualist to some more determinate structural theory, like formism, mechanism, or organicism?

This is the threat that always overhangs contextualism. The best the contextualist can say is, "Catch me if you can!" On his own premises you never can quite catch him, for he can always insist on direct verification (and that means operational satisfaction). He can insist on direct verification even for his own categories, for these he acknowledges are only the strands of a hypothesis which demand operational satisfaction just as the strands of any lesser hypothesis do. But having forced him down to this contradiction in his world theory, you no sooner relax your pressure than his claims spring out once more to the limits of the universe. Perhaps he never exactly contradicts himself (which is more than can be said of any other thorough exponent of a world theory), but when a man proposes a theory so elastic that it can contract to a specious present or expand to the speculative limits of mathematical physics or world history under the exigencies of argument, one wonders about its ultimate adequacy. Possibly we can offer the contextualist this dilemma: Either you must confine yourself to believing only in the facts of direct verification, in which case your theory lacks scope; or if you admit the validity of indirect verification and acquire scope, you must admit that nature has a determinate structure and so fall into the contradiction of both affirming and denying this structure of nature. To this the contextualist's final reply probably is: How can you be so sure that nature is not intrinsically changing and full of novelties?

Chapter XI : Organicism

§1. *The root metaphor of organicism.*—As with contextualism, so with organicism, no ordinary common-sense term offers a safe reference to the root metaphor of the theory. The common term "organism" is too much loaded with biological connotations, too static and cellular, and "integration" is only a little better. Yet there are no preferable terms. With a warning, we shall accordingly adopt these.

Actually, the historic event which is the root metaphor of contextualism is a nearer approximation to the refined root metaphor of organicism than any common-sense term. This is so true that it is tempting to regard these two theories as species of the same theory, one being dispersive and the other integrative. It has occasionally been said that pragmatism is simply idealism with the absolute left out, which in our terms would be to say that contextualism is simply dispersive organicism. But the insistence on integration which is characteristic of organicism makes so great a difference that it is wiser to consider them as two theories. Since they contradict each other on nearly every categorial point, anyone not familiar with them might wonder how they could be thought closely related. The answer is that organicism has to deal mainly with historic processes even while it consistently explains time away, whereas contextualism has to admit integrative structures surrounding and extending through given events even though these structures endanger its categories. Organicism takes time lightly or disparagingly; contextualism takes it seriously. There we have a flat categorial contradiction, and something that cannot be interpreted as a difference of emphasis on certain categories of one view. The root metaphor of organicism always does appear as a process, but it is the *integration* appearing in the process that the organicist works from, and not the *duration* of the process. When the root metaphor reaches its ultimate refinement the organicist believes that the temporal factor disappears. How he can believe this we shall see presently. In the meanwhile let us develop the categories of organicism from the integrative process as this is observed in progress.

§2. *The categories of organicism.*—The organicist believes that every actual event in the world is a more or less concealed organic process. He believes, therefore, that a careful scrutiny of any actual process in the world would exhibit its organic structure, though some of the processes with which we are generally familiar reveal the structure more clearly and openly than others. The categories of organicism consist, on the one hand, in noting the steps involved in the organic process, and, on the other hand, in noting the principal features in the organic structure ultimately achieved or realized. The structure achieved or realized is always the ideal aimed at by the progressive steps of the process.

This opposition between what may be called the progressive categories and the ideal categories is an ineradicable characteristic of organicism, and seems to be the one source of all its difficulties. Ideally, the ideal categories should be the only categories of organicism—and the ardent exponent of this theory with a profound faith in it believes they are,—but without the progressive categories the theory seems rather obviously to lack scope. Yet if the ideal categories are omitted, the progressive categories would inevitably suffer revision in the direction of contextualism, for the root metaphor of "organicism" or "integration" would have been abandoned and the nearest fertile root metaphor would be the historic event. Organicism thus exhibits its basic inadequacy at the start in the very setup of its categories. Why, then, proceed to study this hypothesis? Because its internal contradiction is probably no worse than those hidden away in the other relatively adequate world theories. In this respect organicism differs from them only in wearing its inadequacy on its face.

The opposition of categories just noted is often called by organicists that of Appearance and Reality (the title of one of the classics in the theory). There is a truth in these names. The progressive categories would be Appearance if the ideal categories could monopolize Reality; and, moreover, this would be the situation if the theory were thoroughly adequate. The attitudes implied by these terms indicate the dogmatic organicist's typical way of treating his theory, a way that exposes it unnecessarily to criticism. For by this treatment his theory does not seem to square at all with our ordinary experience. It seems better to be somewhat skeptical of the whole theory, and let Appearance be as real as Reality and so accept the benefits of the insights into the world which the theory as a whole is able to afford. Most of these insights actually come out on the Appearance side, that is, in terms of the progressive categories.

We shall now proceed to name these categories. We shall name seven. They might be more or less, depending on how detailed one wished to be in his exposition of the theory. They are, as we remarked, the features of any organic or integrative process and its achievement. These are: (1) fragments of experience which appear with (2) *nexuses* or connections or implications, which spontaneously lead as a result of the aggravation of (3) *contradictions*, gaps, oppositions, or counteractions to resolution in (4) an *organic whole*, which is found to have been (5) *implicit* in the fragments, and to (6) *transcend* the previous contradictions by means of a coherent totality, which (7) *economizes*, saves, preserves all the original fragments of experience without any loss. The fourth category is the pivotal point of the system and should be included in both the progressive and the ideal sets. It is the goal and final stage of the progressive categories and it is the field for the specification of the ideal categories. So, categories 1 to 4 inclusive constitute the progressive set, and categories 4 to 7 the ideal set. We shall proceed to take up each category in detail. The world theory will automatically exhibit itself by this procedure.

§3. *An illustration.*—But first we need an example to refer to, some illustration in which these categories are pretty clearly exhibited. Let us take for our purpose the history of astronomy. The more complete the history the better, and the reader is invited to look the history up where it can be found in greatest detail. Just here we shall have to be satisfied with a summary in a half a dozen paragraphs.

Astronomy began with a wondering about certain bright spots scattered over the sky. These appearances move in various ways and over great distances, and men wondered about them with mingled admiration and apprehension. Connections presently appeared among them in their related movements, and still further connections were sought to make the movements understandable. The bright, moving appearances began to take on organization. At first the appearances reached out rather far afield for organizing connections with other appearances—with tables, air, mountains, leaves. Anaximenes said the earth is a table-like disk floating upon air. The sun, moon, and planets are fiery disks floating in the air like leaves. "The stars are fixed like nails in the crystalline vault of the heavens." All revolve laterally like a cap or millstone over the earth. The mountains on the northern rim of the earth hide the sun at night and produce darkness.

What was Anaximenes doing here? In a phrase of Plato's, he was trying to "save the appearances," or, more justly—for in an active mind the theoretical imagination works spontaneously,—the appearances through the agency of Anaximenes were trying to save themselves. They came scattered, fragmentary, a new sun every day, a confusion of stars coming and going, planets aimlessly wandering, the surface of the earth cutting these movements off. The movements of the stars led to anticipations contradicted by the movements of the planets. The setting of the sun and the loss of light brought anticipations of eternal darkness contradicted by a rising sun. The steady light of the sun brought anticipations of a fixed object contradicted by the movement and disappearance of the sun. Anticipations of permanence and regularity were contradicted by change and irregularity and, vice versa, expectations of impermanence and irregularity were contradicted by relative permanence and regularity. By an organization of these observations and other observations these contradictions vanished. The northern mountains and a single lateral movement brought the many appearances of the sun into one predictable system, and day no longer contradicted night, but each was consistent with the other, and so was every hour of the day and the night. The planets, moon, and sun were disks floating in the air, the stars were attached to a crystalline vault, whence the steadiness of the stars and the wandering paths of the planets. An organization of heavenly appearances with some earthly appearances saved all the appearances, anticipated some not formerly noticed (that is, predicted verifiable observations), and removed contradictions by including all in a coherent astronomical system. This system, it should be stressed, grew out of the observations and was found in the observations. It was not all sheer fantasy, nor arbitrary convention.

But Anaximenes' system contained contradictions which showed up places where fantasy and convention had entered in; and further observations growing out of Anaximenes' system and out of former observations and out of

more precise observations brought out still further contradictions. Anaximenes' system soon turned out to be
itself rather fragmentary. Anaximenes' mountains, air,
and leaflike disks were discarded, but his crystal sphere
was retained and multiplied. His successors gave a crystal
sphere to the fixed stars, to each planet, to the moon, and
to the sun, and explained the peculiar path of each of these
in terms of the rotation of each sphere in relation to the
earth. When the path of a planet was too complex to be
explained by one sphere, other spheres were interpolated
which carried no bright body, but the motion of which in
one direction or another was compounded with that of the
light-bearing sphere to produce the apparent irregular
path. This system saved all of Anaximenes' observations
and added many more, and freed astronomy from implicit
contradictions which would have appeared from the detailed observations of the properties of air, leaves, and
the like. For aimless as the movements of the planets
seemed at first to be, their regularity was greater than that
of leaves blown in the wind. This crystalline system was
Aristotle's astronomy.

But as more observations were gathered, it appeared
that the paths of the planets were too intricate to be included in any system of solid spheres. The observations
contradicted the possible movements of the spheres. The
crystalline spheres were abandoned, and only their circular motions retained. By multiplying different rates and
directions of these circular motions, by setting the center
of rotation of some of these motions off center (eccentrics),
and by having secondary circular motions ride on the cir-

cumferences of primary circular motions (epicycles), it was possible to describe precisely the observed paths of any heavenly body. This was Ptolemy's system.

But these explanations were enormously complicated, and the more precise the observations the more complicated the explanations. Movements had to be added to movements for every newly observed aberration of a planet. Worse than that, there was no implication or connection from one path or body to another. Every path was isolated from every other, and accurately as each might be described by Ptolemy's cycles, all were fragments, and no predictions from body to body, or path to path, could be made. The geometrical proof that any path which returned upon itself could be described in terms of a sufficiently complex compounding of circular paths in the manner of Ptolemy confirmed the fragmentariness of this mode of systematization. Where everything is possible, nothing is determined or explained. This contradicts the anticipation of predictability and determination that grows out of the regularity of the appearances. Ptolemy's cycles seemed more and more arbitrary, conventional, and abstract. They seemed not to grow intimately out of the observations, as inevitable implications or connections of one with another; they seemed to be simply convenient ways of cataloguing. The enormous and constantly increasing complexity of the explanations of the paths seemed a symptom of the arbitrariness of the mode of connection, as if these Ptolemaic cycles no more belonged to those appearances than Anaximenes' fiery disks floating leaflike in the air.

Copernicus produced an amazing simplification by taking the sun as the center of reference for the cycles of the planets and including the earth as a planet of the sun. This simplification seemed symptomatic of a more highly implicative system for the observations. In this direction, perhaps, lay the actual internal connections of these observations.

Kepler still further simplified the system by converting the circles into ellipses and stating certain empirical laws such as that the planets sweep out equal areas in equal times in their orbit about the sun, which greatly consolidated the mutual implications of the observations of any one planet.

The invention of the telescope in the meantime had greatly increased the precision of observation, and the gross number of observations had increased enormously, especially through the labors of Tycho Brahe. There was, then, a tremendous mass of somewhat loosely connected observations. Within certain limits there was predictability and implicative precision, but beyond these limits only disconnection and fragmentariness. The partial systems and the great mass of observations called for a fuller systematization, for a better understanding of the interconnections which had not yet been achieved and which seemed to demand such an achievement.

Through Newton this achievement was realized. The mode of its realization, however, is almost more important, in the present connection, than the fact. It came about by a convergence of the astronomical system with another system of coherent factual development which had its own history. It came about by the union of astronomy and mechanics into one mutually inclusive system. This resulted from a discovery by Newton that the implications arising from the state of achievement of mechanics at that time were implied by the state of achievement of astronomy at that time. Kepler's fragmentary systematizations of astronomical observations were confirmed and his fragmentary systems all united under Newton's three mechanical laws of motion and his law of gravitation. Moreover, these mechanical laws of motion and gravitation were confirmed and greatly reinforced by the inclusion within their system of the vast mass of factual observations in astronomy. Through these mechanical laws, astronomical observations now acquired determinative implications which to a considerable degree they had lacked ever since the relatively conventional explanations of Ptolemy. Now at last it was possible for groups of astronomical observations to develop significant implications of other formerly unsuspected observations. Something more spectacular than the prediction of an eclipse, or the periodic return of a comet, the Newtonian system predicted and discovered a new planet.

But even the Newtonian system, as we now know, involved some contradictions and led to the system of Einstein. We have gone far enough, however, for our purposes of illustration. This progressive systematization still goes on, and, the organicist believes, will go on as long as there are contradictions or gaps to be resolved or filled in.

We now turn to the application of the organistic categories to this illustration.

§4. *Application of the categories:* (i) *Fragments.*—It should be observed, says the organicist, that the illustration of the previous section is not just one illustration of the application of the organistic categories, but a succession of them. The same integrative process is going on over and over again and always in one direction—in the direction of further integration.

This fact shows that the materials of integration are always relative to the previous integrations. "Fragments," in other words, are relative to the degree of achievement reached. For Anaximenes the fragments were the bright appearances and the segments of their motions. For Kepler the fragments were systems of circular motions. For Newton the fragments were Kepler's laws. Accordingly, the category, fragments, is a sort of negative category which acquires significance in terms of the degree of integration *not* achieved. A fragment is whatever is *not* integrated. The specification of the fragment is always in terms of the integrations in which this fragment ceases to be a fragment. Just what the fragments of motion were which Anaximenes worked upon as data, he himself could not state until he had systematized these data into circular motions, after which he could specify the data he had been working with as segments of the circular movements which integrated the data. So incidentally with all data, according to the organicist. No scientist really knows what are the data he is dealing with until he has the system in which they are integrated. An isolated datum is a fragment. It becomes precise and significant only when it is brought into a coherent system and connected with other data.

Negative as a fragment is, however, in its specification, it has this very positive feature: that it is the thing that is first given. It is not made up; it comes. Those bright appearances in the sky actually appeared. They had an impact and an insistence, even though just *what* they were was not clear. They were the materials of Anaximenes' system. In the progress of integration, each stage necessarily takes as its materials the fragmentary integration of the stage below. In this sense, fragments are always the actual materials of nature. This is a positive contribution of fragments. Moreover, as we shall see from the seventh category, everything that a fragment gives is in some way true of nature. What is not true, however, is the way a fragment gives it, for its way is fragmentary and that, the organicist believes he can show, is not the way of nature. Fragments, therefore, are positive appearances, but only in all that is not fragmentary about them, and what this is can never be found in the fragments but only in the integrations that coherently organize them.

ii) *Nexuses.*—There is another positive factor in fragments, or rather another aspect of their positive nature as materials for organization, and that is their internal drive toward the integrations which complete them. These internal drives are their nexuses.

According to the organicist, facts are not organized from without; they organize themselves. Scientists and philosophers and the common man when he thinks are but the channels of integration and, like the spouts of a fountain, serve best when they interfere least and let the materials take the form implicit in them. It was not Anaximenes,

Aristotle, Ptolemy, Copernicus, Kepler, and Newton who made astronomy. Astronomy made itself through these and other notable men, and their genius consisted in giving access to the facts and clearing away the obstructions of human bias so that the facts could find their own connections. For the connections were really there all the time, working in nature. Newton's integration held among Kepler's fragments as much before Newton made it as after. All the data were there. There was nothing to do but let them come together. Newton's great insight was that transparency of vision which perceived the implications of the data as they were. Had he seen less clearly or tampered with the materials, the synthesis would not have been made: that is, not through him; but it would inevitably have been made soon. This inevitability of connections among fragments, this implication of wholeness contained in them, is what the organicist means by nexus. Every fragment, appearance, datum, fact, he believes, has nexuses. These are immediately discoverable in observation, he thinks, to anyone who looks for them. But better evidence still, perhaps, is the signs of their presence and action in the cumulative integrative progress observable in the history of knowledge.

iii) *Contradictions.* — These nexuses reach out from fragments like tentacles and encounter contradictions for the fragments. The progress of integration is not smooth and continuous, but is a buffeting of fragment against fragment, producing conflict and contradiction which is only resolved in an integration. The nexus of a fragment leads it inevitably into conflict and contradiction with other fragments.

The early organicists, notably Hegel, thought that there was one and only one course of progress from maximum fragmentariness to ultimate integration. His books narrate the tragicomic drama of this fixed and inevitable progress. The drama is comic because the ultimate happy ending is inevitable, but tragic because the path is a path of conflicts and we struggling human beings never reach the final ending. Thesis–antithesis–synthesis is the ever-recurring form in each scene of his drama. A fragment restless in its isolation and "abstractness" is driven by its nexus to a fragment which is its exact opposite and contradictory. These opposed fragments are inevitably connected and inevitably hostile. Each needs and implies the other for its completion, and each is destructive of and contradictory to the other. Thesis and antithesis, they cannot get along without each other and they cannot abide each other. The conflict is finally resolved in an integration, a higher synthesis, which recognizes the claims of each fragment, "transcends" them and harmonizes them in a richer more concrete whole. But presently this whole exhibits an "abstractness" of its own and seeks the whole from which it is abstracted. Its nexus drives it to its own peculiar opposite. These two richer fragments again imply and contradict each other, love and hate each other, demand and try to destroy each other, until a new and still higher and still more concrete synthesis is attained. Whence the same conflict breaks out again; and so on from level to level. But with each level the fragment is richer and more nearly complete, and the progress prefigures the goal where all fragments are united and harmonized and mutually imply one another without residue, so that every fragment finds its completeness in that whole, where is no abstractness, no more fragmentariness, no remaining nexuses flying loose in search of satisfactions, but all tied in within one absolutely concrete coherent organic whole— the Hegelian Absolute.

To the later organicists this drama is a caricature of what actually takes place. There is no single cosmic path to the truth or to the ultimate integration of fragmentary data. There is not one single inevitable opposite for each fragment. The progress of astronomy might have gone along a somewhat different route. There are many paths from error to truth. The thinner, more abstract, more isolated, or the vaguer and more confused the initial facts or fragments of cognition, the greater the variety of ways in which these may seek explanation. As the fragments get richer, the alternatives become fewer. The less we know about anything, the more ways suggest themselves in general for finding out about it. With the observations in Anaximenes' hands, a thousand plausible hypotheses were possible, but with the data in Newton's hands there was probably only one possible synthesis.

Hegel was right, say these later organicists, in the inevitability of the trend of cognition toward a final organization in which all contradictions vanish. He was right in his observation that the nexuses of fragments lead out toward other fragments which develop contradictions and demand coherent resolution. He was right in his idea that these nexuses have a particular attraction for those relevant facts which are peculiarly recalcitrant to harmonization with the facts already gathered. It was the aberrations in the orbit of Uranus, those recalcitrant data which refused to harmonize with the Newtonian laws, that particularly attracted the attention of astronomers and led to the discovery of Neptune. In all these things Hegel was right. But he was wrong and invited undeserved ridicule for the organistic program by his fantastic, arbitrary, and rigid picture of the path of progress.

The nexuses of fragments cannot be regimented or restricted in number; nor is the order of contradictions encountered predetermined. Several lines of progress may go on simultaneously. Aristarchus, for instance, suggested a heliocentric system in astronomy long before Copernicus presented it. Aristarchus' suggestion was perhaps premature, in that it conflicted too strongly with the available data of Greek physics which pointed to the earth as the stable base of physical processes; nevertheless, there appeared the suggestion, and the history of astronomy might have progressed along the lines of Aristarchus rather than those of Aristotle. But Newtonian astronomy was the goal in either case. The goal was predetermined in the structure of the facts, but not the particular path to the goal. The more fragmentary the facts, the greater the number of possible paths, because the greater the number of implied contradictions with apparently relevant facts.

The later organicists are accordingly much more flexible in their descriptions of the organizing process than the earlier ones. They observe that appearances are posited or given. They note that the implications of these appearances lead to contradictions with other appearances, and that these contradictions are resolved in systems which coherently organize both groups of appearances. Beyond this, they do not prescribe the path of knowledge. Nor do they believe they are prescribing anything at all; they are merely pointing out what actually goes on among the facts of the world. Their argument is through and through illustrative. "Look at the facts of astronomy," they say. "Isn't that the way they went?"

What, then, are these contradictions which with nexuses drive on the facts to their fulfillments? Obviously, organicists do not use the terms as equivalent to contradictions in the formal sense of "not both p and not p." Quite true; though this formal expression of contradiction would be accepted by them as the most abstract, and therefore fragmentary, expression of just what they do mean by contradiction. So far as this expression has significance, they say, and is not a succession of mere marks, it signifies some conflict in fact—such as Anaximenes' observation, let us say, that the appearances called the sun both do and do not imply the existence of one object. The sun's similarity from day to day, and the continuity of the appearances from east to west during the day, signify one object. But if the sun were one object and disappeared in the west, then it should rise in the west like a man who disappears into a cave and comes out again. But the sun always rises in the east, so there must be a new sun every day. Yet the sun cannot both be and not be one object. The conflict among these appearances is resolved by observing the structure of the earth and realizing that the sun could go around behind the mountains to the north and come out on the other side in the east. A contradiction, they point out, is always based on a factual conflict. There are, accordingly, as many kinds of contradiction as there are ways in which fragmentary appearances are unresolved.

For instance, an *isolated* appearance is in contradiction with its unfulfilled nexus, or rather the very conception of an isolated appearance is a self-contradiction because an appearance is always an appearance for something and has nexuses. All formistic characters are on this score abstract and self-contradictory. Yellowness never occurs in utter isolation. It is connected with some person or object, or both. As a fact it calls for its setting. To posit it as an isolated fact, therefore, is to contradict its inherent nexus with its setting.

Again, *indeterminateness* is self-contradictory. That was the chief trouble with the Ptolemaic system. The compounding of circles for the orbits of planets was not a determinate implication of the observed positions of the planets. It has been pointed out that the Ptolemaic system has never been disproved. The fact is, says the organicist, it never was proved. The observations of the planets never definitely implied those superimposed circles, any more than they implied spirits to push the planets around. What they do imply, says the organicist, is some determinate system, and this implication is contradicted by the indeterminateness of the Ptolemaic system. Precise and determinate predictions which become verified are for the organicist the best evidence of the truth of the organization of the data that produced the predictions. For verified prediction is the very action of organic implication.

Again, *fusions*, such as the contextualists accept, are self-contradictory. They are another form of indeterminateness. They both assert an independence and deny it. The contradiction is resolved by examining the underlying texture of the fusion and observing that the relative independence of the fusion arises from the organization of materials involved in the texture, and that the texture implies a context.

Again, *conflicting* groups of data like Anaximenes' observations of the sun are contradictory. They both imply a possibility of organization and deny it. Sometimes, as with Anaximenes, a few new observations bridge the gaps and implement the synthesis. At other times, as with Aristotle, new observations exclude the irrelevant leaves and mountains which find their relevant wholes elsewhere, and produce a firmer, completer organization of the remainder. The same happened when Ptolemy excluded the crystalline substance of Aristotle's spheres.

There are as many ways in which fragments may contradict one another as there are modes of conflict, isolation, confusion, and muddledness in the activities of the world. But all these contradictions resolve themselves if the nexuses of the fragments involved are allowed to follow their implications to the integrated wholes in which they belong.

iv) *Organic whole.*—The resolution is always an integration of conflicting fragments. Progress moves from level to level of integration. If we examine these levels, as in the history of astronomy, we shall note that the progress exhibits three main criteria: (1) degrees of inclusiveness,

(2) degrees of determinateness, and (3) degrees of organicity.

The actual number of appearances organized by Anaximenes was comparatively small. His system was not inclusive of many of the facts of the world. The mere bulk of observations increased steadily from level to level of organization in the development of astronomy. One of the remarkable merits of Newton's work was the tremendous added bulk of data brought together by the integration of astronomy and mechanics. Both astronomy and mechanics profited by the synthesis because of the great mass of mutually implicative and mutually confirmatory material.

But the progress of astronomy was also marked by a steadily increasing determinateness of the materials organized. In a way, greater determinateness is but a phase of greater inclusiveness. Increase in the precision of observations generally means also increase in the number of facts observed. The telescope did not simply make observations more precise; it also multiplied their number. Determinateness requires that an organization shall not simply fence in all the relevant facts, but that it shall also penetrate into their details and follow their minutest ramifications.

But neither inclusiveness nor determinateness is sufficient to account for the progress of astronomy. The observations were progressively better integrated. The trend of this integration was in the direction of greater organicity. The principle of organicity can be stated in two ways which are not exactly equivalent but which converge in the end upon the same fact. According to the first statement, an organic whole is such a system that every element within it implies every other. According to the second, it is such a system that an alteration or removal of any element would alter every other element or even destroy the whole system.

On the basis of either of these statements, we may note degrees of organicity or degrees of approach to complete organicity. Some parts of a system may be highly implicative and others less so. An alteration of an element of a system may have serious effects on some parts of the system and negligible effects on others. But so long as a system does hold together with some degree of implicativeness in its elements, or so long as parts of the system are seen to have some effects on other parts, it is in that degree organic.

Now, the organicist suggests that the progress of knowledge—as, for instance, in astronomy—is in the direction of greater and greater inclusiveness, determinativeness, and organicity in the senses defined. For evidence he points to the history of knowledge. Why, for instance, do we unquestionably regard the astronomy of Newton as superior to that of Anaximenes? Because, answers the organicist, it includes vastly more data, because these data are much more determinate, and because these determinate data are so closely integrated that in very large measure they are all mutually implicative, or so interconnected causally that, for instance, the halving of the mass of the sun would upset all of Newton's calculations. In fact, so highly organic was Newton's system that a certain observation on the path of light in the gravitational field of the sun actually did lead to a revision of the whole system in Einstein's terms. This new system is an advance over Newton's because it includes this observation (and a few others which Newton's did not), renders data still more determinate, and still more firmly establishes the mutual implicativeness and interdependency of the data.

Now, the organicist asks us to note that this astronomical system is precisely our present knowledge of cosmic structure. What are the facts of astronomy? Why, precisely the system of Einstein or Newton. There are, no doubt, errors in Einstein's system, as there were in Newton's. How will they be discovered and corrected? Just as physicists and astronomers have corrected Newton's system: by finding new data, tracing out the contradictions among data, finding the integrations of data which resolve these contradictions. As we increase, perfect, and organize these data we get closer and closer to the facts of the case. What, then, may we presume the facts of the case actually to be? Says the organicist, the limit of this series. The limit is clearly defined by the series. It is the all-inclusive, completely determinate system of mutually implicative or causally interdependent data. At the limit, implication and causality would coalesce, for logical necessity would become identified with ultimate fact. This limit of cognition which is absolute fact is often called for short by the organicists, the absolute.

This absolute is the climax and base of organicism. Everything leads up to it and everything is founded upon it. As we said, it is the goal of the progressive categories and the field of specification of the ideal categories. We have been climbing up the progressive categories, and now that we have reached the goal it will pay us to look around.

The first thing, perhaps, to strike us is that in organicism a pure fact is an ideal. For pure fact is the absolute and this is never attained in the partial integrations with which we finite human beings are familiar. Pure fact is the limit approached by the relatively impure facts with which we have commerce. It is an ideal. It follows that the ideal is the real thing. At first this seems like a wild paradox, but then we realize that it is a common enough idea except that the organicist has completely generalized it. For the mechanist also the great machine was of course an ideal of fact so far as human cognition went. We were never acquainted with the great machine, its spatiotemporal frame, its electrons and positrons. These were the basic facts for the mechanist, yet they were sheer ideals of his knowledge so far as his cognition was concerned, for his sensations never got at them. The organicist is better off than the mechanist on this score, because he envisages a continuous bridge from partial evidence to ultimate fact, whereas the mechanist can never get in contact with his ideal fact. To treat fact as ideal, then, is nothing new. All that is new is the thoroughness with which the organicist disparages all evidence except the humanly unattainable goal.

This disparagement, however, is the very basis of his optimism. Here is another paradox. Out of the contradictoriness of all partial facts he finds his evidence for the coherence of all ultimate fact. If there were one isolated fact that was not self-contradictory, the organicist could not carry out his argument for the organicity of fact in the

absolute. He is, therefore, generally dogmatic about the inherent contradictoriness of all experience short of the
absolute.

But his argument is quite strong without any illicit dogmatic appeal. It is stronger than a mere extrapolation of
a historical trend in knowledge to the implied limit, though
such an argument is not to be lightly taken. The real
strength in his argument comes from his analysis of evidence and the cumulative force of this analysis. A datum
is a fragment with a nexus which leads to a contradiction
that is resolved by an integration. This process comes
spontaneously out of the fragment as the very activity of
the nexus. Evidence progressively criticizes itself and exhibits its own degree of reliability and points of itself to
the ultimate structural organization of the world.

The argument from extrapolation is an external formal
argument in which the curve of a set of observations is extended to a limit. But the organistic argument from coherence is an internal material argument by which the
spontaneous integrating activity of evidence is exhibited
as seeking out its inevitable goal in an organicity of fact
which resolves all contradictions. The only way to meet
this argument is to deny the legitimacy of the organistic
critique of evidence. This is very difficult in the face of
the cumulative corroborations of the evidence itself. We
have seen how desperately the contextualist tried to stop
the sweep of this trend toward integration by asserting
the ultimacy of blocking, novelty, fusion, and so forth—
all ways of denying the integrative power, or the cognitive
dissatisfactions, of contradiction,—only in the end to find

that his greatest difficulties arose in his inability, without retreating, to specify the structural features of nature. As for all other theories, their internal contradictions only confirm the organicist's critique of evidence, and he would be triumphant if a basic contradiction did not break out in his own theory. For can he harmonize the organic structure of absolute fact with the fact that evidence as it comes is not absolutely organic?

His best attempts to answer this question lie in an examination of his ideal categories. These ideal categories are the features of any organic whole, and ultimately of the absolute, which, the organicist hopes, explain away any *intrinsic* fragmentariness in nature. He hopes to show that there really are not, never were, and never will be any real fragments or fragmentariness in the universe.

v) *Implicitness.*—Fragments are implicit in the whole in which they are integrated. The point he makes here is that when we find the organic whole in which the contradictions of the fragments are resolved, we acknowledge that these fragments were details in this whole all the time and that their apparent fragmentariness was an error and an illusion. The evidences for this conclusion, he says, are twofold: first, the prospective nexus in the fragment directing us by means of the contradictions it encounters to the place where in fact the fragment belongs in the whole; and second, the retrospective acknowledgment when the whole is attained that this is just where the fragment was, in fact, all the time. The earth was really in the gravitational field of the sun all the time. When Newton exhibited the gravitational relations, these relations, we see, were

all the time implicit in the observations from Anaximenes
to Kepler. Those observations never had any other real
place. The previous astronomers simply failed to see
where they belonged. The observations were never intrinsically contradictory, and the proof of it is that they all
found their coherent places in the Newtonian system.

But, we ask, what about the contradictions themselves,
which the fragments encountered?

vi) *Transcendence.* — These, says the organicist, are
transcended in the integrated whole. The contradictions
were never really contradictions, for in fact they did not
exist. The proof of this is that they all vanish when the
whole is achieved. A detail of a whole taken out of its
organic relations becomes a fragment and seems to involve
all sorts of contradictions. But in fact it simply is never
out of that whole, as our analysis of evidence has shown.
When a fragment is cleared of its errors (which are but
the signs of its being held as a fragment) and exhibits
itself as pure fact in its proper organic relations, then its
contradictions automatically drop off. There are no contradictions of details in an organic whole that has taken
up its details. We actually see this in the relative integrations which we achieve. We have seen how these more and
more nearly approach pure fact. We have seen that complete integration or the absolute is absolutely pure fact.
In absolute fact, then, there are no contradictions, for these
are in absolute fact completely transcended.

But, we object, the feeling of contradiction which we
do in fact have as mere finite human beings not embracing
the absolute, can that be transcended?

vii) *Economy.*—Yes, replies the organicist, that also is a fact and has its place in the absolute. Nothing is lost in the absolute.

How that comes about can be seen in the relative integrations which we have achieved. Show any astronomical facts observed previous to Newton's integration that were not taken up by Newton. All the relevant facts collected by Anaximenes, Aristotle, Aristarchus, Ptolemy, Copernicus, Tycho Brahe, Kepler—all find their place in the system of Newton, the gaps among them filled in, their mutual implications exhibited. Nothing positive is lost, and all contradictions vanish in the realization of how these facts are connected.

To be sure, certain irrelevancies were excluded, such as Anaximenes' leaves and disks and mountains, Aristotle's crystalline material, Ptolemy's epicycles and eccentrics. These irrelevancies would contradict Newton's system. But what, in fact, were these? For, as Newton's system shows, they were not actually implied by the astronomical observations. They are what we familiarly call "psychological interpretations." A psychological interpretation is, of course, also a fact. But the proper place for a psychological interpretation is not in an astronomical system. In a psychological system, however, it is very relevant. That is where most of the facts belong which were dropped out in the progress of astronomy. Psychology also has its history of successive integrations pointing, just as astronomy does, to the ultimate integration of the absolute. The system of psychology has not, however, as yet attained to an integration with the astronomical system. But how whole systems become integrated into a more inclusive system, we have already seen through an excellent illustration of the integration of physics and astronomy. So we can predict that intrinsically the psychological system is integrated with the physico-astronomical system. Just how, we cannot say at the present stage of integration of psychological data. If we knew how, the integration would have been accomplished. But the organistic analysis of evidence shows that in fact that very organization is implicit in the data of both systems.

Now, such being the case, we see that the material sloughed off as irrelevant from the successive astronomical integrations was not actually lost. This material was simply transferred from a system in which it did not belong to another system in which it did belong. Furthermore, eventually the intrinsic connections of this material with the material of the system from which it was excluded will be found in the integration of these systems with each other. So nothing is lost: not the materials, for they find their places in other systems; not even the connections, for when a sufficiently inclusive integration is achieved all the connections that exist in fact will be exhibited.

As to the feelings of contradiction, these also are psychological facts. They are experiences felt by astronomers frustrated in their search for the laws which actually hold among their data. But there is no contradiction in a feeling of contradiction when this is seen in its proper psychological context.

So, concludes the organicist, since the absolute is implicit in all fragments, and in the absolute all contradictions and evidences of fragmentariness are transcended, and in the very nature of the absolute no facts whatever are left out, then in absolute fact there are no fragments.

The argument is plausible. Yet the insistent fragmentariness of every human experience rises up against it. All may be organic in the ideal fact of the absolute, but ignorance and frustration and unsolved problems and the narrow horizons of space and time and the limited span of life are strikingly upon us. These are in flat contradiction to the optimistic serenity of the absolute. The organicist himself admits them in his progressive categories. He admits that as finite living individuals we cannot attain the absolute. Then how can he say that in fact there are no fragments?

The issue comes to a head in the doctrine of time. The fragmentariness of human life clearly has to do with life's being so closely bound up with time. What, for instance, does the organicist say when the contextualist confronts him with what the contextualist believes are the facts of the changing present? This issue for the organicist is that between time and truth.

§5. *Time and truth.*—We have, of course, been examining the organicist's theory of truth throughout our presentation of his categories. Every fragment is a judgment referring to fact, the reference being represented by the nexus. A judgment need not be in words or other conventional symbols, though the formal expression of a judgment is always in terms of verbal or mathematical symbols. Such formal expressions, however, are makeshifts and temporary substitutes for the real judgments which are the fragments meant by the conventional symbols. A concrete fragment and its nexus may be expressed in a sentence with subject and predicate. For instance, the partly systematized fragment of Anaximenes' observations on the sun may be summarized in the sentence, "The sun is a single continuous body." The subject of the sentence refers primarily to the actual facts of the case (the absolute) and secondarily to the best substitute Anaximenes has for these facts, namely, his collection of observations on the sun. His predicate refers to the relations in which he believes these facts stand. He attributes the relations of the predicate to the matter of the subject. The sentence is said to be true if the relations asserted in the predicate are found to hold of the subject. But it is not essentially the sentence that is true, but what the sentence means, that is, the judgment. The sentence is only a substitute for the judgment. If the judgment were not true, neither would the sentence be. Consequently, the organicist is rather skeptical of verbal logic (propositions, sentences, subjects, predicates, p's and q's) and prefers to deal directly with judgments.

Now, a judgment is precisely a fragment and its nexus. And the truth of a judgment consists precisely in the fragment's finding, through its nexus, a whole in which it is free from contradictions. Anaximenes verified his judgment about the sun when he found that his observations fitted into the theory that the sun went around the earth behind the mountains to the north, and that further observations confirmed this judgment. He thereby reached a higher level of judgment. But, as we know, this higher level proved also to be a fragment with a nexus calling for completion. Thus there are degrees of truth. Each level of integration resolves the contradictions of the levels below and so removes the errors that were most serious there. Each level brings about an improvement of judgment. Each level exhibits more truth through the higher integration of the facts. There is more truth in Ptolemy than in Anaximenes, more in Kepler than in Ptolemy, more in Newton than in Kepler. It appears that the criteria of truth are precisely the categorial features of the organic whole—inclusiveness, determinateness, and organicity—and that the ideal of truth is the absolute itself.

This theory of truth is known as the *coherence theory*. It is obviously implied by the categories of organicism and obviously presupposes those categories. In other views coherence may be treated as a gauge of truth but not as its essential nature. In fact, in other views than contextualism coherence is ordinarily confused with consistency, which is, as we know, but the formal shadow of coherence. For consistency is mere formal noncontradiction whereas coherence is the positive organic relatedness of material facts. It follows that the argument sometimes brought against organicism to the effect that there are many self-consistent logical systems, so that consistency is not an ultimate criterion of truth, is irrelevant. It is not formal consistency but material coherence that the organicist sets up as truth. On the basis of his categories this seems to be uniquely determined. His categories and his analysis of evidence may be questioned, but once these are accepted the absolute is inevitable and determinate and without alternatives. For the absolute is fact itself and is completely organic.

The peculiarities of the coherence theory of truth are: (1) Truth is not primarily a relation between symbols and fact or between one fact (such as an image) and another fact. It is not primarily a matter of relation in that sense at all. It is primarily a matter of the amount of fact attained. (2) It follows that there are degrees of truth depending upon the amount of fact attained. (3) It follows that the totality of fact, or the absolute, is true, and is the limit of truth, and the ultimate standard of truth.

Now, these remarks bear directly on the organistic treatment of time, and will show that the difficulties which develop here are endemic to the theory.

We asked what the organicist does when he is confronted with the fact of the specious present. He answers that it is self-contradictory. As a present it implies a past and a future, and not only the little past and future that lie in the span of immediacy, but also the past out of which this span has come and future into which it will go. There are facts off either end, and the full understanding of the present implies these facts.

Admitted; what then? One organicist, Royce, attempted to solve the problem by speculatively enlarging the specious present to the dimensions of the absolute. But the question obstinately returns as, Why are our specious presents so narrow if the real specious present in fact includes the universe?

The commoner treatment is to follow the implications of time gradually out of the immediacy of the specious present. The contradictions of the specious present, the organicist suggests, are partly resolved in the integration of all specious presents into the spatiotemporal field of physics. Then follows the regular organistic critique of the methods of the physical sciences. The contradictions appearing there are the regular formistic, mechanistic, and operational difficulties which we have already studied. Says the organicist, these difficulties are intolerable and suggest a higher integration in which all the immediate data of personal experiences are organically related with the abstract data and hypotheses of the sciences. He is further assisted here by his critique of social institutions and his theory that these have an objectivity independent of the lives and bodies of individuals. Science is envisaged as such a social institution. In this synthesis of science with society two things happen: science is relieved of its abstractness by taking on the substance of an institution actually operating in human experience like a government; and social institutions are lifted out of their historicity, or temporal flow, by being amalgamated with the mathematical laws of physical fields in which time has the character of a dimension.

Now, says the organicist, you see that even within the range of *our* knowledge a careful analysis of time shows that its fugitiveness in terms of crude everyday experience is illusory. Our several specious presents all have their determinate places in the scheme of science as an institution actually governing our social actions. Science and society both show that we are not the isolated things we at first think we are, and to a large extent our interrelations and the connections which hold among our past, present, future, and distant experiences are already well known to us. If it is hard to conceive just how our fugitive present is even now implicative of the whole universe, or if we are not satisfied with the synthesis of science and society which we have attained, we should remind ourselves of the very nature of knowledge and truth as that discovers itself to us. By the very nature of the case, we cannot know the whole truth till the absolute is attained. Our dissatisfaction with our last synthesis is just as it should be, for this also is but a degree of truth and the more keenly we are dissatisfied with it the more rapid our probable progress. Of course, it does not fully answer our problem about time. But it does show the direction of the answer, and we may be assured that in the absolute there is no problem of time, and that all things are organic, and that all things are saved and in their proper places. Since the absolute is the absolute truth, and time and change cannot in the absolute be true, time and change are not true, not real, not facts.

That is the nature of the organicist's answer. Yet for all this increase of knowledge and connectedness, stressed by the organicist—for all our increased power of prediction and historical insight, and our tightening spatial communications,—the specious present obstinately remains the same narrow fugitive thing and gives no signs whatever of bursting its bounds or giving up its suspense and changefulness.

Moreover, suppose the specious present should break bounds and find itself a detail in the wide-open implicative system of the absolute, what would happen to the facts which the very limitations of the specious present appear to create—to suspense, distrust, longing, all forms of desire, frustration, all pain, and perhaps all pleasure, certainly all the pleasures of anticipation and fulfillment? These could not be saved. At least, on the basis of all the evidence we possess (and on what other evidence can we go?) the absolute lacks scope concerning such facts.

Organicism thus requires the progressive categories to give it scope, yet the progressive categories involve time and change and finitude; yet time and change and finitude cannot be true, since only the absolute is true and in the absolute is no time, nor change, nor finitude. Contradiction thus breaks out even in the absolute, since the absolute must include all facts. Organicism thus convicts itself of inadequacy.

Yet it is not much less inadequate, if at all, than the other relatively adequate world theories which we have in our possession. It has added greatly to the wealth of insights and of integral facts. The world would be poorer without the perspectives of organicism. If this view had brought to light nothing else than the doctrine of the creative imagination (which is entirely an organistic doctrine and unknown except in the barest glimmerings before this world view began to emerge), it would have earned a high place in the history of cognition.

PART THREE

Summary, Criticisms, and Answers

Chapter XII : Review and Conclusions

§1. *A review of the argument.*—It remains for us to consider the value for knowledge and practice of our analysis, and also to examine certain questions that arise respecting the correctness of our conclusions.

Let us begin by briefly reviewing the course of the preceding argument.

i) *Rejection of dogmatic claims.*—We first presented reasons for believing that there are no cognitively justifiable claims for dogmatism or for that peculiar dogmatic inversion of dogmatism, utter skepticism. Not only did we show that the usual types of dogmatic claim have fully exhibited their fallaciousness in the course of cognitive history, but also that nothing material is gained for cognition by these claims. The force of dogmatism is entirely noncognitive, and would scarcely ever be appealed to except from an intensity of desire to achieve complete cognitive assurance, or to reach full knowledge of a subject, or simply to win an argument—in advance of the total quantity of evidence needed. A tendency to resort to dogmatism is particularly noticeable in situations where the supply of evidence is scarcest, which in itself should be evidence enough against such claims.

Nevertheless, the desire to know more than one has grounds to know is so strong and pervasive that it is difficult to be convinced of the fallaciousness of dogmatism *in principle*. Historically, few men in any cognitive field, whether in common sense, history, science, or philosophy, have acknowledged the fallaciousness of dogmatism in principle or abstained from its deliberate employment in practice, especially in the two most common forms of an appeal to self-evidence of principle or immediate certainty of fact.

We undertook to point out the fallaciousness of dogmatism in these or in any other forms and to abstain entirely from its employment in practice. We argued that secure knowledge, far from being impossible (as many have held) without a dogmatic basis in certainty or self-evidence, is impossible with any such basis. The security of cognition, we argued, rests on the evidence itself and on its convergence toward belief, not on an intensity of belief in excess of the actual cognitive value of the evidence. And we presented evidence to show that claims of self-evidence or certainty for any cognitive materials are untrustworthy.

From this it does not follow that we are not in possession of trustworthy evidence, but only that the grounds of trustworthiness are not to be attributed to certainty or self-evidence or to any other sort of dogmatic claim. We showed that no cognitive material can justifiably claim exemption from critical scrutiny. There are no "natural rights" in cognition any more than there are in society. Any item of evidence is subject to correction by any other item of evidence, and may in the light of further evidence require revision, refinement, or reinterpretation.

ii) *Affirmation of cognitive value in common sense and dubitanda.*—After our sweeping rejection of dogmatism in all its forms, we undertook to trace cognition back to its sources and thence up to its various refinements or developments. Our first step in this direction was the recognition of common sense or dubitanda.

For many men the resort to dogmatism results from an apprehension that knowledge might have no firm basis, and that if everything is somewhat doubtful (or, more precisely, dubitable) no knowledge is secure. If the evidence did point in this direction, we as cognizers unquestionably ought to follow the evidence and accept the conclusion that knowledge is insecure. But even if this were the conclusion from the evidence, we should find that we did not have anything very serious to fear. For the conclusion that everything is dubitable is not the conclusion of utter skepticism. It does not signify that we know nothing. This, as we showed, is simply inverted dogmatism.

The trend of the evidence was toward something very different, namely, toward the conclusion that, though any single item of evidence is dubitable, the presence of great masses of evidence is highly confirmed. What doubt, or any other cognitive activity, always (Descartes-wise) brings us back to is the realization that some sort of probably pretty rich and complicated thing is being cognized. We never in cognition can sink lower than that. The mass of all this prerefined, preanalytical cognitive material we called common sense, and its various particular items, dubitanda. This, we found, is what all knowledge starts from, however refined it may subsequently become.

Common sense, so described, we thus discovered to be the very secure base of all knowledge. There is no evidence to indicate that common sense will ever fail mankind except as more refined knowledge supplements it. Every item of common sense is highly dubitable and subject to criticism and generally greatly altered by cognitive refinement, but the total collection of these evidences is not highly dubitable. To question common sense as a whole because every item of common sense is highly questionable is to commit the inverse fallacy of composition. Our evidence, we showed, indicates that every item of common sense is a dubitandum, a matter that ought to be doubted in the sense of being subject to rigorous critical scrutiny, but this very same evidence indicates that the totality of common sense itself is, so to speak, not a dubitandum. It is a well-attested fact. All evidence points to it as the ultimate source of our cognitive refinements, and as the lowest legitimate level to which cognition could sink should these refinements fail.

iii) *Corroboration.*—With common sense or dubitanda to start from, we then inquired by what means degrees of doubt could be reduced and more refined knowledge achieved. We found this means in corroboration. The way to improve evidence was to find further evidence to corroborate it. We noted two main types of corroboration, which we called multiplicative and structural.

Multiplicative corroboration consists in attesting to the repetition of the "identical" item of evidence in many different instances. It is the corroboration that results from many different observations of "the same fact" in empirical science or from many different reviewings of the same steps of proof in logic or mathematics. It is, therefore, in a sense social, a corroboration of man with man.

Structural corroboration consists in the convergence of qualitatively different items of evidence in support of a single item. We see its operation in its crudest form in the assembling of "circumstantial evidence," and in its refined form in theories such as those of astronomical mechanics, which have proved cognitively very impressive because of their high predictive powers and their extensive organization of huge masses of diverse, mutually corroborative observations. Structural corroboration requires a theory or hypothesis for the connection of the various items of evidence, and what is said to be corroborated here by the convergence of evidence is not so much the evidence itself as the theory which connects it together. Actually the two assist each other. The theory is progressively confirmed as it successively draws more evidence in, and the various different items of evidence achieve higher and higher corroboration in proportion as more items enter harmoniously into the structure of the theory. Structural corroboration is thus more individual than social. It depends upon the intellectual imagination of a man to conceive a hypothesis which will hold together diverse facts, and his power to demonstrate how diverse facts bear upon one another. It is a corroboration of fact with fact.

iv) *Data.*—We then showed how each of these types of corroboration had its own specific kind of cognitive refinement. The refinement of multiplicative corroboration we called data. The aim here was to obtain items of evidence such that any normal men with a minimum of external information would confirm one another's observations. The pointer reading, we showed, is the consummation of this refinement in empirical evidence, and symbolic substitution its consummation of refinement in logical evidence.

v) *The disposition of positivism.*—We then exhibited a possible conception of cognitive refinement in general—the idea that respectable cognitive materials should be cast in the forms of empirical or logical data. We suggested that this idea of the goal of cognition included most of what has been traditionally meant by positivism.

So far as this judgment was correct, we showed that it is easy to estimate the cognitive validity of positivism. If positivism is undogmatic and merely asserts that the refinements of multiplicative corroboration in terms of data are highly reliable, there is no ground of objection to it. But if it is dogmatic, and asserts that multiplicative corroboration is the only legitimate aim of cognition, and that only empirical data are reliable factual evidence, and only logical data reliable means of theoretical construction, and that all extensive hypotheses are purely conventional, then positivism is exceeding the grounds of evidence available. Our conclusion was that positivism was strong in its assertions but weak in its denials.

There is no adequate evidence, we pointed out, for a denial of the cognitive reliability of structural corroboration on the ground of the reliability of multiplicative corroboration. We pointed out that the converse was also correct: the cognitive claims of multiplicative corroboration cannot be legitimately set aside by those of refined structural corroboration. These two types of corroboration have a certain degree of autonomy. In practice this autonomy produces little difficulty, provided neither type undertakes to eliminate the legitimacy of the other *at the start*. As soon as either gets under way with a considerable body of cognitive material, it is ordinarily glad enough to accept whatever evidence it can get from the other. In general the evidence shows that they are mutually helpful—excellent checks upon one another in the tentative stages of cognition, supporting evidence for one another in the more decisive stages.

vi) *Danda*.—As a result of this criticism of dogmatic positivism, we argued that we had established the cognitive legitimacy and value of structural corroboration and its various refinements in terms of theory and evidence. In order to distinguish the type of evidence refined through structural corroboration from that refined through multiplicative corroboration, we named the former "danda" in distinction from "data."

The characteristic of danda as distinct from data, we showed, consisted in the close dependence of the items of evidence upon the theory which organized them. In structural corroboration the description and precise determination of any item of evidence is qualified by the other items of evidence which bear upon it. The whole structure of evidence hangs together. When the structure is conceived of as wholly abstracted from the evidence, we call it the theory or hypothesis; and when the various items organized by the structure are considered in abstraction from their structure, they are called the evidences for the hypothesis. Actually the two are mutually determinative, and they become more and more so, the more extensive and rigorous the structural corroboration. The term "danda" for the evidential items of structural corroboration connotes this close interdependence of fact and theory in the refinements of structural corroboration. A dandum is what ought to be the precise determination of the evidence presented if it has the structural relationships with the other items of evidence which confirm it; or, abstractly stated, if the theory of the structure of the evidence is true.

It follows that danda for one structural hypothesis will often be incompatible with the danda for another, though the hypotheses nevertheless cover the same general empirical field. That is, the evidences or the facts themselves are found in conflict and are subject to doubt and critical scrutiny even though in the light of the structural hypotheses which support them they frequently appear transparently empirical, certain, and incorrigible. We gave two striking preliminary illustrations of this situation from Dewey and Price, and followed these up subsequently, of course, with extensive illustrations in terms of world hypotheses.

vii) *General criteria of structural corroboration.—* When we have a situation in which danda conflict, it is obviously impossible to solve the difficulty in terms of the facts in question, for the facts are these selfsame conflicting danda. We must turn to a consideration of the presuppositions involved in these particular determinations of the facts, in other words, to a criticism of the structural hypotheses which determine or qualify the danda in question.

We were thus led to ask what criteria could be found for judging the cognitive reliability or adequacy of structural hypotheses. What, in other words, are the general criteria of refinement in terms of structural corroboration?

We found these to be precision and scope. As between two structural hypotheses of supposedly equal scope, the one which had the more precise determination of its danda would be considered the more adequate, since lack of precision indicates lack of evidence to determine the facts in question. And as between two hypotheses supposedly equally precise in the determination of their danda, the one which had the wider scope of corroborative evidence would be considered the more adequate, since it had just that much more evidence in its favor. These two criteria amount in the end to the same thing, namely, a greater quantity of structurally corroborative evidence, that evidence being sought first by looking more closely into a dandum, and second, by looking more widely about a dandum.

Assuming precision for the moment, however, we noticed that the maximum of scope would involve corroboration by all evidence whatever, which would automatically carry with it also complete precision. We thereby get the distinction between restricted and unrestricted structural hypotheses. It becomes clear at once that restricted hypotheses, those which claim to hold only within a limited field of facts, are always in cognitive jeopardy, since they never can tell what evidence may lie outside their field which may be found to bear upon evidence within the field and to conflict with it. Restricted hypotheses have, accordingly, only a restricted cognitive reliability. They demand, for complete justification, the corroboration afforded by unrestricted structural hypotheses. The problem of the determination of degrees of cognitive reliability in terms of structural corroboration thus comes to a head, we argued, in world hypotheses—hypotheses of unrestricted scope, which exclude no evidence as irrelevant on the ground of being outside the field under discussion, and which accept the task of trying to find the bearing of any sort of evidence upon any other if any such bearing can be found.

viii) *Specific criteria of structural corroboration are developed in world hypotheses.*—It then appeared that the specific or detailed criteria for the determination of cognitive validity or reliability in terms of structural corroboration were only developed in a world hypothesis. For these criteria themselves require the maximum possible corroboration, and that means the corroboration afforded by an unrestricted hypothesis. These specific criteria are, of course, the specific theories of truth, perception, reason, scientific method, and the like, associated with a particular world hypothesis. And these specific criteria are as reliable as the world hypothesis which supports them— as reliable as the amount of corroboration they have acquired.

But there are many theories of truth associated with almost as many world hypotheses. The history of cognition, or, more narrowly, the history of philosophy, presents to us hundreds of world hypotheses. Is there any way of simplifying this situation?

There are two ways. The first, which is laborious, we did not refer to, though if any serious error were found in the second it would be the ultimate resort. It is to examine the theories one by one in terms of their degree of structural corroboration. Those which exhibited themselves as particularly inadequate would be rejected in favor of those which were relatively less inadequate. As between a typical mythology, for instance, and any of the classical philosophical systems it is easy to see that the mythology would be rejected, not on the score of its being outdated or alien to our main cultural interests (which the prevalence of "fundamentalism" shows it is not), but solely for comparative lack of structural corroboration.

We did, in fact, make a partial use of this way of rejecting inadequate theories in our examination of animism and mysticism, which we offered as concrete models of inadequacy. These, we observed, could serve as negative standards by which we could judge the relative adequacy of other world theories in terms of the degree of advancement in structural corroboration which these other theories exhibited. The farther away other theories were from these in precision and scope the more reliable we could consider them. All this, of course, would be on the basis of a prior elimination of any dogmatic claims.

This first way of simplifying the situation by comparing world hypotheses as they come, one by one, would undoubtedly lead to the rejection of a great many of these hypotheses, but the number still remaining on our hands might be considerable, provided we had no other clue to reducing them.

The second way is the one which we have followed. It is the way demonstrated in what we have called the root-metaphor theory of the origin and development of world hypotheses. With perserverance, the more plodding first way of successive comparisons should in the end lead to the same result as the second, once claims of dogmatism are eliminated. But the second or root-metaphor way is an effective short cut if it is acceptable, and we have given many reasons for believing that it is.

ix) *The root-metaphor theory as a way of reducing the number of world hypotheses to act as concrete positive standards of cognition.*—The root-metaphor theory is simply a recognition of the fact that there are schools of philosophy, and an attempt to get at the roots of these schools. We argued that the philosophic imagination is not nearly so prolific as many have believed. We showed grounds for believing that there are only seven or eight distinct ways in which men have seriously undertaken to build up unrestricted hypotheses. The appearance of a great number of different world theories arises simply from the great number of combinations that can be made out of the parts of seven or eight complex objects—the world hypotheses we have discussed.

We argued that these seven or eight basic theories are derived from certain masses of empirical evidence, originating in common sense, which become cognitively refined and may be codified into sets of categories that hang together. The concrete evidential source of the categories we called the root metaphor. The categories themselves, we showed, constitute the abstract structure of the theory, and the cognitive power of the categories consists in their capacity to acquire unrestricted structural corroboration.

We argued that, as soon as dogmatic claims are rejected, the theories begin to reveal themselves quite clearly in terms of their corroborative structures. For a categorial set is nothing more nor less than the structural lines of corroboration for the world theory in question. The categories hang together in sets because they mutually corroborate each other through the evidence they gather up. And different sets of categories draw apart from one another precisely because they fail to corroborate one another. Only dogmatic claims of various sorts have blinded philosophers to these corroborative affinities and coagulations of structural theory and fact. Drop dogmatic claims, and the relatively small number of distinct world theories appear of themselves.

This alone is a vast simplification. But the situation is even further simplified by the discovery that out of the seven or eight basic world hypotheses, so derived from their root metaphors, four are to such a degree superior to the others in adequacy that they alone need be seriously considered. These also may some day be superseded, but the present situation, we believe, is one in which these four must be given equal or nearly equal weight in any cognitive judgment or evaluation where we want all the evidence we can get on a matter.

The four world theories formism, mechanism, contextualism, and organicism actually are our four basic concrete standards of judgment and evaluation. They have the highest available degree of structural corroboration.

We, accordingly, gave the skeleton structure of each of these world theories, together with a fairly detailed account of each one's specific theory of truth.

The fact of having four such extensive cognitive standards on a par led us to draw up a set of maxims to guide us in application. Of these the chief one to observe is that of autonomy. Since these four world theories were regarded by us as having about the same degree of adequacy, no one of them can be the judge of the others.

Our general stand, therefore, is for *rational clarity in theory and reasonable eclecticism in practice.*

That an eclecticism should be excluded from within world theories is obvious in the interests of clarity; otherwise, how can one see just where the maximum of structural corroboration lies? If a world theory partly developed in one set of categories is broken in upon by a foreign set of categories, the structure of corroboration is broken up and we cannot clearly see how the evidence lies. For intellectual clarity, therefore, we want our world theories pure and not eclectic.

But for practical application we must be mindful of the judgments of all such rationally justifiable theories. Here each of the four highly adequate theories stands on a par. We wish in matters of serious discussion to have the benefit of all the available evidence and modes of corroboration. In practice, therefore, we shall want to be not rational but reasonable, and to seek, on the matter in question, the judgment supplied from each of these relatively adequate world theories. If there is some difference of judgment, we shall wish to make our decision with all these modes of

might be different degrees of *theory* clarity in theory.

evidence in mind, just as we should make any other decision where the evidence is conflicting. In this way we should be judging in the most reasonable way possible—not dogmatically following only one line of evidence, not perversely ignoring evidence, but sensibly acting on all the evidence available.

As to general knowledge or information about any topic (such as truth, or value, or time, or universals, or relations, or causality, or self, or society), that also is to be gained on the basis of this reasonable postrational eclecticism. Having done all that we can do rationally to organize the evidence on the topic in question in terms of structural corroboration, and finding as a rule that there are four equally justifiable hypotheses explaining the nature of the subject, we shall have the wisdom not to conclude that we know nothing about the topic, but, on the contrary, that we have four alternative theories about it, which supply us with a great deal more information on the subject than any one of them alone could have done.

One such topic is unique: the world itself. About that our knowledge is precisely as concerning any lesser topic. We know a good deal about the world. We have four rather highly adequate theories about it. But we have no single judgment to give as yet. Nevertheless, as we trace the history of cognition over the last twenty-five hundred years we get a definite sense that from different angles our theories are closing in upon the world. The division of the four relatively adequate theories into analytic and synthetic, and each of these divisions into dispersive and integrative (cf. p. 146 above), would be puzzling in its symmetry if it did not suggest the same conclusion. Moreover, multiplicative corroboration is pressing up from below as these four modes of structural corroboration are pressing in from the sides. These various modes of corroboration are, from a certain distance, seen all to be coöperating in a single enterprise. Paradoxically, our very insistence on the autonomy of these modes of corroboration renders their mutual coöperation clearer and more effective than it would otherwise be, for thus they cease to neutralize each other or to get in each other's way. We know a lot about our world, both in its detail and in its general structure, and we have good reason to believe that we shall know a lot more.

§2. *The criticisms.*—Such have been our argument and our conclusions. Now, finally, we must meet certain queries and objections. The following are the principal ones that have come to my attention:

i) Is not positivism an alternative, or possibly *the* alternative, to the specialized world hypotheses, especially in view of the admission that none of these world hypotheses is entirely adequate?

ii) Can any one of the four basic theories exhibited be ascribed to any of the classical philosophers, or, for that matter, to any historical figure at all? If not, how can I assert that I have been studying world theories as objects empirically found in the world?

iii) On what grounds can I maintain that the descriptions I have given of these theories are the *normal* ones? Why would not another disposition or selection of categories for these theories be equally justifiable?

iv) Why are there only four standard theories? Why could they not be subdivided or given any number of varieties or subspecies? And why say there are only seven or eight world theories altogether?

v) Why is there so much insistence on the autonomy and insulation of these world theories? Why not add them all together into one grand theory? Or why not pick out the best elements of each and produce one best theory? Why is there so much resistance to eclecticism within a world theory, especially when in the end a postrational eclecticism is recommended for practical decisions, and for the final survey of our knowledge on any subject?

vi) How practicable is this postrational eclecticism which is recommended? Is it not left pretty much in the air, a prey to the caprice and prejudices of the individual making the decision or summarizing our general knowledge on a subject? Would it not be wiser to produce the best possible single eclectic theory and be done with it?

vii) What about adequacy? Is this not simply another theory of truth which I set up above other theories of truth to legislate over them? How, then, can I establish its superiority to them? And carrying the same line of argument farther, is not this whole root-metaphor philosophy simply my philosophy, one more philosophy in the story of philosophy, and is not the balanced disposition of the four main theories simply my interpretation of the significance of these theories in terms of my philosophy? In a word, am I not just as dogmatic as the men I have been criticizing? Am I not dogmatically setting my philosophy up in preference to any other?

viii) Am I not dogmatically undogmatic? In insisting on this balance of theories am I not just as insistent as any of the men I criticize, who insist on a belief in one theory?

These various queries are, of course, not consistent with one another, but they are all questions that are likely to arise. Most of them represent some misunderstanding of the intent of the argument and so are specially pertinent.

§3. *The answers.*—My answers to the foregoing queries and objections follow.

i) *Is not positivism a genuine alternative to the root-metaphor hypotheses?* Let me state this question at greater length in the words in which it was given to me by one critic: "Although positivism is not a hypothesis respecting the actual nature of the world, since it maintains that this nature is unknowable, does it not remain as a genuine alternative to all the specialized world hypotheses? Can it be refuted or put out of court in any other way than through a consideration of the nature of probability and the application of probability to theories? And does not your view of the inadequacy of all the world hypotheses give it at least a provisional standing?"

My answer is that if positivism is undogmatic it cannot, with the data we have, be a hypothesis respecting the nature of the world either affirmatively or negatively, but can only be an interest in, or a preference for, the results of multiplicative corroboration. It therefore does not assert that the actual nature of the world is unknowable. As soon as positivism makes such an assertion it becomes dogmatic. For on what grounds can positivism make such an assertion? Not on the basis of data obtained, since data themselves do not reject danda. Not on the basis of its conventional hypotheses, since these are just conventions for the organization of data and neither assert nor deny anything. Only, then, on the basis of hidden or disguised danda and suppressed structural hypotheses. Such a positivism asserting that the actual nature of the world is unknowable is dogmatic because it produces data and multiplicative corroboration as its evidence, yet makes an assertion which can be substantiated only through the evidence of danda and structural corroboration.

A dogmatic positivism which is a disguised world theory is, of course, a potential competitor with structural world theories, but only because it is a structural world theory itself with its set of categories by which general assertions and denials can be made. My only criticism of such a positivism is that it should throw off its disguise and its assumed innocence of categorial presuppositions and accompanying danda and stand forth honestly for what it is. Most modern positivists who talk a great deal about "pseudo problems" and various kinds of "nonsense," when examined for their presuppositions, turn out to be somewhat timid mechanists or pragmatists or mechanistic-pragmatic eclectics. Such positivisms, on our analysis, are not genuine alternatives to the structural hypotheses we have described, but simply cases to be diagnosed by these hypotheses with the aid of common sense and the refinements of multiplicative corroboration.

There is, however, one possibility by which an undogmatic positivism might provide a world hypothesis. Suppose the whole body of data should fall together into a

single system on the basis of their own correlated probabilities, or, the other way round, suppose every area of
experience were covered by formulas established by multiplicative corroboration, and that all these formulas
were consistently gathered together in mathematical form,
would not this system be an alternative to the structural
world theories we have been studying? It would, and the
conception of it should be regarded as a genuine possibility. It is the possibility that by means of multiplicative
corroboration alone we might arrive at a precise or fairly
precise determination of any cognitive material whatever,
so that this system through multiplicative corroboration
would achieve an adequacy equal to that of the root-metaphor hypotheses. If any such system were developed, it
would probably supplant the root-metaphor hypotheses,
and this is unquestionably an ideal that many positivists
have had in mind.

There is no reason why the achievement of this ideal
should not be sought. The main point to remember is that
the nearest approximation to such an achievement is at
present in the domain of physics, and it is questionable
whether this achievement would be possible even there
without the assumption and support of the mechanistic
categories. Certainly, in the past, every attempt to extend
the achievement of the physical sciences as a consistent
system beyond the subject matter of these sciences has resulted in some form of root-metaphor hypothesis, usually
mechanism.

There is, moreover, another consideration, and one to
which we have already alluded, namely, that the principle

of multiplicative corroboration itself seems to presuppose strict repetition and hence strict similarity. But similarity is the root metaphor of formism, so that if multiplicative corroboration should develop into a world hypothesis it would seem probable that it would turn out to be a kind of formism. If this is correct, then the consistent development of an undogmatic positivism into a general hypothesis adequate to nature would turn out to be simply one of the root-metaphor hypotheses that we have already considered.

Altogether, the answer to this query is that undogmatic positivism in affirming the independent validity of multiplicative corroboration in the face of structural corroboration is on unassailable ground, but that no general hypothesis of the nature of the world has yet been generated from multiplicative corroboration, and we suspect that none can be so generated that will not turn out to be a structural hypothesis of some type with which we are already familiar. Nevertheless, the possibility cannot be entirely disregarded. Some new type of hypothesis might be generated from this source. As for dogmatic positivism, no more needs to be said about that. It is simply a number of structural categories masquerading as their own denial.

Undogmatic positivism, subject to the qualifications explained, is a genuine alternative to the root-metaphor world theories, but dogmatic positivism is not.

ii) *Can any one of the basic theories be ascribed to a classical philosopher?* Probably not just as described in the text. Nevertheless, the classical philosophers are the men whose writings provided the empirical evidence for the descriptions given in the text. What I maintain is that these theories are what these writers were heading toward in their pursuit of structural corroborations. So far as the root-metaphor theory is correct, this conclusion would follow, as the recent review of the argument has just brought out.

The root-metaphor theory purports to be a descriptive summary of the trends of structural corroboration. The evidence for this descriptive summary is precisely the work of the philosophers, scientists, and others who have sought the establishment of evidence through structural corroboration. This evidence heads up into a small number of distinct types of concrete theories. When once these types are isolated, it is then easy to look back over the history of philosophy and science and see how different men were working with various parts or combinations or stages of these theories and developing them. These theories, in the light of the root-metaphor theory, were literally developing themselves in the work of these philosophers and scientists, by virtue of the very fact that these men were ardently in pursuit of the truth and seeking it in part through the agencies of structural corroboration.

So far as the root-metaphor theory can be supported as an empirical hypothesis for the description of the origin and development of world theories, the theories as here described may be regarded as empirically well founded. They do summarize precisely what philosophers and scientists have been doing in the last twenty-five hundred years in the way of structural corroboration. The rest is simply a matter of historical scholarship to show what interpretations in terms of these theories are to be given to the writings of the historical figures. My assumption is that a history of science or philosophy is a history of cognition, a history of its successes and failures, its instruments, agents, obstructions, and blind alleys; and on this assumption these four theories represent some of the successes of cognition. I certainly do not present them as my inventions or discoveries. They are, I believe, the creative discoveries of many generations of men coöperating in the pursuit of the maximum possible degree of structural corroboration.

If the intent of this criticism is not to question the empirical evidence for the existence of these distinct types of structural corroboration in the course of cognitive history, but only to question the accuracy of the writer's descriptions of them, then that is quite another question, namely, the next.

iii) *On what grounds can I maintain that the descriptions I have given of the four theories are the normal or correct ones?* Naturally, I would not be dogmatic about it. All the evidence is in the reader's hands either directly or by implication. There must surely be granted a great deal of flexibility in the framing of one of these theories. The aim in the text has been simply to describe the theories in the manner that would show them at their best—the manner that carries with it the highest degree of structural corroboration in terms of the maturest development of the root metaphor. There can be plenty of difference of judgment over what is the most adequate statement of one of these theories. The grounds for arguing the case within any one root metaphor, however, are perfectly clear. The presuppositions of the argument are the same for all. It is simply a question of obtaining the maximum of structural corroboration within the limits of these presuppositions, which means within the structural implications of the root metaphor.

iv) *Why are there only four standard theories?* Because there have appeared so far only four root metaphors capable of generating theories with a high degree of structural corroboration. We have just pointed out that within one of these types of theories there may be, and actually are, a variety of descriptions of that type. These may, if we desire, be regarded as different varieties of that genus of theory. But since the aim is to state the theory in its most adequate form, the obviously less adequate forms will not be of any but historical interest. There are an infinity of ways of garbling a theory, but only a few (and ultimately, we may believe, only one) of stating it most adequately. As men mainly interested not in the history of a type of world theory but in its cognitive power, we should naturally try to find it or to state it in its most adequate form. In our statement of the several world theories we have, as a matter of fact, suggested alternative forms—immanent and transcendent formism, for instance, and their combination, discrete and consolidated mechanism, and so on. We have not meant to dictate any standard form. We have merely presented evidence to the effect that the forms we have described are in our judgment the most adequate for their root metaphors in terms of our present information. We have not, strictly speaking, presented four standard world theories. We have merely presented what have seemed to us the best formulations of the four most fruitful root metaphors. These formulations, however, so far as they are accepted, do constitute detailed cognitive criteria.

Why do I give the idea that there have been only seven or eight basic types of world theory altogether? Because those are all the root metaphors I have discovered. Men have made thousands of metaphors, but when these are turned to cognitive use for unrestricted hypotheses they melt down to a very few.

v) *Why is there so much insistence on the autonomy and insulation of world theories?* Because, in the first place, they are derived from distinct root metaphors and, upon the elimination of dogmatic claims, just naturally seek out their own distinct lines of structural corroboration, gathering their categories together into distinct clusters which reject one another. And because, in the second place, that is the only way to keep our thinking and the interrelations of our evidence clear.

Having got our thinking and our evidence clear, however, then it is essential in the recognition of all cognitive claims to recognize diverse claims, no matter how irreconcilable. Hence the insistence upon the exclusion of eclecticism within world theories, and at the same time the recommendation to make a reasonable use of it in estimating the results of world theories.

vi) *How practicable is this postrational eclecticism?* We have, of course, distinguished it from irrational eclecticism. And that distinction is just the answer to this question. The dangers of eclecticism arise from its interference with the processes of structural corroboration. There is no cognitive profit in an eclectic world theory (cf. p. 104, above). Our postrational eclecticism is simply the recognition of the equal or nearly equal adequacy of a number of world theories and a recommendation that we do not fall into the dogmatism of neglecting any one of them.

As to the objection that the weighting of the different judgments of different world theories for practical action would open the way for prejudice and caprice, the answer is that the ignoring of these diverse judgments would be still more prejudicial and capricious. Unfortunately there is no way of overcoming ignorance but through more knowledge. It is highly practicable to be as fully and clearly aware of our ignorance as of our knowledge. Four good lights cast fewer shadows than one when the sun is hid, but a man has to do his own walking.

Apart from practice and the urgency of making decisions on the basis of such evidence as we have, this postrational eclecticism produces no problem at all. About any subject, such as truth, we simply inquire what is the judgment of each one of these world hypotheses on this subject. We come out commonly with four different theories about the matter. What we know about the subject, then, is that there are four well-corroborated alternative world theories about it which describe it in detail thus, thus, thus, and thus. Our postrational eclecticism consists simply in holding these four theories in suspended judgment as constituting the sum of our knowledge on the subject.

This point is so important for our treatment of cognitive matters that it deserves expansion. Let us take the subject of "truth" as our illustration. For "truth," it may be recalled, was the concept which we agreed to follow through each world hypothesis as an example of the interpretive effect of different sets of categories on a relatively identical field of "fact." Moreover, we courted this example because it would bring to a head the question of the cognitive value of the hypotheses themselves—for "truth" is the common name given to what is prized in cognition.

Following this concept through from the beginning, we should want to know what it roughly referred to in common sense so as to get an idea of what the common mass of fact is that is subsequently refined. We should like a common-sense definition of truth. It would presumably be something to the effect of "telling just what happened" as opposed to a lie or an error which would be "intentionally or unintentionally saying what did not happen."

This field of rough common-sense material was then refined into multiplicative agreement for data; and for danda into various structural theories of the nature of cognitive value—into infallible authority for animism, immediate certainty for mysticism, correspondence for formism, nominalism or causal-adjustment theory for mechanism, operationalism for contextualism, and coherence for organicism.

We notice that each world hypothesis has a quite distinct interpretation of the nature of truth, and that the interpretation implied by data and multiplicative corroboration is different still.

We notice also that infallible authority and immediate certainty are the criteria of truth supported by two theories which we found to be highly inadequate. We thus obtain another reason for disallowing the validity of these criteria of truth. The inadequacy of those two supporting hypotheses systematically confirms the great weakness of these conceptions of truth. What it amounts to, of course, is this: that in animism and mysticism these tests of truth have a chance to work themselves out for all they are worth, and the result is a chaos of imprecision in the one and a pitiful scope in the other—being two ways of piling up contradictions in these two cognitive standards' own terms. These conceptions of truth, then, in terms of infallibility and immediate certainty can be rejected as being inadequately supported and lacking in structural corroboration.

Now, in order to avoid the postrational eclecticism which is being objected to in the present criticism, the following question must be raised and answered affirmatively: Can the remaining interpretations of truth, which are supported by relatively adequate world theories, be harmonized or amalgamated into one interpretation that will do justice to them all? But the answer is, No, not in a manner that will be acceptable to them all. Let us try.

Suppose we begin with the correspondence theory. In terms of this theory the other three theories of truth become subsidiary criteria of considerable reliability. The nominalistic theory of the causal adjustment of an organism's attitude to its environment becomes an interesting observation of what actually happens when an organism's beliefs correspond with environmental conditions. Consequently, the well-adjusted activity of an organism in its environment is, for a formist, a good sign that the implied beliefs are in correspondence with the environmental objects responded to. But it is only a good sign, and does not guarantee correspondence or truth, and therefore requires more rigorous confirmation. Likewise for the operational theory. The smooth working of a hypothesis becomes for a formist a good sign of its truth, but does not guarantee truth proper or correspondence. As for coherence, this seems to involve for the formist a certain confusion between fact and logical consistency. If this confusion is cleared up and fact is definitely distinguished from description of fact, then we see, says the formist, that the self-consistency of a description of fact is a necessary requirement for a true description, but, of course, it does not guarantee the truth of the description, for many self-consistent descriptions do not correspond with the facts they refer to.

Try the mechanistic causal-adjustment theory. On this view, whatever is meant by correspondence can be nothing but the causal adjustment of a description (which itself is nothing but a physiological reaction set) with the environment responded to. Anything else implied in correspondence is a hypostatization of a name. Operationalism, for a mechanist, is a halfhearted causal nominalism which has failed to look into the causes for the working of hypotheses. It is correct as far as it goes. Coherence is a muddled view, but the self-consistency of a description is a good negative criterion which often saves a scientist from the necessity of putting his hypotheses to the experimental test.

Try operationalism. On this view, correspondence becomes the hypostatization of convergent activities, which as means of integrating instrumental textures are conducive to the solution of problems; but convergent activities do not guarantee the solution of a problem, and so cannot constitute the truth of a hypothesis. Mechanistic nominalism, says the operationalist, is correct in its insistence upon the close interaction of an organism with its environment, but it tends to hypostatize the organisms and environmental structures into static fixed entities beyond all empirical justification. Coherence, for the operationalist, is the inevitable result of the successful solution of a problem. A workable hypothesis always brings about an integration among a group of activities which previously had been blocked. But the coherence view exaggerates the necessity of organicity and in the end hypostatizes the principle of organicity. The coherence view, says the operationalist, confuses the *nature* of truth as the verification and the successful working of a hypothesis with the *results* of truth, which are an integration of activities toward a desired end.

Try the coherence theory. On this view, correspondence represents a rather low degree of coherence. It contains some truth, for it has some organizing capacity. But its inner contradictions and fragmentariness are patent. The causal-adjustment theory is not much better, involving, as it does, the mechanistic opposition of mind and matter. But so far as it indicates the extensive integration of matter it is a movement forward toward a higher degree of truth. Operationalism, says the organicist, contains a great deal of truth and fails only in not accepting the full implications of its own method. It arbitrarily restricts truth to the temporal integrations of sporadic problematic activities. This arbitrary restriction is self-contradictory, says the organicist, and implies in itself the coherence theory, which alone resolves the contradictions involved.

None of these theories of truth gives way to the others. Nevertheless, this survey gives a more balanced and informed conception of the subject than could be got in any other manner. We see that there is much to be said for each of these theories of truth, that they cannot be successfully amalgamated in one view that will do full justice to them all, that they are a great refinement upon the rough common-sense conception, and that they are much more adequate than the animistic and mystic conceptions. This is what I mean by postrational eclecticism, or by being reasonable with the results of rational procedures. It is entirely practicable.

vii) *What about adequacy?* Is not this simply another theory of truth clapped on top of the theories just considered? Clearly not, as the preceding survey shows. We have no theory of truth to supersede or legislate over the four most adequate ones we have just considered. That is why we recommended a postrational reasonableness. Adequacy means nothing but degree of structural corroboration, and for the details of what this means there is no authority but the actual world theories which have achieved such corroboration.

As to the further question, whether the root-metaphor theory was not a world theory itself, or one of the already described world theories pretending to be a neutral, it is almost a sufficient reply to record that the root-metaphor theory has been accused by various persons of being every one of these world theories except animism and mysticism.

Actually it is, as remarked earlier, nothing but a short-cut method for getting at the smallest number of world theories having a high degree of structural corroboration. If the root-metaphor theory is in error, we are simply thrown back upon the more laborious way of testing structural corroboration. But I have tried to show by my very exposition of these theories in terms of their root metaphors that there is a good deal of evidence for the truth of the root-metaphor theory. My contention is that as soon as the claims of dogmatism have been dissipated, this root-metaphor theory of structural corroboration appears of itself, just as the natural contours of a landscape appear as soon as the morning mists are burned away.

viii) *Am I not dogmatically undogmatic?* I leave that for the reader to judge from the evidence.